A Big Fat Crisis

A BIG FAT CRISIS

*The Hidden Forces Behind the Obesity Epidemic—
and How We Can End It*

Deborah A. Cohen, MD

NATION
BOOKS
New York

Published by Nation Books, A Member of the Perseus Books Group
116 East 16th Street, 8th Floor
New York, NY 10003

Nation Books is a co-publishing venture of the Nation Institute and the Perseus Books Group.

Books published by Nation Books are available at special discounts for bulk purchases in the United States by corporations, institutions, and other organizations. For more information, please contact the Special Markets Department at the Perseus Books Group, 2300 Chestnut Street, Suite 200, Philadelphia, PA 19103, or call (800) 255-1514, or e-mail special.markets@perseusbooks.com.

Library of Congress Cataloging-in-Publication Data

Cohen, Deborah (Deborah Ann)
  A big fat crisis : the hidden forces behind the obesity epidemic - and how we can end it / Deborah A. Cohen, MD, MPH.
    pages cm
  Includes bibliographical references and index.
    ISBN 978-1-56858-967-1 (hardback) — ISBN 978-1-56858-965-7 (e-book) 1. Obesity—United States. 2. Obesity—Government policy—United States. 3. Obesity—United States—Prevention. 4. Overweight persons—United States—Social aspects. 5. Public health—United States—Planning. I. Title.
  RA645.O23C64 2014
  362.1963'98—dc23
                                                                                    2013024389

Contents

To my mother, Sheila Fried Cohen

"Obesity shows how abundance, through cheapness, variety, novelty, and choice, could make a mockery of the rational consumer, how it enticed only in order to humiliate."

—*Avner Offer*

Introduction

I am one of the 97 percent of Americans who find it difficult to routinely eat a healthy diet and get sufficient exercise.[1] I have been fortunate not to have serious weight issues, but according to the US Departments of Agriculture and Health and Human Services' Dietary Guidelines for Americans, I am still supposed to eat a wide variety of fruits, vegetables, and whole grains; limit my consumption of meat; and drink the equivalent of three cups of milk every day. And because my cholesterol is high, it has to be skim milk. Hypertension runs in my family, so I also need to limit my salt intake.

If you think that maintaining a healthy lifestyle would be easy for me because I am trained as a medical doctor and conduct research on diet and physical activity, you couldn't be more wrong. Adhering to this kind of healthy diet is neither easy nor fun. You pretty much have to cook everything from scratch, and whether you work outside of the home or are a stay-at-home parent, it's no picnic finding the ingredients and the time to prepare tasty, balanced meals. In every supermarket I visit, the items are scattered everywhere in no logical pattern that I can understand. I often have to ask for help to locate what I need. Does the store have any low-salt canned beans? Or will I have to buy them dried, soak them overnight, and then boil them for hours?

When I do find the right aisle, I am never sure which item to choose from the dozens of available varieties. Which cereals really have less sugar and more fiber? Should I get the multigrain, whole wheat, or rice flour pasta? What about chips? Are the baked chips or the ones with the flax and sesame seeds really good for me? There are so many products, and I just don't have the patience to read every label.

It was especially difficult to be a wise consumer when I had to take my kids grocery shopping with me, whether they were four or fourteen. As a mom, I not only had to figure out what to buy for my family but also had to remove more than half of what my kids managed to sneak in the cart before I got to the checkout—chips, sodas, and sugar-frosted cereals. Now that my kids are older and I tend to shop alone, I have a hard time resisting the premium dark chocolate candy bars at the cash register. Yum! Should I get the large bar or the three-pack of small ones?

And my family hates to eat at home all the time. (Boring!) Once in a while I give in and take them out to a restaurant, even though it is next to impossible to find a meal away from home that is both healthy and delicious. Last week we went to a Mexican restaurant called El Torito, conveniently located a few blocks from our house. The menu listed the calorie count next to every entrée, as mandated by a recent California law that requires all restaurants with twenty or more outlets to list calories prominently on menus and menu boards. Although this theoretically should have helped me choose something healthy, I could find hardly any meals under nine hundred calories. And that's not including the free chips and salsa, the margaritas, or dessert. Forget about trying to find skim milk, fruit, or a low-salt option—it's just not on the menu.

(El Torito is not an exception, by the way. According to recent research, fewer than 4 percent of restaurant meals meet the latest USDA guidelines for sodium, fat, and saturated fat.[2])

What about exercise? That should be easier than finding a healthy meal, because it only involves carving out thirty minutes five days each week. But it somehow doesn't work out that way. Although I could take more breaks and be more active during the day, or even walk around the block a few times, other things always seem to take priority. Deadlines for completing projects, the needs of my family, and the lure of a good movie after a tiresome day at work keep me in a chair, in a car, and on a couch.

Should I blame myself for my failure to make healthy choices?

Should I hold myself responsible for eating too much chocolate? For my untoned, sagging biceps and belly? Should you? When we're on our own, who else is there to blame?

⸺⸺⸺

Because I have many family members and friends who are overweight or obese,* my interest in addressing the epidemic is both personal and professional. Unlike most medical doctors who see patients for a living, I specialize in public health. Rather than helping individuals with their medical problems, I study entire populations, trying to pinpoint why people engage in behaviors that lead to ill health. With board certification in public health and preventive medicine, as well as a master's degree in epidemiology—the study of the incidence, distribution, and control of disease across a population—I have spent more than twenty-five years studying why people engage in risky, unhealthy behaviors like smoking, drinking too much, having sex without a condom, eating too much, and exercising too little. For the past twelve years, as a scientist at the RAND Corporation, my focus has been on the obesity epidemic and how we can reverse it.

There are plenty of guidelines intended to help people figure out what to eat. The Dietary Guidelines for Americans, a consensus on what people should and shouldn't eat to stave off obesity and diet-related chronic diseases, haven't changed much in the past fifteen years. Even if you've never read them, you can probably guess what they say: eat your fruits and vegetables and go easy on sweet, salty, and fatty foods. Not very complicated, yet only 3 percent of Americans faithfully adhere to the recommendations.[3]

Similarly, the recommendation for physical activity has remained constant for nearly twenty years. Adults should get at least 2.5 hours of moderate exercise every week (e.g., thirty minutes five times per week), and children should get sixty minutes every day.[4] Yet fewer than

---

* To meet the technical definition of "overweight," the ratio of one's weight to the square of one's height (kilograms/meters^2) must be equal to or greater than twenty-five but less than thirty. One is obese when the ratio is equal to or greater than thirty. For example, a five-foot-eight person who weighs more than 164 pounds is overweight; if that person weighed 197 pounds or greater, he would be classified as obese.

5 percent of adults and less than half of all children exercise enough to achieve these modest goals.[5]

As a result of not meeting either the diet or physical activity guidelines, two out of three adults and one out of three children in this country are overweight or obese.[6] Although in theory we know what to do to optimize our health—eat reasonable portions of nutrient-rich food and exercise regularly—in practice we don't do it.

This gulf between our knowledge and our actions has long plagued me. As a physician and public health researcher who has studied obesity for more than a decade, I am especially aware of what I *should be* eating and how much I *should be* exercising. And I'm especially aware of the consequences of being obese: higher rates of diabetes, heart disease, hypertension, osteoporosis, and even cancer. Still, like most Americans, I find that this understanding only goes so far. It doesn't dissuade me from eating more sweets than I should, and it doesn't propel me to go jogging after a long day of work. I want to be healthier and stronger, I want to live longer and continue to lead an active lifestyle for years to come, but I fail to take the necessary steps to make this happen. And so do most Americans.

From a rational perspective, the motivation to eat well is clear. Research suggests that

- Being obese doubles one's risk of dying prematurely.[7]
- Eating too many trans fats increases the risk of coronary artery disease by 23 percent.[8]
- Eating too little fiber increases the risk of colon cancer by 18 percent.[9]
- Drinking one sugar-sweetened beverage every day increases the risk of diabetes by 83 percent in women.[10]
- Excess dietary salt is believed to be responsible for 62 percent of all strokes.[11]

The research demonstrating the harms from eating too much food, especially too much sugar, is becoming increasingly clear and graphic. The Pennington Biomedical Research Center in Baton Rouge, Louisiana, whose mission is to tackle nutrition-related problems, recently showed how healthy people can develop risk factors for heart disease and diabetes merely by being fed too much.

To precisely measure what happens to the overfed body, Pennington scientist Alok Gupta recruited fourteen healthy volunteers, with no hypertension, no diabetes, no heart disease, and a normal waist size, and had them eat all their food at Pennington for two months. During this time they were poked, prodded, and observed to see what was going on internally when the calories in their diet were increased.

In the first week the volunteers spent an entire day in a metabolic chamber to have their daily energy requirements assessed. They had biopsies to measure the size of their fat cells and MRIs to measure the volume of all their fat, including the fat in their internal organs as well as the fat stored under the skin and around the waist. After quantifying the volunteers' total body fat, total body muscle mass, and total body water, Gupta measured the fat in their livers and the fat around their lower legs and in the calf muscles. He measured the baseline functioning of all their organs—the liver, the pancreas, and all the hormones related to eating, like insulin and leptin. He also measured inflammation in the blood and tested how well the blood vessels function by seeing how quickly blood vessels in a single finger recovered after the circulation was cut off for five minutes. And for seven days, while the volunteers wore an accelerometer to record how active they were, their blood pressure was also measured every thirty minutes.

Then, every day for the following seven weeks, the volunteers were served 40 percent more calories than needed to maintain their current weight. As they stuffed themselves, the measurements continued to record what happened to their organs, blood pressure, hormones, fat cells, muscles, and blood vessels.

On average, the group gained more than sixteen pounds, their body fat increased by 2 percent, and their waists grew more than three inches. Extra fat was deposited in organs rather than in muscle, especially in the liver. The average fat cell size grew by 54 percent.

Indicators of systemwide inflammation increased by 29–50 percent. Fasting blood sugar (an indicator of diabetes), cholesterol, and insulin resistance all increased. Blood pressure and heart rate went up and blood vessel functioning capacity was reduced by about 21 percent—altogether demonstrating a significant increase in factors associated with heart disease.

At the end of seven weeks, most of the volunteers still felt fine and had measures that remained within the normal range. But it was very clear that continuing the trajectory would have led to serious problems.

Although most people understand that being overweight or obese puts them at a greater risk for all kinds of diseases, especially life-threatening ones, on a day-to-day basis the consequences seem pretty remote. The body changes happen gradually, and without these detailed measures they often go undetected. Moreover, even if we put on two pounds per week, we generally don't get any obviously recognizable symptoms letting us know that any internal damage is occurring. Most people put on one to two pounds per year, so it would take more than eight years to match what the Pennington volunteers gained in eight weeks.

Although there is no doubt that obesity increases the risk of a wide variety of medical problems, what is less well understood is why people eat too much even though they are aware of the negative consequences.

The conventional wisdom is that obesity is the expression of individual weakness, gluttony, and/or lack of personal responsibility. Some claim that the current epidemic, therefore, indicates that a substantial portion of the population has lost all sense of self-control while the rest are intentionally choosing to become fat.[12] This is where I am extremely skeptical.

The increase in obesity cannot simply be an isolated matter of lack of self-control. Why? If the absolute loss of self-control was responsible for the obesity epidemic, it would mean that people in this country had more willpower thirty years ago, when the rate of obesity was half of what it is today. It would mean that people in countries with lower rates of obesity like Japan, Costa Rica, Sweden, and Finland are more controlled, more responsible, and perhaps even morally superior to Americans. Is that plausible?

The fact is, the majority of people who are overweight appear to have plenty of self-control in most other areas of their lives. They have completed school and earned college or higher degrees; they maintain full- or part-time jobs, arrive at work on time, complete their assignments, raise successful children, vote, volunteer, and contribute to society in many ways. Few get into trouble with the law or are violent, impulsive, or irresponsible in ways that demonstrate low self-control.

Based on my own research, as well as the latest insights from behavioral economics, psychology, cognitive science, and the social sciences, the pages that follow describe the surprising forces behind the obesity epidemic and how we, as a nation, can overcome them.

My conclusions contradict conventional wisdom and widely held expert opinion, and go against our intuitive belief that people are fully in control of what they eat. They suggest that our basic assumptions about human nature and how our DNA is hardwired must be changed. Accepting that humans face limitations that interfere with self-control represents, in short, a paradigm shift in how we approach the problem of obesity—and the solution.

Specifically, *A Big Fat Crisis* argues that the obesity epidemic is the product of two forces:

(1) Immutable aspects of human nature, namely the fundamental limits of self-control, the inflexible decision-making strategy of the brain's noncognitive system, and the automatic and unconscious way that we are hardwired to eat; and

(2) A completely transformed food environment, by which I mean all the food-related elements of our surroundings, including grocery stores, restaurants, prices, portion sizes, availability, marketing, and advertising.

The book focuses in equal measure on human nature, with its irrational and unconscious decision-making process when it comes to eating, and the modern food environment, which puts cheap, high-calorie, low-nutrient foods at our disposal in a way that is unprecedented in human history. Drawing on cutting-edge research from a variety of disciplines, I argue that the current discussion surrounding obesity, with its primary focus on individual responsibility and self-control, demonstrates a fundamental misunderstanding of human nature. We are biologically designed to overeat when presented with the opportunity (that is, to eat more than we need in order to ensure our survival); most of us have a shockingly limited capacity to deliberately and consistently regulate our eating behaviors; our eating behaviors are not a matter of thoughtful, mindful decision-making, but instead happen automatically, without our full awareness.

Nevertheless, we assume that most people are rational and that we ourselves are even more rational than others. We see ourselves as powerful agents who decide what we will or will not do on a daily basis, particularly when it comes to our basic preferences, like how we spend our time and what we consume. We believe that we all have the capacity to control what and how much we eat. Although researchers in behavioral economics, cognitive science, and psychology have begun to poke holes in the rational-actor theory of human behavior, most of us still cling to this notion of omnipotence when it comes to food. If you're being honest, I bet you blame yourself when you are unable to resist temptation—and probably hold overweight individuals accountable for their size.

If the limitations of human nature explain why we are prone to make unhealthy choices, the modern food environment practically assaults us wherever we go. The number of restaurants in America has more than doubled since 1977, and is still growing.[13] The number of vending machines has also increased exponentially. When I was a child, vending machines were a rarity, and they usually sold either gumballs or cigarettes. Today, vending machines are in practically every office building, gas station, and public venue in the country. Advertising, too, has become increasingly sophisticated and insidious, so much so that we might not even recognize it as advertising: movie scenes feature actors eating name-brand foods, and the judges on *American Idol* sip Cokes as they dole out their scores. *A Big Fat Crisis* argues that the modern food environment is the largest determinant of our behavior—and what we need to focus on if we are going to end the obesity epidemic.

Finally, the last section of the book offers concrete solutions, arguing that the most important and modifiable steps in the chain of events that leads to obesity are at the point of purchase and the point of consumption—the supply side of the problem. I contend that we need regulations standardizing portion sizes in restaurants and laws prohibiting the sale of candy at all cash registers. We must demand that restaurants offer balanced meals as alternatives to the standard fare that increases our risk of chronic disease. We have to apply to unhealthy foods the kinds of regulations that have been successful in limiting alcohol consumption—a prohibition on "two for one" specials, for example, and limitations on "all you can eat" promotions.

Because some of my ideas may come across as overly intrusive or inordinately dismissive of the importance of personal responsibility, I describe several historical examples of even larger public health initiatives that were initially derided but eventually embraced. Two hundred years ago, for example, societies throughout the world had no regulations governing environmental conditions. The result was recurrent epidemics of infectious disease, including cholera, typhoid, tuberculosis, and gastroenteritis. At that time, prohibiting people from tossing garbage and human waste out the window and mandating indoor plumbing seemed like an invasion of privacy and an attack on individual rights. Prohibiting butchers from dumping animal carcasses and their entrails on the public streets was considered undue interference with private business. Implementing regulatory controls required long, contentious political battles. Now, because we recognize that integrated sewer systems and restrictions on dumping protect us from infectious disease and exposure to toxic chemicals, we find it hard to sympathize with those who resist these kinds of environmental regulations.

Like cholera and typhoid in the nineteenth century, obesity is the twenty-first century's public health crisis. Our major approach of exhorting individuals to be more responsible is just not working. Ending obesity requires solutions that transcend individual behavior.

In the 2012 US presidential campaign, Bill Clinton summarized two perspectives on governance. He juxtaposed one philosophy, "We're all in this together," a view that indicates that as a society we must take steps to care for one another, with the diametrically opposite view, "You're on your own," which suggests that each person has to make his or her own way in the world, without any special help or protections from an unfettered marketplace.

In my view, the reason we have the obesity epidemic is because we've been on our own for way too long. Change begins with a fresh perspective and a clearer vision of what we need to do. Let me take you on a journey through the obesity epidemic and show you how we can end it.

PART I

Human Nature and Food

1

It's Not Your Fault

"After 6 months of diet success, I can't control how much I eat. I am a 6'2" tall 19-year-old man. Since May 2008, I lost 50 lbs. from 210 lb to 160 lb. Now, in the last two weeks, I just can't control how much I eat. Some days, it's ~2000 calories and other days 4000. Because of that, I put on 10 lbs in two weeks. I am pretty much in depression right now. I can't think about anything else. What is wrong with me?"[1]

"I feel so out of control. I think I am doing good and then the cheetos call my name or a burger and fries from McDonald's. I do not need this kind of food. I need healthy food, but there are days that I cannot help myself. Mostly when I am away from my family like when I am at work. I think of different things I can eat and it does not help that I work at a grocery store where I have access to all kinds of junk food and things. But you would think I would eat fruit or veggies at the store, but no not me I get in this kinda trance like state, thinking I am hungry and on the hunt for something that tastes good. I cannot seem to stop this."[2]

"I eat. A lot more than I should. I'll just finish eating a meal, and suddenly, I want more, but I don't want just any food. I crave junk food. I know that I should start to eat less and exercise more, but I can't find the motivation. When I think about how unhealthy this is for my body, I just eat more. It's gotten to the point where it's hard for me to control. Please help."[3]

Struggling with obesity is not a rare, personal story—it is the problem of our time. More than 150 million Americans are overweight or obese, and across the globe an estimated 1.5 billion are affected.[4] One-quarter to one-third of all cancers can be attributed to obesity.[5] Being overweight and/or obese is also a strong risk factor for type 2 diabetes, heart disease, hypertension, joint and back pain, and a host of other medical problems.[6] The diseases associated with obesity cost our medical system an estimated $147 billion per year.[7]

Even beyond the physical toll of obesity, the emotional pain makes this condition difficult to bear. Not only are overweight and obese people stigmatized by others, but those who struggle with their weight often stigmatize themselves—they feel inferior, ashamed, unhappy, and even depressed. One obese colleague told me that she felt like a blob; mortified by her condition, she started to withdraw from others. She and others like her believe their lack of self-control is an inherent character flaw they may never be able to overcome.

The perceived link between lack of self-discipline and obesity has become so strong that overweight or obese people are often judged as less competent than their thinner peers. US Surgeon General Regina Benjamin was initially criticized for being overweight. What credibility would a health expert have if she couldn't practice a healthy lifestyle? When New Jersey Governor Chris Christie first began exploring a run for the presidency, his ample girth led many to question his fitness for office. To defuse the charge, he joked about his size by eating a doughnut on the *Late Show with David Letterman.* However, more recently, he admitted to getting LapBand surgery to help control his weight.

Yet the stereotypical view of obesity—that it is a marker of low self-control, deep character flaws, or serious psychopathology—is plain wrong. Yes, dozens of studies—some of which I will explore in the next chapter—show that overweight and obese adults have much more trouble resisting food than their thinner peers. Obese adults have more problems with self-regulation, they are more impulsive, they have higher levels of urgency, they lack perseverance, and they are more sensitive to rewards.[8] This is neither novel nor particularly helpful to the two-thirds of American adults who are already overweight or obese.

What is needed is an entirely new way to think about and frame the obesity epidemic. We must recognize that an individual's ability to resist overeating is limited when excess food is constantly available. Why else would so many people have trouble controlling their weight? If it was so easy to maintain a normal weight and everyone had the capacity, then logically, many more people would have a normal weight. Why suffer the stigma of being overweight? Why rack up chronic diseases that make us feel miserable and force us to take medications if we didn't need to?

Everyone wants to believe that we all can accomplish whatever we want, if only we try hard enough. Unfortunately, no matter how hard many of us try, we cannot always achieve our goals. Most of us will never be movie stars, rock stars, prima ballerinas, astronauts, the president, or even president of our local parent-teacher organization.

That is because talent, skill, intelligence, and even self-control tend to be distributed across our population like a bell curve. Most of us are average, and by definition only 5 percent of us are at the top 5 percent of anything. We tend to think of a glass as half full rather than half empty, yet the sad truth is that half of us are below average. Although we expect to be treated equally by others and have equal rights under the law, our abilities are anything but equal.

More than that, each person's abilities vary over time and across the day. In the morning some of us are fresh and energetic, but others get their best work done late at night. The point is that no matter how competent we are, there are days and times when all of us are less competent. Sometimes we feel happy or sad, and these feelings influence our behaviors too. We are not machines, and we do not perform the same way all the time. One quality we can count on is variability. Although some may seem to be able to navigate through the modern world effortlessly without putting on an extra ounce or missing a single day of exercise, this does not prove that everyone has the same capacity.

Because our moods and desires change throughout the day, many people claim their weight problem is the result of emotional eating. They say they eat when they are stressed, lonely, or anxious—whenever they are not at their best. Yet others claim they eat too much when they are happy.

Catherine Morgan, a writer, nurse, and mother, wrote this confession on her blog:

> Are you an emotional eater? If it's any consolation, you're not alone.
> I have to confess. . . . I am an emotional eater. When I'm upset I eat.
> When I'm stressed I eat. When I'm worried I eat. And let's be clear,
> these are the times I have uncontrollable urges to eat junk (candy, cookies, ice cream), all the stuff I know is bad for me. I could be eating
> healthy for months, then something upsets me, and it's all over.
>
> The crazy thing about being an emotional eater is that you know that
> eating isn't going to make what you're upset about any better, but you
> do it anyway. In fact, you know that eating the junk that you're craving
> is actually going to contribute to making you feel worse, but you do it
> anyway.[9]

When we have a problem, we usually find a plausible reason to explain it. We look to psychological explanations for our behaviors because we don't have a way to see the big picture of what is really causing us to eat more than we need.

The conventional advice for those who suffer from "emotional eating" is first to recognize the triggers and then to find distractions to avoid eating. The medical website WebMD recommends the following alternatives to counter emotional eating impulses: "Read a good book or magazine or listen to music, go for a walk or jog, take a bubble bath, do deep breathing exercises, play cards or a board game, talk to a friend, do housework, laundry or yard work, wash the car, write a letter, or do any other pleasurable or necessary activity until the urge to eat passes." The article continues: "If distraction doesn't work, try relaxation exercises, meditation, or individual or group counseling."[10]

But could emotional issues really be responsible for the population-wide epidemic of obesity? Do people in modern times experience more emotional stresses or more intense feelings than in the past? Do people in the United States have more emotional issues than those in countries with lower rates of obesity, like Sweden, Ethiopia, or India? Probably not.

During the Great Depression, a lot more people suffered a great deal more stress than we do today, but there was no obesity epidemic in the 1930s. People couldn't afford a lot of food, and so they had to resort to other ways to deal with stress. The reason we can eat too much today, whether or not we are under stress, is because food is affordable and available in large quantities.

The obesity epidemic is the result of the unique interplay between human nature and the contemporary food environment. Three aspects of human nature make it impossible for most of us to remain in control of what and how much we eat consistently, day in and day out. These are:

- *Limited self-control.* Whether we try to study all night, watch a marathon of movies, or hold back tears when we are upset, most of us can control ourselves up to a certain point. Eventually, we all get tired and have to rest. When we are fatigued, we tend to choose foods we know we should avoid and we eat too much of them.
- *Limited cognitive capacity.* We usually reserve our cognitive processing system, the part of our brain that handles thoughtful planning and long-term problem solving, since it is easily depleted. When it comes to eating, we tend to rely on our noncognitive processing system, which guides our food choices based on superficial characteristics like size, color, brand, or price. This noncognitive system is primarily responsible for poor dietary choices.
- *Automatic functioning.* Eating is an automatic process that does not require our full attention and awareness. Driven by our survival instinct, we respond reflexively and rapidly to opportunities to obtain and consume as many calories as we can get our hands on. Automaticity is primarily responsible for overeating.

Today, the food environment assaults us at every turn in ways we cannot ignore, stimulating us to feel hungry or at least to think about eating. From the displays of candy at cash registers in supermarkets, hardware stores, and even clothing stores to the constant product placements of soda and junk food on television and at the movies, it's difficult to have anything on our minds except our next meal or snack. And when we do sit down to eat, most of us cannot easily limit the amount we consume per meal if too much food is available. That's what happens when we dine out. According to Dr. Lisa Young and Dr. Marion Nestle, experts on the impact of supersized meals, most restaurants serve two to five times the calories we need.[11]

But this also doesn't mean we are gluttons. Most of us are not eating supersized meals, dozens of candy bars, or gallons of ice cream every day. It doesn't take much to go into a positive energy balance in which we eat more than we burn, so our bodies convert the extra calories into fat for use at a later time. An extra soda, an extra slice of cheese, an extra handful of chips can accumulate into an extra pound or two slowly, in ways that are difficult to notice, especially when we are routinely confronted with larger quantities of food than we need.

The food environment has become a tsunami. If it doesn't drown us, it waterlogs even the strongest of swimmers, who have to exert more energy, be more alert and more conscientious than ever before just to stay afloat. Indeed, given the evolution and limitations of human nature, there is simply no way for most of us to avoid succumbing to the enticements to eat that we are bombarded with ceaselessly.

Americans today are no different from Americans of thirty years ago, when obesity affected one in six instead of the current rate of one in three. Physiologically, our capacity for self-control has not shrunk over the past several decades. Instead, the changing conditions of our modern world have ramped up requirements for self-control to such an extent that more and more of us are simply no longer up to the challenge.

The next chapter addresses the limits of self-control head-on.

2

The Limits of Self-Control

In 1994 Dr. Rena Wing, Professor of Psychiatry and Human Behavior at Brown Medical School, and Dr. James Hill, Professor of Pediatrics and Medicine at the University of Colorado, Denver, started the National Weight Control Registry (NWCR). Because losing weight and keeping it off is so rare, they wanted to see if they could pinpoint exactly what explained the success of those who were able to shed pounds and maintain a lower weight. The NWCR is conducted online; those who want to participate can sign up and share their stories. The only requirement is that registry members have to have lost at least thirty pounds and kept it off for at least one year. The registry periodically asks its volunteer participants to fill out questionnaires that track their behavior over time.

For almost twenty years Wing and Hill have been studying some five thousand successful dieters, of whom 80 percent are women and 20 percent are men. The "average" woman in NWCR's registry is forty-five years old and currently weighs 145 pounds, while the "average" man is forty-nine and currently weighs 190 pounds. They have lost an average of sixty-six pounds each and kept it off for five and a half years. Most lost weight with the help of a program—like Weight Watchers or Jenny Craig—but 45 percent lost the weight on their own.

What are these people doing to keep the extra weight off? What do they know that the rest of us don't? The answer might surprise you. Seventy-eight percent of them eat breakfast every day. Seventy-five percent weigh themselves at least once a week. Sixty-two percent watch fewer than ten hours of television per week. And 90 percent exercise, on average, about one hour per day.[1]

None of this sounds like magic, or like anything particularly special. Millions of Americans already know that they should exercise more, watch less TV, and eat at mealtimes and not in between. But millions of Americans have *not* had similar success, or any success at all, when it comes to losing weight. Does this study explain how these men and women were able to change their habits—to actually follow through and stick to the healthier routines we all know we should be following? No. What it tells us is that there is no secret weapon in the fight against fat. What it tells us is that people who can stick to a healthy routine are the exception rather than the rule.

Although the NWCR is a collection of people who represent the "exceptions," who are self-selected and therefore not representative, we can learn more about the obesity epidemic by examining a group of people selected to be representative of a larger population. In 1976, with funding from the National Institutes of Health, a team of researchers led by Frank Speizer from Harvard Medical School chose to follow a cohort of registered nurses. The researchers believed the nurses, given their advanced training, would be able to provide very accurate reports of health-related issues, like symptoms, dietary habits, and other medical-related problems. By studying nurses over time, researchers hoped that they could provide insight into which behaviors and exposures might lead to or protect against a variety of long-term chronic diseases.

The study solicited married registered nurses, age thirty to fifty-five, living in the eleven most populous states. Approximately 122,000 nurses out of a pool of 170,000 responded.[2]

You might think that because nurses know more than the average person about health, they would tend to be healthier than the rest of us. Yet between 1976 and 2005, the number of overweight study participants doubled, while the number of obese participants tripled—a pattern very similar to changes in the rest of the population. By 2005 only 44 percent could be classified as having a normal weight. Excluding nurses who were pregnant or had cancer or other serious medical problems, fewer than 3 percent reported losing at least 10 percent of their weight. Of the entire group of nurses, fewer than one in three hundred were able to lose and then maintain the 10 percent weight loss for four years.[3] So even among a group of people who are supposed to be experts in health issues, only a small fraction were able to reduce and maintain a lower weight. Like most of us, the nurses could not stick to a diet, even when armed with the necessary information and the best of intentions.

Why do nurses seem to be no better off than the rest of us? If you asked them for diet advice, they could probably list all the things that should be done and could tell you which foods are healthy and which to avoid. Like the advice that all experts give, the solutions they would mention would sound simple and feasible.

But how simple is following a diet? When people first decide to go on a diet, they are optimistic and think it should not be a problem. The typical advice is to restrict intake: say no to specific types of foods that are not considered healthy and are readily identifiable (like candy, cookies, pastries, sugary sodas, and salty snacks such as chips and other deep-fried foods with lots of oil and grease), and the excess weight should disappear. Some experts go further and offer a wide variety of tips and advice to help—use smaller plates, eat slowly, cut your portions in half, substitute lower-calorie foods for higher-, etc. In fact, nearly all diets work if people follow them. When a diet doesn't work, it's usually because of one of two things: the dieters are not following the diet and are aware of it, or the dieters are not following the diet but believe that they are following it.

My father had a problem controlling his weight his entire adult life. He was a dentist. He knew everything one needs to know to be able to control weight. Yet, as educated and intelligent as he was, he struggled and mostly gave up trying to be slim. He was short, about five foot six, and he weighed more than two hundred pounds; he should have weighed about 140 pounds or less. He would lose ten, twenty, even forty pounds with a new diet that he would follow for as long as six months. At one point, I remember, my mother prepared plain rice, a plain chicken breast, and broccoli for him every night for months and months, and he began shedding the weight. But it didn't last long. He fell off the wagon and returned to his old habits of going to work, dining out for lunch, coming home, having dinner and watching TV, and going back to the kitchen every night for a midnight snack.

My father knew what he had to do, and he knew when he failed to follow his diet, yet somehow he could not maintain it. He felt better when he lost weight, and he felt worse when he gained it back. He suffered constantly because of his weight. He had hypertension and had to take medications that made him depressed and sapped his energy. He was always worried about his health. Yet these risks, fears, and his knowledge were not enough to lead him to control his diet.

Dieting: The Forever Time Horizon

Whether it's Atkins, South Beach, or Paleo, diets involve restricting intake for long periods of time and limiting the quantity of calories consumed, especially calories from foods with few nutrients. If you restrict yourself long enough, the excess weight should disappear. Here is the difficulty. Few are able to stick to a diet for more than six months.

Dr. Robert Jeffery, a professor at the University of Minnesota and a national expert in weight control, and his colleagues have tried to identify why people give up on their diets.[4] They followed dieters for a year and found that after a few months, people's experience of the benefits and rewards of dieting tended to peter out. The dieters might have received compliments for losing weight and improving their appearance at the beginning, or appreciated that their clothes fit better, but this seemed to be less noticeable later on. Even more surprising, people did not see a significant relationship between their weight loss and the time and effort they put into losing weight.

One of the problems with dieting is that our bodies respond slowly to changes in calorie consumption, unlike the instantaneous responses we get upon touching a hot stove. If we touch fire, we learn immediately to stay away or protect our hands. But if we eat an extra chocolate chip cookie every day, a scale may not register that we gained weight until a month later, so that immediate negative feedback and the associated learning experience are not there. Instead, we get immediate positive feedback from sugar, chocolate, and fat, so we tend to view chocolate chip cookies in a very positive light and learn to desire them. Instant feedback is a wonderful behavioral learning technique when it comes to promoting eating, but it is not very useful as a tool to support dieting.

Can We Control Self-Control?

Because self-control seems so central to diet and obesity, I began to investigate the scientific literature on the subject. After reading hundreds of papers on the topic, I learned something astonishing: when it comes to eating, self-control is not what we generally believe it to be—a reflection of an individual's character, upbringing, and moral strength. Instead, everyone faces limits in his or her ability to maintain self-control in the face of too much food. Our capacity for self-control varies by the moment, depending on whether we have just solved a difficult problem or met another demand. Moreover, self-control is often irrelevant when it comes to food, because we can be influenced to overeat by environmental cues we cannot consciously recognize. In many cases we may never get the opportunity to exercise self-control, even if we otherwise have it in abundance.

Self-control has been closely tied to health, well-being, and general success in life. This association has led multiple researchers to investigate its development over the life cycle. Obviously, a newborn lacks self-control entirely. But when does self-control start to develop? And why do some people have more than others? Is it a consequence of one's upbringing?

A couple of recent scientific studies point to early childhood for the onset of self-control failure. In one study, Drs. Lori Francis and Elizabeth Susman, professors at Penn State University, followed more than one thousand children from age three to twelve.[5] At ages three and five, they tested the children's capacity for self-control. In the first test at age three, the children were shown how much fun it is to play with Ski Boat Croc, a small plastic toy boat on wheels with a crocodile at the steering wheel pulling another crocodile behind on water skis.

After spending a few minutes pulling the toy back and forth, the children were told not to touch the toy or play with it while the interviewer left the room for about two and a half minutes. However, the children were allowed to play with other toys in the room instead. Children who couldn't wait more than seventy-five seconds before touching the Ski Boat Croc toy failed the test. Forty-five percent failed.

In a second test, the same children at age five were asked to pick their favorite snack from among three choices: M&M's, animal crackers, and pretzels. Then a small pile and a large pile of that snack were placed in front of the children. If the children wanted to eat the snack right away, they could have the small pile. But if they could wait three and a half minutes, they could get the large pile. Again, nearly 45 percent failed to wait. Only 36 percent were able to wait long enough at ages three and five to pass both tests of self-control. By age twelve, those who had failed both tests had higher rates of weight gain than those who had passed both.

Another long-term study looking at the relationship between the early capacity for self-control and obesity weighed and measured 805 children at age four. In this study the researchers didn't directly test the children's ability to restrain themselves, but instead asked their mothers how well they thought their children would be able to delay gratification. The children of mothers who reported that they were unable to delay gratification at age four had a 29 percent increased risk of being overweight by age eleven.[6]

What do these studies suggest? In every case the researchers claim the implications are that we need to work harder to teach our children better self-control at an early age or they will become out-of-control adults. But how hard would parents need to work? What would they have to do?

Would parents have to adopt the strict child-rearing methods advocated by Amy Chua in her book *Battle Hymn of the Tiger Mother*? Do we need rigid schedules and routines, vigilantly limiting the foods we bring home, controlling where our children dine out, and cautiously planning each and every calorie they consume?

Two experts in child development and obesity, Drs. Leann Birch and Jennifer Fisher, suggest the opposite. Attempts to restrict and control children's eating appear to exacerbate the problems of self-control, poor diet, and obesity.[7] If parents force their children to eat fruits and vegetables and constantly say no to foods high in sugar and fat, children learn to value these forbidden foods and hate fruits and vegetables.[8]

A study that followed girls from age seven to fifteen supported this observation. At seven, the girls were asked about parental restrictiveness with food. "If you ask for a snack, does Mommy let you have it?" By fifteen, girls who had earlier said their parents were more restrictive became heavier than those who had said their parents were more permissive. The implication is that children may be better able to learn self-control when parents do not closely monitor them but allow them to make unfettered choices. (Of course, the researchers caution that unhealthy foods should only be available in limited quantities.)

These studies seem to point to misguided child-rearing practices as a potentially important contributor to obesity. But could child-rearing practices be responsible for adult obesity? Most adults become overweight well after they reach adulthood. People typically gain weight gradually, over decades, with the average American gaining only one to two pounds per year. While child-rearing practices may matter, they probably only contribute to a very small fraction of the obesity epidemic.

Another concept closely related to self-control is "executive functioning," also called "executive capacity," which represents our ability to make wise choices. These terms are largely used in the fields of neuroscience and psychology. Executive functioning abilities develop as we mature, and they have been shown to be closely related to how much self-control we have as children.

A long-term study investigating the trajectory of self-control followed 946 twins.[9] Given that some of the twins were identical (monozygotic), meaning they shared the exact same genetic material, and the rest were fraternal (dizygotic), genetically different, it was possible for the researchers to distinguish between factors that appeared to be inherited and those that were the result of child-rearing practices.

When the twins were toddlers, at fourteen, twenty, twenty-four, and thirty-six months, they were challenged with a self-restraint test to avoid touching a glitter wand for at least thirty seconds. Later, at ages sixteen and seventeen the same twins were given a barrage of tests to study their executive functioning. Just as in the previous studies, the youth who showed more self-control as children had higher executive functioning in late adolescence.

While the researchers found that absolute levels of self-control increased with development, the children's relative abilities to restrain themselves were fairly stable over time. Because the identical twins were more similar in their capacity for self-control than the dizygotic/fraternal twins, genetics were deemed primarily responsible for self-control and executive functioning, a finding that contradicted the popular belief that the aptitude for self-control was chiefly due to training.

Many psychologists believe that within limits, the overall capacity for people to restrain themselves is a permanent, relatively irremediable trait. An individual can improve to a degree, but someone who has been born with genes associated with low self-control will never be able to develop the capacity for self-control of someone who was endowed with more favorable genes.

A long-term follow-up of ninety-two four-year-old children followed over forty years lends substantial support to the conclusion that self-control is a stable trait that doesn't change over time.[10] The study was initiated in the 1970s, when the four-year-olds participated in tests of their ability to delay gratification (by resisting a marshmallow). There are cute videos on YouTube showing how some of the kids handled the challenge.[11] Some were able to withstand the temptation by covering their eyes, while others were not so successful and surreptitiously licked the marshmallow or took tiny bites.

Later, as adults in their twenties and thirties, they were again tested on self-control abilities. Those who had lower self-control at age four also performed poorly as adults, and similarly, those with higher self-control as children performed better. Recently, nearly sixty of these ninety-two individuals, now in their forties, were called back again, and this time, they underwent brain scans as they participated in another self-control experiment.[12] A different part of the brain was activated among the group with lower self-control than among those with higher self-control, suggesting that the brains of those with high and low self-control are wired differently. This finding signifies important differences in brain functioning that may not be easily changed.

Accepting that we might not be able to substantially increase our self-control abilities may be difficult, whether or not we personally have trouble controlling our weight. Most of us don't see ourselves as limited. After all, there are so many self-help books that promise we can improve ourselves in every area of self-control—from anger management to reducing procrastination. Why would we bother to make New Year's resolutions if we didn't believe we could follow through?

When it comes to eating, we don't see ourselves as automatons being hypnotized by food cues and unable to refuse. And we have the experience of making our own decisions. We think we understand ourselves, and we have the sense that we really can control ourselves if we want to.

The capacity for self-control seems to depend on what has to be resisted. People have trouble inhibiting themselves only when they would otherwise want to engage in a particular behavior. But eating is one of those universal behaviors that is challenging to most people's capacity for self-control, regardless of how well they might score on scientific tests of executive capacity.

We typically think of self-control as an internal struggle that we have to fight within ourselves. If there is no struggle, then we don't think we are using any self-control. For some, controlling the consumption of all foods may be a challenge, while for others, only particular foods may be difficult to resist. If you dislike apple pie, then you don't have to use any self-control to prevent yourself from eating it. On the other hand, if you hate vegetables, then it would take a great deal of self-control to make yourself eat them.

Dr. Wilhelm Hofmann, an Assistant Professor of Behavioral Science at the University of Chicago, specializes in the study of self-control. He recently conducted a study to try to understand how often people have problems with self-control. He recruited 206 adults and asked them to carry a BlackBerry with them fourteen hours a day, for seven consecutive days. The BlackBerries were programmed to prompt participants to answer questions at least seven times a day about their desires, the strength of their desires, and whether they tried to resist acting on these desires.[13]

Hofmann found that, in general, the participants felt some kind of desire or want during half their waking hours. About 28 percent of the time, they said they wanted to eat. Next, about 10 percent of the time, they wanted to sleep. After that, about 9 percent of the time, they just wanted something to drink other than coffee or alcohol. Coffee was desired 3 percent of the time, and alcohol another 3 percent of the time. Not surprisingly, the participants only wanted to engage in sports or exercise 2.6 percent of the time. Thus, the desire to eat occurred more than ten times as often as the desire to exercise.

Furthermore, when people desired something, about half the time these desires came into direct conflict with other goals, values, or motivations. Maybe they wanted to sleep or relax, for example, but they were at the office and had to work. Yet when there was no feeling of conflict and they wanted to do something, such as write a thank-you note or practice playing a musical instrument, people were only able to follow through and do what they desired about 70 percent of the time. But when there was a conflict and they would have preferred not to do something, like smoke a cigarette or have a drink, they failed to control themselves, on average, one out of every six times. Self-control was worst when it came to media activities, like watching television or using the computer. About 42 percent of the time, they failed to turn off the power buttons when they knew they should have been doing something else. They failed to control their eating nearly 25 percent of the time. However, they had little trouble resisting sports participation, sexual urges, or the desire to spend money. The study also showed that within a given day, the more people tried to resist an urge, the lower their ability to control themselves as time went on.

You might be able to pass on the drinks and appetizers, and pick a healthy entrée, but when the dessert cart rolls in, all bets are off.

Self-Control Fatigues Like a Muscle

In the 1990s social psychologist Roy Baumeister and his colleagues conducted several studies on self-control. They were the first to note that self-control tends to deteriorate over time, in the same way a muscle fatigues with repeated exertion. One of their studies showed the consequence of resisting available food.

Three groups of people were asked to participate in a taste perception test. All groups were told to skip a meal before the experiment and to make sure they had not eaten for at least three hours. The laboratory room had a display of freshly baked chocolate chip cookies and chocolate candies and another display of red and white radishes. The first group was assigned to taste the cookies and candies. The second group was assigned to taste the radishes, and was specifically told not to eat any of the cookies or candies, which were meant for the first group. The participants who tasted the radishes were asked to eat at least two or three. Similarly, those assigned to the treats were asked to eat at least two or three cookies or a handful of the small candies. Both groups were asked to wait at least fifteen minutes to allow the sensory memory of the food to fade and at the same time to do an unrelated problem-solving task. A third group (the control group) did not have to wait in the room with the food displays, and was asked to work on the problem-solving task right away. The researchers then looked at how well the three groups did with the problem-solving task.[14]

The group with no food in the waiting room worked the longest in trying to solve the puzzle, an average of twenty-one minutes. The group that was allowed to eat the cookies and candy gave up after nineteen minutes, while the group that had to refuse the treats gave up after eight minutes. Why did they give up so quickly? "I was tired" and "I didn't feel like it" were the common responses. No one in the group was able to see a connection between having to use a lot of energy to resist the lure of the cookies and the rapidity with which they tired in their subsequent task.

In a similar experiment, conducted by social psychologists Kathleen Vohs and Todd Heatherton, thirty-six women considered chronic dieters were asked to watch an emotional scene from the movie *Terms of Endearment*.[15] Half were asked to control their emotions and suppress their feelings, while the other half were asked to act naturally. After the movie the subjects participated in an ice cream taste test. They were told to eat as much ice cream as they wanted. Those who had been asked to suppress their emotions ate 55 percent more ice cream than those who had been asked to act naturally. Controlling emotions appeared to deplete their ability to exercise self-control immediately afterward, and they ended up gorging on the ice cream.

Several studies have even suggested that people who attempt to diet run the risk of getting even fatter over the long run. Another twin study—one following Finnish twins over twenty-five years—convincingly demonstrated this unintended consequence.[16] Researchers followed 4,129 individual twins, most of whom were born from 1975 to 1979. The twins who made a concerted effort to lose at least ten pounds ran a greater risk of becoming overweight. By comparing the weight differences between monozygotic and dizygotic twins, one of whom tried to lose weight while the other didn't (comparing the genetic factors versus nongenetic factors), they found that although a large part of the weight gain appeared to be genetic, a smaller portion was attributable to dieting itself.

In today's world, dieting and its many demands are beyond the capacity of most. It is not just hard manual labor that tires us. Decision-making, thinking, concentrating, and exerting self-control to resist food use up our limited mental energy. Having too many options, whether it's the variety of snacks, candy bars, or breakfast cereals that take up entire aisles in supercenters, can make decisions more difficult, sometimes leading to cognitive overload and poor choices.[17] And the available options continue to multiply on a daily basis.

Our ability to make active, thoughtful decisions is a type of self-control. It fatigues, but it can be renewed after rest. When we exhaust our reserves, we typically function on "default," hardwired behaviors that automatically lead us to the "easy" choices that do not require self-control. When it comes to energy balance, our default behaviors are to eat as much as we can when food is available, and to rest as much as we can when we don't have to be physically active to obtain food.

Glucose, the sugar in our blood that supplies calories to our cells and organs, plays an important role in self-control. When we make careful, thoughtful decisions and control our impulsive behaviors, we burn glucose. Per ounce of body weight, our brain consumes more sugar than any other organ in the body. It constitutes 2 percent of body mass but consumes 20–25 percent of the body's calories.[18]

In another study of self-control, one group of sixty subjects was given a drink of lemonade made with real sugar, while another group of sixty participants was provided with lemonade made with an artificial sweetener with no calories. Afterward, half the participants in each of the two groups were asked to perform a task that required self-control, to avoid looking at distracting words on a video monitor. All 120 participants were then asked to make some choices that depended on thoughtful reasoning. Those who got the lemonade with real sugar made the best choices, and those who were served the lemonade with artificial sweetener did the worst.[19] The work required by the self-control task depleted the brain's cognitive-processing capacity, handicapping those whose blood sugar was not replenished.

Cognitive, controlled, effortful processes like those for decision-making and dealing with novel situations appear to be highly susceptible to fluctuations in glucose. The change in blood glucose is quite subtle. In a similar lemonade study the glucose level of each participant before being asked to control eye gaze and not look at distracting words was, on average, 107 mg/dL. After doing the task, the average glucose level fell to 101 mg/dL.[20] As a doctor I would say there is no clinically significant difference between those two levels of glucose, and that both represent a normally functioning pancreas and insulin response. Yet these subtle differences distinguished those with higher performances from those with lower. This phenomenon is likely to explain why children who eat breakfast do better in school than those who skip it. One study showed that the sooner children took tests after they were fed, the better they did.[21]

The irony is that the more someone tries to control herself by avoiding tempting food, the more the brain uses up the available sugar and the more difficult it is to continue to exercise self-control. The lower our blood sugar is, the more likely we are to choose foods high in sugar and fat. Any one instance of self-control is relatively easy, but it appears that continuous demands for self-control will be self-defeating.

Likewise, when shopping, we are constantly comparing and making trade-offs, since we have to choose one item over another. The number and difficulty of the choices we have to make affect how depleted and vulnerable we will become. When we make larger trade-offs, we tend to become more mentally fatigued. For instance, in one study, participants were asked to choose between two different memory sticks and then select a snack, a chocolate chip cookie or a yogurt. After making a large trade-off by choosing between a relatively cheap, low-capacity 64MB memory stick and an expensive, high-capacity 3GB one, study participants were more likely to choose a chocolate chip cookie over a yogurt than participants who were asked to choose between memory sticks that differed only slightly in price and storage capacity.[22] Yet irrespective of the magnitude of the trade-offs, the more choices we have to make in a short period of time, the more depleted we become and the more vulnerable we are to temptations.[23]

Maintaining self-control when shopping may be especially challenging for people with a low income. Dean Spears, a Princeton University PhD candidate, conducted an experiment in India in which he randomized participants to be "rich" or "poor."[24] (By American standards of income, all the participants would be considered very poor.) Those in the "rich" group could choose two of three items, which they could have for free, while those in the "poor" group could choose only one for free. Afterward, all the participants were asked to squeeze a handgrip for as long as they could—a test of self-control. The rich group significantly outlasted the poor group. Spears also had a control group in which "poor" and "rich" participants were randomly assigned to receive one or two items, but they did not get to make the choice themselves. Their performance on the self-control tests was significantly better than that of the "poor" participants who had to make the choice themselves.

For decades, economists have recognized that being poor is associated with more self-control challenges. The demands of large trade-offs and the subsequent depletion of self-control may be among the mechanisms that explain, in part, why low-income groups have higher rates of obesity. If you have only $10, for example, and what you want to buy costs $15, you have to give something up. Having to make difficult trade-offs is highly depleting, leaving individuals more vulnerable to automatic, impulsive behaviors. This difficulty has nothing to do with character or personality—it is situational.

Regardless of whether people are rich or poor, to lose a substantial amount of weight, people need to resist food multiple times per day, rule out many options, and make large trade-offs every day of the week, every week of the year, for many years. In the current environment, with temptations everywhere, the mental effort needed to lose weight is enormous.

For most, dieting will not be the answer to weight control. Dieting will be frustrating and disappointing. It's clear that the few, who seem to be able to completely change their lifestyle, lose weight, and keep it off, are pretty exceptional. If it were easy and common, we wouldn't need testimonials that a diet program worked.

A dieter's eating behavior tends to become abnormal over time, usually after some experience with successful self-control at the beginning of the effort. As dieting continues, the desire to eat may become greater, although dieters show no differences in the actual enjoyment of food compared to nondieters.[25] Dieters will usually go through periods when, instead of inhibiting their eating, they break down and eat too much, certainly more than a person who isn't dieting would eat in the same circumstance. Some dieters call the lapses in self-control "what-the-hell" reasoning—if they experience a single lapse, they may let go completely and find themselves bingeing.[26]

There are other downsides to applying self-control for weight loss. Many people who are dieting have been found to have trouble making decisions, and they tend to perform poorly on tests of executive capacity.[27] If we improve self-control in one area, we often sacrifice it in another area. That is why people who try to quit smoking often gain weight. By directing their limited capacity for self-control toward refusing cigarettes, smokers have less capacity to refuse food.[28] Similarly, if we try to control something like our emotions, we might not be able to refuse alcohol.

The physiological constraints of what our brains can handle cannot be easily altered. There are limits as to how many decisions, choices, challenges, and stresses we can actively address in one day. The advice not to sweat the small stuff allows us to marshal our limited resources for the important decisions.

When you think about it, it seems obvious that our ability to exert self-control for long periods of time is limited.[29] At some point, we can no longer hold up a weight, stay alert, or continue to move. We need to rest. We need to relax. We need a break. It takes energy to resist, to fight, and to refuse. The energy to maintain self-control has to come from somewhere, and when we use it to withstand the forces that cause us to eat too much, we deplete our energy reserves and have less energy available for other activities and tasks.[30]

And it isn't just our efforts to avoid or resist food that deplete our reserves of willpower. Controlling our emotions when interacting with demanding partners, refraining from making impulse purchases, and abstaining from sexual behavior or drug and alcohol use can all deplete our self-control and lead us to make immediate, reflexive responses that preclude self-restraint.[31] When we are depleted and have a choice between easy and difficult behaviors, we typically choose the one that is easiest and most convenient; that causes the least exertion, analysis, and work; and that provides the most immediate short-term pleasure or reward.

Could that be a doughnut or a Frappuccino?

3

The Overwhelmed Brain

As we learned in the last chapter, the limits of self-control are key factors in our poor eating habits. One reason self-control is limited is because the capacity of the brain's information-processing system is relatively minuscule.

Scientists generally agree that our brain has two operating systems: a cognitive system and a noncognitive system. The cognitive system requires conscious awareness; it is reflective and deliberate. It can perform mathematical computations, make novel decisions, and engage in long-term planning and "out-of-the-box" thinking.[1] It operates, on average, less than 5 percent of the time and is the internal resource responsible for self-control.

The other 95 percent of the time, our noncognitive system is in control. Impulsive and immediate—and following well-established rules and patterns—it is responsible for quick, automatic decision-making. The noncognitive system is often emotionally charged and responds to external signals, cues, information, signs, or symbols. When a person is under stress, tired, preoccupied, or overwhelmed with too much information, noncognitive processing dominates over thoughtful decision-making.[2] Put more simply, when we are overloaded, we tend to make decisions impulsively. And when it comes to food, impulsivity typically leads to nutritionally poor choices and what we perceive as a loss of self-control.

We can think of our brain as being engaged in a constant ebb and flow between deliberate and automatic processing. Sometimes it is more of a fight between two mismatched warriors, like David and Goliath. David represents the small, nimble, and smart cognitive force that has to face a massive, primitive, noncognitive giant that is in charge most of the time. Goliath is unflagging and never sleeps. Sometimes David can win, but it is nearly impossible for him to win all the time. David can be distracted, he can be worn down, and he needs to sleep. This is not a single battle but an eternal struggle.

Limited Processing Capacity and Food Choices

To illustrate how the cognitive and noncognitive systems interrelate, psychologists Baba Shiv and Alexander Fedorikhin developed an experiment that looked at the kind of decisions people make when their cognitive systems are occupied (also called a "cognitive load"), compared to when they have less to think about.[3] In this study 165 participants were asked to memorize either a two- or seven-digit number (the same length as a phone number without the area code). After they were shown the number briefly on an index card, they were asked to memorize it and then select a ticket for a snack, which was supposed to be a token reward for participating in the study. The participants got to choose either a piece of chocolate cake or a fruit salad. After they selected the ticket, they had to disclose the number they memorized and then complete a final questionnaire about the factors that influenced their choice of snack. Presented with the sentence "My final decision about which snack to choose was driven by . . ." they were asked to choose between "my thoughts or feelings," "my willpower or desire," "my prudent self or my impulsive self," "the rational side or the emotional side," and "my head or my heart."

Among participants who had to memorize the two-digit number, 41 percent chose the chocolate cake, while among those who memorized the seven-digit number, 63 percent chose chocolate cake, a 50 percent difference. Those who had to memorize the seven-digit number said their decision was influenced more by their emotional, impulsive side than by their rational, prudent side. The researchers concluded that the group memorizing the longer number had less available brainpower to carefully consider the items, and resorted to impulse.[4]

Given how taxed the average person is by the stresses of his or her job and family life—stresses that far exceed having to memorize a seven-digit number—our tendency to take mental shortcuts when it comes to figuring out what to eat is understandable. Is it any wonder that we sometimes choose cake over fruit? Before we do, does it cross our minds that one bite of cake might have five times the calories of a bite of fruit? Probably not.

The part of the brain that governs conscious awareness is relatively small and processes only forty to sixty bits per second, the equivalent of a short sentence.[5] The brain's entire processing capacity, however, which includes the visual system as well as the unconscious, automatic system, is estimated to process eleven million bits per second. This is faster than a sophisticated computer and about five hundred thousand times the power of our conscious awareness.

To better appreciate how small our David is compared to our Goliath, look at the grid in Figure 1. If this 50 × 50 grid represents the entire cognitive capacity of all the neurons of the human brain (Goliath), the single dark square represents an amount about two hundred times larger than the cognitive capacity of our conscious awareness (David).

Why is Goliath so large compared to David? Goliath has to direct all the minutiae of every gesture, movement, action, and reaction. Goliath gets us out of bed, moves our arms and legs just the right amount so we don't fall over, and alternates our fingers back and forth to efficiently scratch that itch on our scalp. Goliath makes sure that when we walk from the house to the car, we lift our feet just so high to ascend the correct distance from the ground. When we get in the car, Goliath ensures that we elegantly maneuver to a sitting position without bumping our head, and that we find the brake and gas pedal. Goliath is simultaneously processing all that our senses experience—the sights of the road ahead, the sounds of the freeway, the smells of the new air freshener, the aftertaste of coffee, the wind against our cheeks. As Goliath is navigating the journey, David, however, is focused on a very

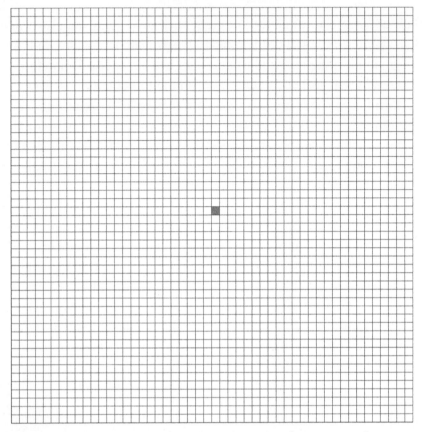

FIGURE 1. *Noncognitive processing capacity versus the capacity of conscious awareness. Because the ratio of noncognitive processing capacity to the capacity of conscious awareness is 500,000:1, the gray square represents 200× the capacity of human conscious awareness compared to the rest of the brain.*

narrow set of goals: what to get Mom for Mother's Day, which movie to see this weekend, whether Goliath automatically locked the front door, and whether David should go back home and check.

Distractions and Eating

Because our cognitive capacity is so limited, most of us can do or think about only one thing at a time. If we multitask, we can consciously direct only one of the tasks, while the other is handled automatically.

In an experiment conducted by French researchers France Bellisle and Anne-Marie Dalix, a group of forty-one healthy, normal-weight women were asked to come to the laboratory weekly for four weeks.[6]

The first week they were asked to eat a meal alone. The following week they had to eat while listening to a description of the food's tastes and textures. The third week they were asked to eat while listening to a detective story. And the fourth week they were asked to eat the meal with three other women. The meal was exactly the same each visit. The women ate the same amount at every meal except when they had to listen to the detective story. On that occasion, they ate an average of seventy-two calories more—even though they rated their levels of hunger exactly the same on all four occasions.

Listening to the detective story was the only situation in which the women's attention was directed away from their food. In the first instance, there was nothing else but the food to attend to; in the second, they were directed to focus on the sensual qualities of the food. When dining in company, they would have watched the other women and might have felt like they were being watched, possibly making them more self-conscious of what they were eating. The lesson: when we don't pay close attention to the food on our plates, it is easy to eat too much.

Memory and Eating

Although distractions can lead to overeating, the limits of our memory also contribute to eating too much. When amnesiacs with no short-term memories were offered meals in quick succession, even just one minute apart, they kept on eating and consumed full plates each time. Afterward, they reported no change in their feelings of hunger because they didn't remember that they had already eaten.[7]

In studies to test how important memory is for people without amnesia, British researcher Suzanne Higgs found that when subjects were prompted to remember their last meal, they ate less. She discovered this by having participants come to her lab for lunch at 12:30 p.m. and then again at 3 p.m. for a biscuit taste test.[8] For lunch, participants were given pizza and asked to rate it as well as their own feelings of hunger and fullness. In the afternoon, they were again asked to rate their hunger, fullness, and desire to eat. Half the group was then asked to think about the pizza they had for lunch and write down their thoughts about it, while the other half was simply asked to write down whatever thoughts they wanted. Afterward, both groups were presented with three plates full of different types of biscuits and asked to taste and rate them. After eating, the researchers measured how full the participants felt and how much they ate.

The group that did not write about the lunch ate more of the biscuits but rated their fullness, hunger, and desire to eat the same as the other group. Yet the other group consumed 21 percent less of the biscuits.

Dieting also requires a good memory because it demands that people keep track of how much they eat. But most people don't do this very well, and there are multiple reasons why. Even if we have a good memory, if we eat while multitasking, it's possible we won't remember that we ate at all. Another common barrier to keeping track of our food is that we may not know what's in the food or how much we are eating, especially if we aren't the ones preparing and serving it. And if people can't tell how much they are eating, it's no surprise that researchers also have considerable difficulty in measuring what and how much people eat.

Until now, there has been no objective way to measure what people eat other than to keep them locked up in a laboratory, measuring all the food they are served and subtracting what they leave on their plates. Outside the laboratory, when people have unlimited choices, they eat different foods in varying amounts at different times. Therefore, what a person reports eating over the course of a single day may not reflect what he or she eats over a week, a month, or a year.

Not only do researchers measuring diet have to overcome the challenge of variability; they also have to overcome inherent limitations in memory and attention. How accurately can people remember what and how much they ate over time?

To help figure out the best way to measure what and how much people eat, scientists have to be able to verify whether people are really eating what they say they are. One method to verify people's food consumption is to draw their blood and collect samples of their urine to test the concentration of various nutrients. If people really ate what they say they did, we should be able to see some of the food by-products or nutrients that were absorbed. These nutrients are called biomarkers.

In one of these investigations, the Observing Protein and Energy Nutrition (OPEN) Study, funded by the National Cancer Institute, researchers assessed how well people could remember and report what they usually eat. Almost five hundred participants were asked to fill out a food frequency questionnaire detailing exactly how often they ate a serving of each of the foods listed. Based on their responses, researchers calculated the average daily calories consumed. Beyond this questionnaire, study participants were also asked to recall what they had eaten in the previous twenty-four hours. Their reported consumption on both the food frequency questionnaire and the twenty-four-hour recall was checked against blood and urine biomarkers, which indicated the amount of protein and calories actually consumed.

Compared to what the biomarkers showed, the food frequency questionnaire suggested that both men and women underreported what they ate by more than 30 percent. This enormous calorie gap is, in part, due to the inability of the food frequency questionnaire to accurately reflect what is eaten. Nevertheless, even when reporting the foods they ate in the last twenty-four hours, which depends on short-term memory, participants still underestimated the quantity of food eaten by up to 20 percent. Given that, on average, women consumed 2,277 calories per day, their underestimates ranged from 358 calories at best to 872 calories at worst. The range of men's underestimates was even wider: from 337 calories on the twenty-four-hour recall to 1,031 on the food frequency questionnaire. These "missing" calories could easily represent an entire meal. In general, overweight individuals tended to underreport more than those of normal weight. This is probably part of the reason they are more likely to be overweight in the first place: if they cannot recognize that they are consuming too much, they cannot easily limit their intake.

Rationalizing Our Behaviors

If people were truly rational, they would act in their own best interest. While there are probably some who like being fat, most people would prefer not to be. There are also plenty of people who know eating too much will make them fat but prefer eating excessively over maintaining a normal weight. However, there is an even larger group of people who know they eat too much and would prefer to eat less so they can lower or maintain their weight.

Like many people, my father had a habit of watching television before he went to sleep at night. During commercial breaks he went to the kitchen to grab a bite to eat. There wasn't any junk food in the house—he just made himself a sandwich. Although he knew he should have skipped this snacking to control his weight, he said he felt hungry. He recognized that he did not need to eat for his survival, but the urge to snack was uncontrollable, a consequence of all the stress he faced from his job and family. Eating, he believed, helped him cope with the stress.

In hindsight, the source of his hunger was probably the sight of food advertisements or people eating on television. Current research has shown that people who spend more time watching television are more likely to be overweight or obese.[9] A school-based intervention among third and fourth graders and a home-based intervention to reduce screen time among adolescents were both found to be effective in helping the children and teens lose weight.[10] Yet twenty to thirty years ago, it was not widely appreciated how famishing food images can be. Instead, my father rationalized his behavior and joked that if he didn't overeat to cope with his stress, he might find himself doing something much more dangerous, like driving too fast, gambling, or womanizing.

When the reality of a situation is different from what we expect or desire, we often adjust our attitudes so they are more consistent with our experience. We alter our attitudes the most when we believe that we are in control or that we did something of our own volition. If we eat too much, we may believe it is because we are hungry. If we eat something that ordinarily we wouldn't like, we may begin to like it. Typically we don't remember we previously had a different opinion and don't recognize that we changed it as a result of the change in our behavior.

Cognitive dissonance is the psychological term for the situation that leads people to rationalize their behaviors. As our experience clashes with expectations, we somehow adjust (as my father did to try to explain his overeating) to reduce uncomfortable feelings and adapt our preferences. We can make these adaptations automatically, and we might not realize that our changes in preference were influenced by the situation.

Psychologist Timothy Wilson has called hidden influences "mental contamination," a process whereby people's judgments, emotions, or behaviors are influenced by mental processing that is unconscious or uncontrollable.[11] People don't realize that they are being affected. For example, although we may not admit it, our judgments of others are frequently influenced by the other person's appearance. If they are attractive, we may like them more; if they are reading, we might think they are smart. We categorize others instantaneously and make all kinds of assumptions that influence our attitudes and decisions. We often think that nothing influences us and that our opinions are our own. But we may also wrongly think we are influenced by factors that don't influence us at all.

Although we may not recognize the triggers of all the behaviors that we engage in, we tend to think that other people (but not us) are affected by outside influences. It's called the "third-person effect." You and I believe that we are completely independent and that no one else can change our viewpoints. But other people are suckers and can be taken in.[12]

Some people might be able to recognize their own behavioral triggers, if they pay close attention or if someone points them out. But most of us have a limited cognitive capacity that precludes our ability to recognize the true reasons for our choices. The fact is that most of us are influenced every day by different cues and triggers in the environment. Even when these are pointed out, we often deny that they actually influence us.

There is no easy way to keep track of what we eat, and our ability to do so is further diminished when we multitask. Activities like driving, watching TV, or talking on the phone draw our attention away from the food and beverages we are consuming. If we watch the latest episode of *Game of Thrones* while we eat, odds are we will have little memory of how much we ate.

And little differences here and there really add up. Consider this: the average individual weight gain of twenty-two pounds over the past thirty years in the United States can be explained by a person eating just an extra seven calories per day.[13] If most of us lack the brainpower to keep track of seven hundred calories per day, how can we possibly notice seven?

4

Eating Is Automatic

Imagine going to a meeting where cookies are served. It shouldn't be hard to picture; cookies are a common incentive to get people to attend meetings. As you enter the conference room, your eyes scan the room, then fixate on the plate of chocolate chip cookies on the side table next to the coffee. This is especially likely to happen if you're on a diet or if you've recently decided not to snack between meals.

You might think, "Uh-oh. Better sit far away from those cookies!" You might hope other people will eat them all, so you won't have to think about them anymore.

No such luck. Someone grabs the plate and starts to pass it around the conference table. When that temptation-laden plate stops in front of you, can you pass it on without taking one? If you do manage to resist, will you be wishing throughout the meeting that you had taken one? Can you ignore any remaining cookies on the plate and still concentrate on what's happening in the meeting? Will you go over and take one during the break?

How hard is it to say no to a cookie?

Our senses were designed to work automatically and reflexively. From an evolutionary point of view, our senses give us an edge to defend ourselves from threats from predators, as well as to alert us to opportunities such as new food sources. In every setting we visit, our eyes automatically rove our surroundings. We orient our attention to anything that moves. If we hear a loud noise, we reflexively turn to investigate its source. The smell of smoke repels us, but the sweet aroma of freshly baked bread or the smell of grilling onions will stimulate the flow of our digestive juices. After signals are picked up by any one of our senses, the messages are directly transmitted to our muscles.

We have the capacity to respond immediately and unconsciously. The signal to our muscles travels about half a second faster than it takes for the signals to reach our conscious awareness. When it comes to matters of survival—fleeing from enemies and finding food—we are designed to act first and think later. If we hesitate, we risk losing our dinner to others or, worse, becoming dinner.

The Great Behavior Debate

There is a great deal of controversy about the role of conscious awareness in behavior. Some scientists believe that all behaviors are essentially automatic and that our conscious awareness is merely an "epiphenomenon"—just a curiosity of evolution that has no causal impact on our behaviors.[1]

More than thirty years ago, Benjamin Libet, a scientist from the University of California, San Francisco, conducted a groundbreaking experiment. He invited subjects to participate in a trial that timed the sequence between an action and awareness of the action. If an action is caused by an intention, he reasoned, a person should be aware of it before engaging in it.

Libet hooked subjects up to an electroencephalogram (EEG) machine to measure brain activity (i.e., awareness) and an electromyogram (EMG) machine to measure activity in an arm muscle. He instructed participants to flex their fingers or wrist. Surprisingly, the machines showed that subjects moved their arms and fingers before there was an EEG spike to show brain activity, which, presumably, would indicate awareness. There was a half-second delay between the onset of the action and the subject's awareness of the action.[2] Figure 2 illustrates the sequence of what occurs when we perceive something in our environment and respond.[3]

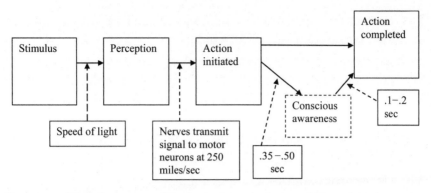

FIGURE 2. *Time Sequence of Brain Activity, Action, and Conscious Awareness*

Conscious awareness of our behavior appears to be activated *after* we begin an action in a secondary, indirect way, almost as an afterthought. Nevertheless, we usually have the feeling that our conscious intentions direct our actions.

Imagine a scene with a cat on a sidewalk, and the sidewalk is adjacent to a doughnut shop. When we observe the scene, we selectively focus on some of the elements. If the cat is moving, most people will look at the cat, because the eye gravitates toward moving images more than toward stationary ones. Yet parts of the brain outside conscious awareness will notice the doughnut shop. The brain might send a signal that could make the person looking at the cat start to feel hungry. Only after these hunger feelings start, the spectator might consciously notice the doughnut shop, but he may not realize it was the doughnut shop that caused the hunger.

A multitude of psychological experiments have also shown that our behaviors can be influenced by subliminal triggers—images too brief to enter our conscious awareness.[4] Yet we are frequently blind to behavioral triggers even when they are not subliminal.[5] Often, we simply don't recognize the factors that activate our behaviors, even when they are in plain sight. We're tricked into thinking that outside or contextual cues have nothing to do with our actions.

But as Libet's findings show, the belief that we are in complete conscious control of everything we do is wrong. It is rare when we come up with an idea first and then act on it. More often than not, it's the other way around: we act, and then try to come up with a plausible reason to explain or justify why we did it.

Even though there is a great deal of evidence suggesting that we don't consciously control much of what we do, many scientists find there is an important role for our conscious awareness. Some argue that consciousness has an integrative function: it's useful for recalling past events and connecting abstract ideas to actions.[6] Nevertheless, our everyday existence and most routine, mundane activities are dominated by nonconscious processing, a human attribute that largely explains why people find it very difficult to consistently limit how much they eat when too much food is available.

Captivated by Food

Which of these images grabs more of your attention?

Eye-tracking equipment has demonstrated that we automatically pay more attention to food images than to nonfood images.[7] Moreover, we have a greater attraction to "vice" foods that are high in fat and sugar than to healthier "virtue" foods such as fruits and vegetables.

Just how fast do we respond when food is in sight? Researchers at the California Institute of Technology conducted an experiment to find out.[8] First, participants reviewed a list of fifty snacks and candies and ranked their favorites. Then images of two randomly selected snacks from the list—for example, Kit Kats and Mars bars—were flashed side by side in front of study participants for twenty milliseconds. Participants were asked to choose their preferred snack as quickly as possible, with the knowledge that they would be given one of their choices to eat after the experiment. They spent less than one-third of a second making a decision and were able to correctly identify which snack they had ranked higher more than 50 percent of the time.

To see if participants could be even more accurate, the researchers then asked them to make sure they were certain before making their choice. Accuracy improved to 73 percent, with the average decision taking less than half a second (404 milliseconds).[9]

In a study examining shopping behaviors, Manoj Thomas and his colleagues timed how long it took 151 subjects to decide whether to buy "vice" foods compared to healthier foods. The researchers found that buying decisions were made in less than a second, and the reaction times were even quicker and more automatic for the unhealthy foods (574 milliseconds for "vice" foods compared to 619 milliseconds for "virtue" products).[10] Obviously, not much thought goes into decisions made that quickly.

Decisions about food can be so quick that no real conscious effort or direction seems to be involved. One of the preeminent researchers in the field of social psychology, Yale Professor John Bargh, refers to this kind of rapid reaction and decision-making process as "automaticity." An automatic behavior, as Bargh describes it, is any activity we engage in without conscious direction, effort, intention, or control. For something to be considered automatic, it only has to meet these criteria some of the time. For example, walking can be considered an automatic behavior. Although we may use our conscious awareness to get up and start walking, once we are walking we do not need to use our conscious awareness to direct the right foot in front of the left, then move the left foot in front of the right. We can do this automatically. This frees up our conscious awareness to pay attention to other things.

Similarly, we can eat without paying any attention to the food in front of us. Although we are watching television, reading the newspaper, talking with a friend, or even driving, we can still manage to put food in our mouths, drink, chew, and swallow. Sometimes we may not even remember what or how much we ate. We may not even recall the taste. We may only realize we are done when the food is gone. We know we have been eating, but the details, the movements of food to mouth, seem to happen on their own, without thought or deliberation. You've probably had the experience of unwittingly finishing a pint of ice cream or a bag of chips.

In addition to this kind of mindless or unconscious eating, etched into our DNA is the mantra "Eat available food," a survival imperative passed on through evolution. Just as our eyes are captivated by food, our brains are wired to respond to food by secreting a neurohormone called dopamine.[11] Dopamine is believed to be responsible for the urge to act on our desires. According to Dr. Nora Volkow, a renowned researcher on addiction and Director of the National Institute on Drug Abuse, "The message that you get when dopamine is liberated in [the brain] is that you need to get into action to achieve a certain goal. It is a powerful motivator. It is extremely hard to overcome these impulses with sheer willpower."[12]

Dopamine is intimately tied to our natural opioid system, which gives us a sense of pleasure and well-being. Dopamine secretion is also automatically triggered by novelty; something that is unusual and unique, that stands out from the average, creates cravings and desire, be it food or drug. This means we are hardwired to enjoy eating, which stands to reason from an evolutionary point of view. If we didn't have the drive to obtain food coupled with the pleasure of eating it, the human species would not have survived.

Because eating is second only to breathing as a critical survival behavior, it tends to be more automatic and more automatically stimulated than any other behavior we engage in. That's why eating is not a rational behavior. It's not an advanced cognitive behavior like studying for a test, memorizing facts, understanding and manipulating sophisticated mathematical equations, painting a portrait, or writing a book. It's a primitive one: instinctual, hardwired, and in many ways uncontrollable. The desire to eat can be easily triggered just by an image flashing as we drive by (the billboard depicting the juicy burger, the neon sign shaped like an ice cream cone), or even by sounds we associate with food (the rustle of candy wrappers, the pop of a soda can tab). Even if we have insight into these triggers, we may not be able to resist them. We can easily be influenced to eat too much.

The Triggers All Around Us

For most everyday behaviors, automaticity plays a much larger role than is generally appreciated, and cues, signs, symbols, situations—in fact, most of what goes on around us—trigger automatic behavioral responses. In the 1960s psychologist Roger Barker developed the concept of "behavioral settings," the idea that the environment guides individual behavior. He noted that two different people's behaviors are more similar in one setting than one person's behavior is in two different settings.[13] For example, when two people are sitting in a classroom at 10 a.m., they will probably behave similarly, quietly listening to the instructor. But the attentive behavior of one of those individuals at 10 a.m. in the classroom compared to the same individual's behavior at 9 p.m. in a dance hall—when she is moving around the floor vigorously, shaking her hips and arms, singing with the music—couldn't be more different. The settings we are in dictate our behaviors more than we do ourselves.

The food environment sets expectations and guides behavior based upon the availability and presentation of food. For example, nearly all people automatically eat more when they are served more.[14] This phenomenon has been proven with hundreds of people of multiple age groups and types—children, adolescents, college students, adults, thin people, and fat people—and in both laboratory settings and natural settings such as restaurants.[15] In each experiment, all the available food is first measured, then the food that remains after eating is subtracted to calculate exactly how much participants consumed.[16]

In a food consumption study of thirty four-year-olds, not only was the usual food weighing done, but researchers also counted how many bites the children took.[17] Regardless of what portion size the children were offered, they took the same number of bites during the meal. Those with the larger portions just took bigger bites, putting more food in their mouths per bite. Children given double the usual portion size of the entrée ate 25 percent more food by volume, consuming 15 percent more calories than children who got the regular-size portions. Children were not aware that the portion size had been increased, and they did not compensate for eating more of the entrée by eating less of the accompanying foods.

The researchers did a follow-up study on decreasing portions: if they reduced the calories in the meal, would the children eat more to compensate? They reduced the amount of pasta in an entrée and added more pureed cauliflower and broccoli. The kids ate more vegetables and did not compensate by eating more of the other foods. And 79 percent of the children said the lower-calorie entrée tasted better![18]

Adults, too, tend to eat in proportion to what they are served. David Levitsky and Trisha Youn from Cornell University recruited thirteen college students for a study to see what would happen when the students were served more food than they usually ate.[19] First, they asked the students to help themselves to a buffet lunch of soup, pasta, bread, and ice cream on a Monday, Wednesday, and Friday. Researchers weighed the lunches and determined what the typical average portion size would be. The following week, they fed one group exactly the same amount as the self-served portions, the second group 25 percent more, and the third group 50 percent more. No surprise: the groups served the most ate the most.

When seventy-five adults were offered six-inch, eight-inch, ten-inch, and twelve-inch sandwiches in another study, they also ate more when served the larger sizes.[20] However, even though people served the twelve-inch sandwiches ate the most, there was no difference afterward as to how they rated how hungry or full they felt compared to those who ate the eight- and ten-inch sandwiches. In addition, when asked to rate how large their sandwich was, the women eating the ten-inch sandwiches rated the size the same as did the women eating the twelve-inch sandwiches. Misperceiving the size of food is quite common.

Dr. Barbara Rolls of Penn State University, one of the most prominent researchers in the area of portion sizes and weight control, wanted to see how long people would sustain eating larger portion sizes. She had twenty-three participants come to her laboratory to eat all their food for eleven days in a row, not once but twice, for a total of twenty-two days.[21] During one of the eleven-day sessions, she served standard portions of food. During the other eleven-day session, she served the participants 50 percent more of everything.

Previous studies had suggested that after a couple of days, people would naturally begin to compensate and eat less. But no such compensation was seen. For eleven days in a row, the participants ate an average of 423 more calories per day when they were served larger portions.

What is most surprising about this series of studies was participants' consistent lack of insight and awareness of portion sizes. In one study comparing how much people ate when they were served four different portion sizes of macaroni, more than half of the fifty-one participants didn't even notice that the portion sizes were different.[22] Nor did they experience different degrees of hunger and satiety from eating different-sized portions.

Larger Portions = Larger People

Many of us are aware that the portion sizes served in restaurants have increased over the past thirty years and that bulk packaging of the foods in warehouse supermarkets has become larger. There is no doubt that the increased portion sizes bear responsibility for a significant part of the obesity epidemic.

Also, as our society has grown more affluent, families are eating out more often: today nearly half of our food dollars are spent on meals away from home. What do we get now from a restaurant that we wouldn't have gotten thirty or more years ago? In 1955, a McDonald's burger weighed 1.6 ounces. Today, the burgers come in four sizes, with the larger ones being four ounces (quarter-pound) or eight ounces (half-pound). At a sit-down restaurant like Howard Johnson's, a burger in the 1970s weighed 3.5 ounces. Today it weighs either five ounces or eight ounces.

When sodas were introduced in 1916, the volume was 6.5 ounces per single serving. Now sodas are typically served in no less than twelve-ounce sizes, but sixteen-, twenty-, and even thirty-four-ounce sizes are intended as single servings. Size inflation occurs not just with fast food; it also affects items like bagels, muffins, cookies, steaks, pasta, and pizza.[23]

In 1986, a study measured the portion sizes of breakfast, lunch, and dinner foods that college students selected from a buffet. When the study was repeated twenty years later, college students served themselves considerably more cereal, more milk on the cereal, more orange juice and fruit salad, but less tossed salad.[24] Size inflation has changed the judgment of portion norms.

With the increase in portion sizes since the 1970s, the typical restaurant meal now provides significantly more calories than are needed.[25] Although fast food restaurants are commonly blamed for contributing to obesity, sit-down restaurants may be even more guilty. Before the 2011 California state mandate to label calories, the Spicy Buffalo Chicken Melt at Denny's had 930 calories, and the Fabulous French Toast Platter had 1,261 calories. At Applebee's, the Crispy Orange Skillet with rice, veggies, and noodles had 1,706 calories, and the Southwest Philly Roll-up with sour cream, salsa, and fries had 2,231 calories.

At sit-down restaurants, too, we may be more likely to order desserts, an important source of excess calories with almost no nutritional benefits (Applebee's Blue Ribbon Brownie has 1,600 calories). With calorie menu labeling, many outlets have modestly reduced the number of calories per serving.[26] But with unlimited free refills of high-calorie items like sodas, taco chips, bread, rolls, and butter, we still get far more calories than we need in most casual dining venues.

And More Calories per Bite

It's not just that restaurants serve larger portions today than in the past; they also use more high-calorie ingredients, like butter and oil, than most people use when they cook at home. Everyone knows that a pound of butter has many more calories than a pound of broccoli. That's because butter has greater energy density—the number of calories per unit of weight. The butter is more energy-dense because it is composed of fat, which has nine calories per gram. In contrast, broccoli is mostly made of water, which has zero calories per gram.

We might think the Caesar salad is a good choice, but the dressing is mostly made of fat, so the salad might even have more calories than the burger and fries. The brown rice seems healthy, but some restaurants add a lot of butter, possibly more than doubling its calories. Even if we think we know which foods to eat, we still have limited ability to judge calories, if they aren't listed and if we don't know all the ingredients that were added in the preparation.

Automatic Judgments About Size

Which Has More Water?

Determining the size and volume of the food and drinks we consume is difficult. Look at the two glasses above. Which do you think has more water?

Although most people would guess that the taller glass holds more liquid than the shorter glass, in reality, they contain the same amount. Accurate volume judgments are complicated processes that require knowing the geometric formulas for volume as well as the height, width, and depth of the container. People automatically, and often incorrectly, use the height of an object to assess the volume, even though width and depth are equally important measures.[27]

Just how much can our eyes deceive our stomachs? Priya Raghubir and Aradhna Krishna, professors in the business schools of NYU (previously at UC Berkeley) and the University of Michigan, respectively, developed a series of experiments to find out. In one study, forty people were shown twenty-seven different cylindrical containers of varied height and width, all filled with water. Some jars were short and fat. Others were tall and thin. But they all had the same volume of water inside. As expected, most participants thought that the taller cups contained more water. But when the cups were half-filled with the same volume of water and participants were asked to drink the water from both cups, most thought they drank less from the tall cup than from the shorter cup. The illusion is likely a contrast between what was expected and what was experienced.

Our incorrect perceptions about volume lead us to consume more than we think. The larger we perceive the size of a container to be, the less we think we may have consumed from it; thus, people tend to consume more from larger containers. In another experiment Raghubir and Krishna showed how this happens by giving people different-sized cups. When the participants were told to drink as much as they wanted, those with larger glasses drank more.

These researchers did another experiment to see whether people preferred larger or smaller cups. They placed different-sized glasses on a table and asked fifty-three people to choose one for a drink. Most spontaneously chose the taller cup. In a follow-up study in which participants were asked which cup they preferred, again the majority preferred the taller glass. This behavior also holds true for packaged goods at stores: people tend to choose packages that look larger, even when they contain the same amount as smaller packages.

Efforts have been made to train people to become better judges of portion sizes, but there are significant limitations to how much most people can learn and retain.[28] In particular, people have a very difficult time estimating the volume of foods that are amorphous—that is, they take the shape of the container they are in. These include foods like jam, mayonnaise, applesauce, and pudding. In one study, even after participants received intensive training, the average estimates of a container of popcorn were off by more than 60 percent, and of rice by more than 30 percent.

We don't do much better when it comes to beverages. When glasses had ice in them, even after training, people had difficulty estimating the amount of drink in the glass, unless the glass was full of ice. (In that case, the rule of thumb is that the liquid is about half of the glass's volume.)

What about estimating the size of a pizza? How much bigger are the second and third pizzas compared to the first?

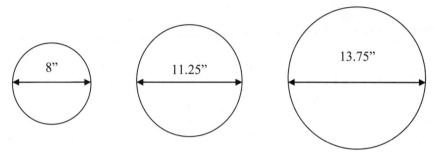

FIGURE 3. *We usually estimate size based on one dimension.*

Although most people know the formula for the area of a circle is πr^2, the calculation is neither easy nor automatic. So we don't easily grasp that the medium pizza is twice the size of the smallest and the largest pizza is three times the size of the smallest. (The pizza sizes in the illustration, from left to right, are 50, 100, and 150 square inches.)

In some studies, training in judging portion sizes either doesn't help or doesn't last. When tested again several weeks later, people didn't remember what they'd learned and made the same mistakes they'd made before. In one weight loss study of 177 people, most initially lost weight when they had meals with the correct portion sizes delivered to them for eighteen months.[29] Although they had a better understanding of portion sizes than participants whose meals weren't delivered, they ended up regaining the weight they had lost and ultimately fared no better than those without the portion training and meal delivery.

Variety Makes Us Eat More

Although portion sizes influence how much we eat, so does the variety of food available. Professor Barbara Rolls prepared three types of pasta—spaghetti, bowties, and macaroni—and studied how much subjects consumed when offered pasta of one shape compared to being offered all three shapes.[30] Each serving was prepared to have exactly the same calories and the same ingredients, so the only difference was the shape of the noodle. One group was offered three courses of spaghetti, a second group was offered three courses of bowtie noodles, a third group was offered three courses of macaroni, and a fourth group was given a different shape for each of the three courses (spaghetti, followed by bowties, followed by macaroni).

It turned out that just changing the shape of the pasta increased participants' appetites! They ate 14 percent more when offered three different shapes of pasta compared to one. And of course, the participants in the study had no idea how much they were eating, that the different shapes of the food encouraged them to eat more, or that getting only one shape made them eat less.

The same type of experiment has since been repeated with different kinds of foods and different groups of participants, all with the same result: when people have more variety, they eat more.[31]

To better understand how variety stimulates more eating, scientists have asked participants to rate food every minute they eat. As people continue to eat the same food and they get full, the sense that the food is pleasant decreases. The pleasantness of a food starts to decline within the first five minutes of eating. This is called "sensory-specific satiety."[32] However, when a different food is offered, pleasantness ratings increase for the new food. If the food differs only in flavor or appearance, people may eat only slightly more, like the 14 percent increase in the pasta study. If the food has a different texture, content, and flavor, increases in consumption have been up to 40 percent.[33]

The Role of Repetition and Novelty

Remember that knock-knock joke where the answer to "Who's there?" is "Banana," not once but at least a dozen times? Finally, the answer to "Who's there?" becomes "Orange." "Orange who?" "Orange you glad I didn't say banana again?"

The joke is an example of how people respond to boring repetition, which can apply to food as well. We would get very tired of having even the most delicious meal over and over again. When something different comes along, we're grateful for the novelty. Variety not only affects our ratings of foods' pleasantness; it also increases how much we salivate.[34]

In one study, children between the ages of nine and twelve had cotton balls placed in their mouths to measure their saliva. Then, for one minute, half of a fresh Wendy's cheeseburger was placed on a table one inch from each child's mouth, at the height of his or her lower lip. The children were asked to look at the burger, smell the burger, and think about eating the burger, but they were told they could not eat the burger. After one minute the researchers took the burger away, took out the cotton balls, and gave the kids a one-minute break. Then they put in new cotton balls; placed the burger one inch from the children's mouths again; and asked them to look at it, smell it, and think about eating it, but not to touch it. Again, after one minute the researchers removed the food and took out the cotton balls. They repeated this procedure seven times to measure the amount of saliva the cotton rolls absorbed. For the eighth time, half the group was presented with a portion of Wendy's french fries while the other half once again had to look, smell, and think about the cheeseburger. With each of the first seven trials, the amount of salivation decreased substantially. However, in the last trial, salivation among the group shown the french fries sky-rocketed to reach almost the same level measured the first time they saw the cheeseburger.*

Sensory-specific satiety, getting tired of the taste of a particular food, occurs not only because one's stomach is full but also because of habituation, which means we get so used to something that we begin to register a response sooner than we did previously, resulting in eating less. Sensory-specific satiety can develop when people simply smell a food, or chew the food over and over without swallowing.[35] In one study, participants were asked to drink as much orange juice or coffee as they wanted, until they felt full. However, half the group was first asked to rinse their mouths with the drink and not swallow it. Those who did the rinsing procedure drank less than those who did not—so

---

* When the study was over, they finally let the kids eat the burgers!

sensory-specific satiety occurs whether or not we actually eat the food. Eating the same old thing quickly reduces our motivation to continue eating. Variety delays satiation and encourages and prepares our body in many ways to continue to accept and crave food.

The attraction to food variety affects all people. In one intensive experiment, six lean and six overweight men were asked to stay in a residential laboratory for nine days.[36] During this time they were given access to five types of food (considered a low level of variety), ten types of food (a medium level of variety), or fifteen types of food (a high level of variety). All the men ate more calories when they had access to the high variety of foods. The lean men gained weight when they had a high variety of foods. The overweight men lost the most weight with the lowest variety of foods. Similarly, soldiers given "meal, ready-to-eat" (MRE) rations tend to lose weight, partly because of the monotony of eating the same foods day after day.[37]

The food industry is very aware of people's attraction to variety, and as a consequence it introduces more than ten thousand new processed food products annually into US markets.[38] These foods tend to be high in sugar and fat, so they pack a double punch, exploiting not only our natural attraction to novelty and variety but also our preferences for these energy-dense ingredients. Picture the cookie aisle in the supermarket—how many varieties of Oreos are there? The Oreo website shows forty-seven different products. You can get chocolate-covered Oreos, Oreos with purple creme, Oreos in mini sizes, or Oreos stuffed with double creme. You can even get Oreos made with organic flour and sugar.

How many different types of Pop-Tarts are in the cereal/breakfast aisle? I counted thirty-six on the manufacturer's website, including Barbie Pop-Tarts, Vanilla Milkshake Pop-Tarts, and Pop-Tarts made with whole-grain wheat and brown sugar and cinnamon-toasted with icing.

The food variety in our environment is now so great that it may actually be turning normal-weight people into dieters. It's likely that many of us find ourselves exhausted by the end of the day from just seeing all the variety and having to refuse, resist, or try to ignore it. Variety has positive consequences when it comes to fruits, vegetables, and whole grains, because we get more nutrients with fewer calories. But eating too many foods that are high in sugar and fat may lead to chronic diseases.

Other People Can Make Us Unconsciously Eat More

Remember the game Simon Says? While demonstrating the moves, the leader shouts out the commands: "Simon says, Touch your face. . . . Simon says, Touch your nose. . . . Simon says, Touch your knees. . . . Simon says, Touch your shoulders." Everyone has to do what Simon says. Players are eliminated if they mimic the leader when he doesn't preface the command with "Simon says." But the leader can also trick the players by doing different things than what he says. He might say, "Simon says touch your mouth" while touching his waist. It's surprisingly easy to imitate the action rather than follow the verbal direction.

Our ability to move our bodies and copy what we see is much faster than our ability to hear what someone says, process the information, and then act on it. Mimicking is an automatic behavior like eating. In fact, it is a normal and important part of development and growth; children learn to talk by imitating the sounds they hear. We sometimes unknowingly copy the motions and movements that we see others perform—yawning, scratching, crossing arms, and leaning.[39] So it should be no surprise that we automatically copy others' eating behaviors as well.

Several studies have demonstrated that our tendency to automatically mimic others affects how much we eat. In an ice cream taste test, participants were paired with someone they thought was another study subject but who was actually a lab assistant instructed to behave in one of two ways.[40] Half the time, the lab assistant was instructed to "spoon large quantities of ice cream into her bowl and eat rapidly and hungrily, with great enthusiasm." For the other half, the assistant was told to "spoon small quantities of ice cream into her bowl and taste it delicately and slowly." Participants were told not to pay attention to or wait for the other person to finish and that they could taste as much of the ice cream as they wanted and take as long as they needed to complete the taste test. After rating the ice creams, they also had to estimate how much they had eaten and how much their tasting partner (the lab assistant) had eaten. The experimenters then weighed the remaining ice cream and calculated how much each participant had actually consumed.

When the lab assistant ate a large amount of ice cream, the participants also ate more—almost double the amount eaten when the lab assistant ate a small portion, and 50 percent more than when participants did not have a tasting partner.

When participants were asked how much ice cream they thought they'd consumed, they were actually quite good at judging. However, when asked how much they thought the lab assistant had eaten, they said they had no idea and vehemently denied paying attention to the other person. Moreover, none of the participants thought that the other person influenced how much they ate.

We mimic other people's eating behaviors in many more situations than we realize. The more people there are at a dinner table, the more each person eats. For example, with two diners, each eats 33 percent more than if he or she ate alone; three diners typically eat 47 percent more; four, 58 percent more; and so on. With seven companions, people eat nearly double what they would have eaten alone.[41] If we have finished eating and we see another person still eating, we may unconsciously mimic the other person and take another bite. With more people at the table, we stay longer and we eat more.

Our mimicking tendency goes beyond simple unconscious imitation—it can even change our preferences.[42] In one experiment conducted at Duke University, 147 students were asked to participate in a study about advertisements and memory. However, the real purpose was to study mimicry and awareness of mimicry. Three days before the study, the students were asked to fill out a questionnaire regarding which snack they liked the best. At the time of the study, the students and the experimenter, who was shown on a videotape, both had two bowls of snacks in front of them: one filled with animal crackers and the other filled with goldfish snack crackers. The experimenter told the students they could help themselves to the snacks at any point. With half of the students, every ten to twenty seconds, the experimenter would eat an animal cracker. With the remaining half, he would eat the goldfish. The researchers videotaped the students and later counted how much of each snack the participants ate. Afterward, the students were again asked to complete a questionnaire that included answering which snacks they liked best.

Not only were the students more likely to eat the same snacks as the experimenter, but they also reported liking the snack they ate more than the one they didn't. They claimed they had always preferred that specific snack, yet when the researchers compared the snack preferences the students had listed three days before with those chosen during the experiment, they did not always match.

In another Duke University study, instead of seeing whether participants unconsciously mimicked the experimenter, the experimenter purposely mimicked the participants and then observed whether mimicking influenced how much the participants ate.[43] What they found was astonishing.

The participants were told that the study was about impression formation and how new products might be perceived. The researchers said they were testing a new drink called Vigor and that the participants would get an opportunity to taste and rate the drink at the end of the study. There was a highly scripted interaction in which participants were asked their opinions about drinks and, in particular, sports drinks. For half of the group, the experimenter mimicked the participants, copying their mannerisms such as posture, leg crossing, arm and hand movements, and face and hair touching. In addition, after a question was asked, the experimenter would repeat the participant's answer verbatim. In contrast, for the other half of the group, the experimenter "anti-mimicked" the participants: if the participant slouched, the experimenter stood straight; if the participant crossed her legs, the experimenter kept both feet on the floor. And instead of repeating participants' answers verbatim, the experimenter said something like, "OK, I got your views on that one."

Mimicking made a significant difference in the participants' preferences and responses to the drink. Not only did they report enjoying the drink more when they were mimicked, they also drank nearly 60 percent more. They also said they would be more likely to buy Vigor and were more likely to think that the marketing would be successful. Moreover, the participants were completely unaware that they were being mimicked, and of course they had no clue that this could have influenced their rating of the drink or how much they drank.

Mimicry may even play a role in immigrants' assimilation in their adopted countries. The longer immigrants stay in a new country, the more their health patterns and diseases become like those of their adopted country. If the changes don't happen in the first generation of immigrants, they most certainly occur in the second generation. For example, when Asians move to America, they typically gain weight and eat differently from their families in places like Japan and China.

As I was growing up, the food served in my house was always plain and bland. My mother never added spices, except sometimes on hot summer days. She thought that salting our food would prevent us from becoming dehydrated in the sun. Until I left home for college, I had never tasted any food that was peppery or pungent.

You can imagine the difficulty I faced when, during college, I spent a year in India, in a city far from the main tourist spots catering to Western tastes. My first experience of Indian food was quite an unpleasant shock. I could not tolerate any of the hot spices, and many of the other flavors seemed strange and disagreeable. The savory pickles seemed foul, and many of the vegetables and curries looked plain nasty. At first, all I could eat were yogurt and rice. But yogurt and rice weren't going to sustain me for an entire year. So I kept trying the foods in small quantities. Gradually, I learned to appreciate the exotic flavors and hot spices. By the time I left India, I couldn't remember what had tasted so terrible. I came to like Indian food so much that today I choose it over American food at every opportunity.

I learned to like the food that was available to eat. All people have this ability to one degree or another. Part of this is related to mimicry, in that we sometimes automatically and other times intentionally act to fit in. We adapt—and being able to do so is a matter of survival. We will usually adjust to whatever situation we face, and we will most likely come to satisfactory terms and accommodations, if not actual happiness about it. In fact, for most of us, it may be harder to maintain dissatisfaction with our circumstances than to gradually adjust and accept them, especially when we believe we have no other choice. We have a natural ability to make the best of our reality. When the conditions around us change, most of us assimilate.

In 1957, Vance Packard wrote *The Hidden Persuaders,* in which he warned of the techniques advertisers were using to create demand for products. He described what seemed to be advertisers' ability to influence people's preferences and behaviors in a way that was below their capacity to recognize. At that time, the evidence was anecdotal, and there were no controlled studies that allowed us to identify the magnitude of the impact of marketing techniques on individual behavior. But now there are hundreds of studies that document how simple changes in the design, content, format, and layout of stores, displays, advertisements, packaging, and images make significant differences in how people automatically respond. Those in the food industry, as in other industries, have applied these techniques to their products and sales campaigns. They have increased the frequency and location of messages about food and dramatically altered food accessibility, availability, and variety. Most of the time, we just don't notice. We simply adapt.

We don't go through life with access to a master plan revealing how our environment has been arranged and rearranged so that it constantly guides our perceptions and actions. When it comes to shopping wisely at a supermarket or eating healthfully at a restaurant, we are handicapped by our built-in responses and tendencies. If we want to lose a few pounds, we might know that we really don't want to eat cookies from a plate that's in arm's reach. But when we find ourselves eating them, we have no explanation other than to blame our imagined lack of willpower. We might believe that we consciously and willfully make these and other choices of our own volition. But science shows we may not be in control of all our behaviors.

Our limited self-control, our bounded ability to perceive our environment and to recognize behavioral triggers, and our hard-wired drive to eat more than we need are the immutable human factors that underlie our poor dietary behaviors.

There is now a mismatch between our evolutionary roots and our contemporary food environment. Far from ensuring our survival, our instincts—designed to function in a less toxic food environment—now threaten our well-being as they compel us to take advantage of the cheap calories that surround us.

PART II

The Food Environment

5

Abundant and Cheap

In the late 1970s, just before the obesity epidemic started to accelerate, I was attending medical school at the University of Pennsylvania. I lived off campus and either walked or rode my bike to school every day. I typically had breakfast at home, packed a lunch, and made dinner for myself at home. There weren't many places to eat on campus—a few dining halls with limited hours for students on meal plans—and only a few small greasy-spoon restaurants nearby. On my way home, I passed a coffee shop, a deli, and a pizza place; there were no fast food chains within walking distance. There was a supermarket across the street from my apartment, and although it closed at 7 every night, stayed open for only half the day on Saturday, and was closed on Sunday, I never went hungry. When I graduated in 1981, my weight was the same as it had been when I entered medical school.

In the summer of 2008—twenty-seven years later—I strolled through campus for the first time since I graduated. The difference was astounding. Now, on the same walk from the center of campus to my old apartment, there is an abundance of food outlets and cafes. The University of Pennsylvania boasts sixty-one places to eat within walking distance of campus. More than a dozen food outlets are housed within classroom buildings on campus. There's even a coffee shop in the school's main library. (This would have been a sacrilege during my college days, given the strict no-food policy in university libraries.) More than that, now there's a Chick-fil-A, Subway, Jamba Juice, Top This (a burger and fries outlet), and Starbucks on Locust Walk, the main pedestrian thoroughfare crossing university grounds. Students who live on campus and use the meal plan have the option of spending their dining dollars at these places as well as at a Savory restaurant, Einstein Bros. Bagels, a C3 convenience store, and five different dining halls. There's a new building in the Wharton School with an Au Bon Pain on the first floor and a cafe for MBAs on the second.

Campus dining services also feature what they call "fresh air food plazas," which allow food trucks and carts on or adjacent to campus. According to the university's website, at the corner of Thirty-Seventh and Walnut Streets there are Bento Box Japanese Foods, a Quaker Shaker Lunch Truck, Ali Baba, George's Super Lunch, Kim's Oriental Foods, Indian Foods, Trong's Fresh Fruit Salad, and Pamela & Andreas Crepes Cart. The website boasts that "vending activity around the Penn campus has exploded to include more than 90 trucks, carts, and tables selling various foods and other products. And vendors, responding to the Penn community's appetite for inexpensive, convenient foods, are currently doing an estimated $12 million in annual business according to a recent study."

If the vending trucks don't satisfy students' appetites, perhaps Insomnia Cookies will do the trick. Started by Penn undergrads in 2003, the company serves a wide variety of cookies to hungry undergrads at fifteen other campuses. Available from 8 p.m. to 2 a.m., the cookies can be ordered online and delivered to students' dorm rooms. According to its website, "Insomnia Cookies was born out of our dislike of heavy meals late at night, our love of food delivery, and our realization that by the time we got hungry at night, nothing was open." With varieties including Sugar, Chocolate Chunk, Peanut Butter Cup, White Chocolate Macadamia, Oatmeal Raisin, M&M, Double Chocolate Chunk, and Ménage à Trois (a cookie with three flavors), the cookies are hardly a light, nutritious alternative to the greasy fare available elsewhere.

With the cookies, the convenient fast food places and cafes, and the open-air plaza of food trucks and vendors—not to mention the all-you-can-eat buffets at the university's multiple dining halls—should we be surprised that college students today gain three to ten pounds in their first year away from home?[1]

The dramatic changes in the food environment at my alma mater mirror the thirty-year transformation of the American food environment as a whole, and I strongly believe that these changes are the direct cause of the obesity epidemic. In this short period of time, three important things have happened: the relative price of food has declined, especially for high-calorie foods filled with fat and sugar; food has become increasingly accessible; and cues to eat are more salient as advertising has become increasingly sophisticated and ubiquitous. Together, these three changes have made it possible for people to eat as much as they can, whether or not they intend to do so.

Lower Relative Prices

The major accomplishment of the Green Revolution, the wide-sweeping technological transformation of agriculture since 1945, was to increase the productivity of cereals, rice, wheat, and maize, staples for much of the world.[2] Improvements in plant breeding, the creation of genetically modified plants resistant to pests, as well as new cultivation techniques and better fertilizers, improved crop yields substantially. Before the Green Revolution the maximum yield potential of rice was four tons per hectare. After improving the variety and adding fertilizer, the yield went up to ten tons per hectare. In addition, the growth duration was reduced from 150–180 days to 110 days, making it possible to plant two cycles of crops rather than just one in a year. Yield was also improved by developing disease-resistant varieties that could tolerate problems with soils, temperatures, and insects. The increase in rice production has resulted in a decrease in cost; on average, people are paying 40 percent less (adjusted for inflation) for rice now than they did in the mid-1960s.[3] The consequence? The Green Revolution has saved millions of lives across the globe.

In the United States, technological advances in food processing lowered the cost of transforming cheaper corn, potatoes, and wheat into snacks like chips and pastries. Improvements in food chemistry and packaging made it possible to maintain crispness and taste for months after preparation, increasing the shelf life of snack foods.

The downside, however, is that the increase in food availability has made overeating affordable to most of us. Consider the facts: in the 1920s, the average American family spent 25 percent of its income on food. In 2011, we spent only 9.8 percent.[4] And because we spend relatively less on food, more people can afford the convenience of having others cook it for us. In 1966, 24 percent of total food expenses went toward food prepared away from home; in 2011 that number was 49 percent.[5] And even though we are spending less of our overall budget on food, we are consuming more calories. According to Dr. Barry Popkin, Professor of Nutrition at the University of North Carolina, in 1977–1978 the average American consumed 1,803 calories per day. From 2003 to 2006 we ate 2,374 calories per day, a daily increase of 571 calories.

Still, a common refrain many of us hear is that healthy food is too expensive. Dr. Adam Drewnowski of the University of Washington points to the relatively high prices of fruits, vegetables, and lean meats compared to the cheap prices of foods like hot dogs, sodas, and other fast foods as the reason people with low incomes tend to have higher rates of obesity than do wealthier individuals.[6] Yet if high costs were the main problem rather than hardwired automatic behaviors and environmental triggers that interfere with self-control, people with limited resources could save money by eating less. To the contrary, the problem is that we can afford to eat too many calories—and are often incapable of resisting the opportunity.

Yet if only the cost of the ingredients is considered, it is still cheaper to eat at home than to go to a fast food restaurant, especially for a family with many mouths to feed. To save money, one must purchase quantities larger than needed for one person, and items have to be prepared from scratch. But with a freezer and refrigerator, nothing should go to waste. Although we commonly hear that it is cheaper to eat fast food than to cook at home, going out is about convenience and/or the desire to be taken care of, not price.

The following table itemizes the cost of a fast food meal and compares it to the cost of a similar home-prepared meal. The home-cooked meal is both healthier and cheaper.

Dinner Out			Dinner at Home		
Item	McDonald's*		Item	Supermarket Cost	Single-Serving Cost
Hamburger (regular) Hamburger (1/4 lb.) Cheeseburger (Dollar menu)	$2.69 $3.69 $1.00		Turkey burger on whole-wheat bun	Ground turkey, $2.69/lb. (5–8 servings); Whole-wheat buns, $3 for 8	34–54 cents (2–3 oz.) (Costco) 38 cents (Von's)
Fries (small)	$1.29		Baked potato	$3.89/10 lbs. (enough for 25 servings)	16 cents/0.4 lbs. (1 medium potato)
Soda (small)	$1.29		Milk	$2.99/gallon (16 servings)	19 cents
Total (lowest possible for burger, fries, and soda)	$3.58		Total		$1.07–$1.27
Meal Combo	$5.79				

* Price on Oct. 6, 2012, at McDonald's in Wal-Mart, Riverside, CA

FIGURE 4. *The Cost of Fast Food vs. a Similar Meal at Home*

My RAND colleague Jill Luoto, an economist, argues that this is an unfair comparison, because I haven't accounted for the time it takes to prepare the food—and time is money. But I would argue back that it takes me more time to go out to eat than to prepare food at home. To go out, I have to either walk at least fifteen minutes to get to a fast food outlet or restaurant or get in a car, navigate through traffic, find parking or wait in a drive-through line to be served, place my order, wait for it to be prepared and served, pay the bill, and then retrace my steps to get back home. Not including ordering, waiting for the food, and eating, the round-trip transportation alone takes at least thirty minutes—as long as or longer than it would take me to put a burger in a pan, a potato in the microwave or oven, cook, and even clean the pan afterward and put the dishes in the dishwasher.

What about the time it takes to shop for the food? Considering that it is possible to buy in bulk and store food in the refrigerator or freezer, and that the haul from an hour's shopping can provide meals for a week or two, shopping time does not add much to the calculation, maybe two to three minutes per meal.

So why do fewer people cook at home than they did thirty years ago? It's because the costs to eat out are not that high. If we couldn't afford to eat out, we would make the effort to master cooking at home.

Greater Accessibility of Food

Along with the real decrease in food cost, in the 1980s the amount of calories available per person increased by about 15 percent compared to 1970, with a disproportionate increase in grain-based foods (per capita carbohydrate availability increased by 27 percent).[7]

Although a common belief is that agricultural subsidies are responsible for the low price of ingredients used in grain-based snack foods, processed foods, and drinks with added sugars, like high-fructose corn syrup, there is little hard evidence to support that. In fact, the reason that crop subsidies were introduced in the first place was to keep the cost of grains high, rather than make them cheap. When farmers had a bumper crop and there was abundant grain to sell, the price kept going down, so a crop ended up costing the farmers more to grow than they could sell it for.[8] Government subsidies persuaded many farmers to grow less so the market would not be flooded with grain, keeping the price at a level where farmers wouldn't go bankrupt.

Although the economics of farming have changed substantially since subsidies were first introduced, recent analyses suggest that even if subsidies were removed, the change in the price of commodities might have an impact of less than 0.5 percent in the average calories consumed.[9] This is because the cost of the products sold has little to do with the cost of the raw ingredients—often packaging, marketing, and labor cost many times more than the ingredients. It has also been argued that removing all subsidies, including barriers to imports of sugar and dairy products, might lead to greater levels of food consumption, as people might shift to foods that have even higher calories than what they consume now.[10]

In my view, the most important force behind the increase in consumption of calories and nutrients like carbohydrates is the aggressive nature of the food industry and its highly forceful snack sector.

When I was a child in the early 1960s, my family seldom had snack foods in the house. Only on special occasions, like for birthday parties or entertaining, did foods like soda or potato chips appear. One of my earliest memories of our local grocery store, the A&P, was when my mother sent me there to buy a bag of potato chips to serve company she was expecting. I loved being asked to do these types of errands, because my mom would give me some money and I could show off my newly gained arithmetic skills at the register, figuring out exactly what the change would be before the cashier did. I remember skipping to the store and looking up and down all the aisles trying to find the potato chips. I didn't know where they were, because this was not an item we usually bought.

Finally, I asked the store manager where they were. He led me to the back of the store and pointed to the last aisle. There, on the bottom shelf, were a few bags of Wise potato chips. Not too many people bought them, so they were not in the most convenient spot.

Those days are long gone, and making appealing, crunchy snack foods highly visible and accessible is now the name of the game. Indeed, companies pay substantial "slotting fees" or "trade promotion fees" to ensure that their goods are front and center, on special floor displays, or at the end of an aisle where people can notice them right away. Not only have snack foods gained increasing prominence in supermarkets, but they are almost everywhere we go.

Moreover, a large percentage of retail outlets that do not sell food as their primary business now have food available as "impulse buys" at the cash register, as an add-on to their other merchandise, or in vending machines. The types of food sold in nonfood establishments like gas stations, hardware stores, bookstores, car washes, office buildings, and clothing stores are largely cookies, candies, chips, and sodas.

Today, larger supermarkets and warehouse stores are becoming more prevalent. Just twenty years ago, nearly 90 percent of purchases of food for the home were made in traditional grocery stores. Today, grocery store purchases account for 69 percent of at-home food purchases, and 21 percent are obtained from nontraditional food stores like Costco, Target, and Wal-Mart, where people can buy more food in bulk quantities.[11]

Despite all the new types of outlets and the changes in products, packaging, and access, the quality of the American diet has not improved over the past thirty years.[12]

Increasing Cues to Eat

As obesity has climbed over the past thirty years, the time devoted to television commercials has also grown considerably, while the length of the typical commercial has shrunk. The typical ad length has decreased from sixty to fifteen seconds. Recently, with more people using ad-skipping technology like TiVo, ads are being made as short as five seconds, so people using the ad-skipping device will still see the five-second spot when they bounce back to the program.

This means that we are being exposed to more products and more information packed into smaller amounts of time. As we are asked to absorb more, our cognitive systems may become overwhelmed, leading us to process more information with our noncognitive system. Thus, we may be reacting more automatically and less deliberately, without understanding why.

Beyond the different manipulations of commercial time, advertisers are increasingly using "product placements," integrating a particular branded product into television programs and movies, for example, by having the actors drinking Coke, like the judges on *American Idol*. A watershed moment in the use of product placement in American cinema was Steven Spielberg's use of Reese's Pieces as a prop in the movie *E.T.*—which gave the candies a 65 percent spike in sales.

Advertisers have increasingly targeted children, who now view about sixty-five messages from television advertising each day (about half are for food), along with many additional marketing messages from websites and in retail stores.[13] In 2005, the National Academies' Institute of Medicine found that food advertising affects children's food choices, food purchase requests, diets, and health.[14]

In a study of children's exposure to food advertising, Sarah Speers and colleagues from Yale's Rudd Center, an institute devoted to reversing the global spread of obesity, analyzed Nielsen data on television programming in 2008.[15] Food, beverage, and restaurant brands appeared a total of thirty-five thousand times within primetime. Regular soft drinks, traditional restaurants (i.e., not quick-serve), and energy/sports drinks made up 60 percent of all brand appearances. Coca-Cola products were seen 198 times by the average child and 269 times by the average adolescent during primetime shows over the year, accounting for 70 percent of child exposure and 61 percent of adolescent exposure to brand appearances, with *American Idol* accounting for more than 95 percent of these exposures.

Unhealthy food ads are also targeted more heavily toward minorities. Researchers compared the number of food-related commercials shown on primetime shows with African American characters to those on primetime shows with predominantly white characters.[16] Not only did the shows targeting African Americans air 66 percent more commercials about food (4.8 spots for a thirty-minute show versus 2.9 ads for white audiences), but 30 percent of the food commercials for African Americans were about candy and chocolate versus only 14 percent for white audiences; 13 percent advertised soda during primetime targeting blacks versus only 2 percent for shows targeting white audiences.[17]

Overall, the food industry spent a staggering $9.65 billion on food advertising in 2009, and nearly $1.8 billion of that was directed at children and teens.[18] Over the past decade, companies have moved beyond traditional media and product placements and are increasingly shifting their advertising dollars to the Internet, digital marketing, advergames, advertising on video games and movie DVDs, cellphone and other mobile media, and word-of-mouth viral marketing.[19] Internet and mobile media can attract substantial audiences. In one month alone, McDonald's websites saw seven hundred thousand visitors, half of whom were under twelve. Cereal manufacturers like Kellogg's have smartphone apps for their products; General Mills offers kids virtual adventures starring Lucky the Leprechaun, with 227,000 visitors per month.[20]

Everyone can recognize changes in food prices, increased food accessibility, and increased food advertising, but many fail to see the connection between these changes and why we are eating too much. These changes didn't happen by accident, nor were they developed as a plot or conspiracy to make people fat. They are only about increasing profits.

The profit motive has infected even nonprofit and public institutions like hospitals, schools, colleges, universities, and our military—all presumably concerned about the health and well-being of their clients, enrollees, and personnel. Because they get a percentage of sales when their captive audiences eat too much in company cafeterias or buy junk foods from on-site vending machines, these nonprofit institutions may be undermining the very people they want to help.

The food industry is not putting a gun to our heads to make us eat too much. It doesn't have to. It is simply taking advantage of our natural interest in food and our innate instincts to survive.

6

A Food Desert? Try a Swamp

Last fall, while speaking to a group of community leaders on the South Side of Chicago, Michelle Obama said, "In so many neighborhoods, if people want to buy a head of lettuce or salad or some fruit for their kid's lunch, they have to take two or three buses, maybe pay for a taxicab, in order to do it." As part of her anti-obesity campaign, Mrs. Obama was highlighting the much-trumpeted relationship between obesity and "food deserts"—communities or neighborhoods where healthy food is unavailable or prohibitively expensive.

Through the Healthy Food Financing Initiative, $400 million will be spent to bring grocery stores and other healthy food retailers to underresourced urban and rural communities across America where people live more than a mile from a supermarket and do not have access to a vehicle.[1] The goal is to eliminate such food deserts within a seven-year period. Although a variety of solutions have been proposed, from farmers' markets to street vendors, the one that has grabbed the popular imagination is to put large, full-service supermarkets in every neighborhood lacking one.

Supermarkets are considered places that provide the breadth and depth of options that people need to stay healthy, including large assortments of fresh fruits and vegetables. Moreover, a variety of studies have found a strong correlation between distance to a supermarket and the prevalence of obesity.

Yet this correlation does not explain why 67 percent of Americans are overweight or obese, since only 4.1 percent of Americans live in food deserts.[2] In my view, the problem is less about access to healthy food than it is about being inundated with too much unhealthy food.

In most communities, we can count on finding food 24/7. We all live in a food swamp. I use that term not only to refer to the proliferation of food outlets and the growth of big-box stores featuring bulk packaging, like Sam's Club and Costco, but also to describe how outlets market their wares.

For example, take Kroger's Food 4 Less, a large chain of 145 "price impact" warehouse stores in four US states, mostly concentrated in California. Although Food 4 Less has a substantial section of very reasonably priced fresh fruits and vegetables, much of the store is filled with aisles of junk food and prepared foods with too much salt, sugar, and fat. Right at the entrance one must run a gauntlet of cases and cases of juices, Chips Ahoy cookies, Coca-Cola, Sprite, Sunkist orange soda, Squirt, and 7Up stacked high on either side of the aisle, and guess what? They are always on sale. Three for $10. Four for $11. Fifty-count snack packs of thick and hearty tortilla chips for $10.98. A special floor display of Hostess Zingers at two for $5 dead-center in the middle of the pathway. "Save on Big Packs" is plastered on all the shelves, right over the deal on a twenty-four-pack of Instant Lunch noodles for $6.98.

As you move through the store, the end aisle displays contain more Coca-Cola and Chips Ahoy, along with Cup Noodles, BBQ chips, doughnuts, Cap'n Crunch, Pepsi, Orange Crush, Mountain Dew, and Doritos, not to mention aisles devoted exclusively to even more chips and sodas. In the front of the store, before you approach the area for checkout, there are special displays of M&M's, single-serving packages of pastries, Reese's candies, and Nestlé Crunch bars. And if your diet goals weren't already hijacked, there is an extensive display of candy bars and smaller bags of chips right next to the cash register, at about eye level for a seven-year-old.

Today, the real estate in most supermarkets may be largely controlled by vendors who pay to have their goods displayed in specific cases in particular locations, like end aisle and floor displays or at the cash register. That's because people are automatically attracted to special displays, and when they are, they buy more of the products. Research shows there is something about the arrangement of the goods and the way end aisle displays stand out that people cannot ignore. The effect is so powerful that an estimated 30 percent of all store sales are from these end aisle displays.[3] In fact, supermarkets now make more money selling their shelf space to vendors than they do selling their products to customers. Although the emphasis on "junk food" is greater in stores that serve low-income populations than in higher-income areas, higher-end outlets simply promote more expensive "gourmet" junk food.

This kind of store placement is such a successful strategy that non-food establishments like gas stations, hardware stores, bookstores, car washes, and clothing stores—an estimated 41 percent of all retail businesses—now have junk food available at their cash registers too.[4] At Macy's you can find Godiva chocolates in the lingerie department and premium chocolate bars at the men's department cash register. One clerk informed me that the candy bars sell very well, as many people add these $3 bars onto their purchases of $40 shirts or $60 jeans.

The food industry doesn't need fancy scientific experiments to figure out that people are more likely to be tempted at the end of a shopping trip or to buy more from the end aisle displays. They can just look at their sales receipts.

Another common belief is that fast food is the primary cause of obesity. In line with that thinking, in 2008 the Los Angeles City Council passed a temporary ban on new fast food restaurants in South Central Los Angeles, a low-income area claimed to have too many fast food outlets and too few supermarkets.

To verify this claim, my colleague Dr. Roland Sturm and I studied the number of food retail outlets in Los Angeles. We counted all the food outlets based upon the total population, a per capita measure, as well as based upon the neighborhood's miles of roadway, a measure of exposure. Our thinking was that opportunities to purchase food are dependent on whether we pass by grocery stores, supermarkets, and restaurants as we go about our daily routines, rather than how many people live in a neighborhood. Looking at South Central LA in this manner, we discovered that compared to wealthier areas like the west side of LA, there were a similar number of fast food outlets but nearly double the number of convenience stores and seven times the number of small groceries, where there are usually some fresh fruits and vegetables, but where foods like chips, soda, and candy tend to dominate.

The fact is, we are very seldom in a situation where there is nothing to eat. We would have to be pretty far out in the wild, perhaps in the middle of one of our national parks. This observation is not just anecdotal: in a ten-year period, from 1986 to 1996, the number of commercial food establishments in the United States increased by 78 percent, fast food outlets by 85 percent, and restaurants and lunchrooms by 62 percent.[5] And in the past forty years, the total number of restaurants in this country has tripled.

Restaurants, including fast food outlets, have also figured out how to get their customers to buy (and eat) more than they intend, not only by serving larger portion sizes but also by altering the way they present and bundle their products. The ubiquitous combo meal is no accident: it has been finely developed and bred for success.

Kathryn Sharpe from the University of Virginia and Richard Staelin from Duke University's business school conducted a careful study to figure out why customers are so attracted to combo meals.[6] They asked 215 adults from all over America who eat at a fast food restaurant at least once a month to participate in an experiment in which they had to indicate what they would buy if they stopped at nine different fast food outlets (all serving burgers, fries, and sodas on their menus) on a cross-country trip. At each of these outlets the menu was configured in different ways. In some of the restaurants the food was bundled as a "combo" meal; in other scenarios, if you wanted all three options, you would have to order them each à la carte. On some menus, the price of the combo meal was placed right next to the price of the entrée alone, so the customers could directly compare the two choices. Drink sizes and food prices were varied.

Sharpe and Staelin found that when meals were bundled, the number of people who bought fries increased by 15 percent and people ended up with larger quantities of soda, together resulting in an average increase of 110–130 calories per meal. Bundling was effective primarily because it lowered the number of decisions customers had to make and it made them more aware of prices, especially when the format of the menu presented the à la carte price right next to the bundled price. So getting the three items for less than when purchasing each separately may have been automatically perceived as a bargain that could not be missed, even though the customers would actually be spending more than if the combo wasn't available.

"Combo meals" are only one of the many potential traps in our modern food swamp. Just like a real swamp, the food swamp can be dazzling, its vastness overwhelming, its thoroughfares tricky to navigate, its inhabitants quite dangerous.

The next chapter describes how the variety of marketing techniques may influence you without your being able to recognize it.

7

Marketing Obesity

On a blog for moms, Joyce Slaton described her horror when her young child began parroting a television commercial for Slushy Magic that claimed the machine turned drinks into slushies by using "snowflake science." This event transformed her from a person who was against limiting advertising to kids to an advocate for greater advertising controls.[1]

Although it's common to hear complaints like Slaton's about how advertisers are unfairly targeting children, who are gullible and overly trusting, the reality is that we have to be just as worried about how advertising influences adults. Children may be more vulnerable to overt advertising messages, but adults are also highly impressionable; and like children, adults are often unable to protect themselves.

We don't perceive adults as vulnerable, though, because they have well-developed cognitive abilities. We expect adults to be able to see through any glitzy subterfuge and to transcend appeals to glamour, in contrast to children, who usually cannot distinguish ads from programming until they are between ages four and eight. Nevertheless, even adults may have difficulty when the breaks between programming and the ads aren't clearly defined or when infomercials look like talk shows.

Advertising encourages impulsive behaviors, which children work on mastering from birth. As anyone with a teenager knows, during adolescence impulse control may regress and defense against advertising may be particularly difficult. At the same time, adolescence is the period when we first begin to have an understanding of complex concepts. But there is a huge variation in teens' sophistication: some are able to analyze advertising mechanisms as early as twelve, while others still fail to see behind even the most superficial and transparent advertisements at eighteen.

What about adults? Our greatest vulnerability to advertising, regardless of age or development, is through our noncognitive processing, when we impulsively react to superficial appearances, gestures, and sounds, and fail to analyze the information carefully. We know that automatic responses to images, like brands and symbols, begin as early as age two. One study showed that children ages three to five, not old enough to read, recognized and understood the significance of brands and characters like Ronald McDonald.[2] Both children and adults respond automatically to colors, variety, size, logos, and icons. Yet children may not respond as strongly as adults to symbols or brands because they are less exposed. Their lack of experience is a barrier that can initially protect them from advertising. But it is just a matter of time until they are sufficiently exposed and the brands become meaningful.

The ability to override automatic responses begins during the teen years. Despite having the theoretical capacity to inhibit noncognitive processing, teens and adults seldom do. Moreover, as discussed in Part I, everyone's ability to make cognitive rather than automatic decisions is constrained by other demands on attention.

Increasingly, marketers develop advertisements that can get under our skins by capitalizing on noncognitive, automatic processing. One way they can learn how to do this is by using advanced technology—like eye-tracking equipment. As a website from a company that offers eye-tracking services claims,

> When the consumer is ready to buy, it is the package that sells the product, setting it apart from the competition. Our company offers testing of live package and shelf displays or simulations. Proprietary software developed by our company allows users to view a simulated shelf display, select a package off the shelf and rotate it to view all sides. Analyses

include how the consumer scans the shelf, what packages are noticed, when and for how long, and how the target package is viewed.

Eye tracking is a particularly useful tool when it comes to developing ads, logos, packaging, and other aspects of presentation, such as the color and designs on a can of soda or a package of chips—products that often depend on consumers' impulsive responses. Eye tracking enables advertisers to see exactly how consumers view a particular advertisement or product, whether it's a new bar of antibacterial soap, a caffeine-laden energy drink, or a gluten-free frozen pizza. Market researchers will have hundreds of consumers view products or ads to be sure that they will get a positive response before they recommend that a company invest a lot in production or promotions.

Here's how it works: market researchers hire consumers to be their test subjects. Participants are asked either to wear a special pair of eyeglasses on which a tiny camera is mounted or to look at a computer screen that precisely measures where they are looking. Participants are then shown images of new products, packaging, logos, or ads. They don't have to answer any questions as they gaze at the images on the screen, because the eye-tracking equipment objectively documents where they are looking and how long their gaze stays fixed on something. (Incidentally, even if you did ask consumers what they were looking at, their reports would be of little use—people often have no idea what their eyeballs are doing at any given moment. This is because eye gaze is not fully controllable, and we consciously perceive only a fraction of the world around us.)

The researchers will manipulate the position, color, and size of fonts and images, and then study how people view the objects. By playing around with placement, they can optimize attention. For example, just switching elements of an advertisement from the right side to the left or from the top to the bottom can make a substantial difference in how long people fixate on the brand name, the text, and the pictures.

Although eye movements have been studied for more than a hundred years, only since the 1970s has the technology become sufficiently sophisticated for scientists to study how eye movements predict behaviors. Eye tracking has revealed an important finding: the more attention people pay to a particular product, the more likely they are to buy it.[3]

That minor pictorial changes can have major effects is not unusual. Eye tracking reveals, for example, that font size can affect sales. In one study, researchers measured the amount of time consumers focused on different sections of a supermarket advertising circular. People looked at larger fonts longer, such that a 1 percent increase in font size was associated with a 0.9 percent increase in duration of attention. Attention, in turn, was directly associated with increased sales of the products described in larger fonts. Appealing to reason is not necessary to influence what we choose and consume—we may only need to supersize the font.[4]

But it's not just the font size that matters—style also counts. When the color and typeface of a product logo are congruent with the product, people can more easily recognize and recall the product.[5] For example, the font *Palatino Italic* is often judged as feminine, bright, quiet, and light, while **Braggadocio** is judged as masculine, rough, and strong. Somehow, the angle of the lines, their delicacy or thickness, suggests different qualities that can influence our opinions of a product. **Cooper Black,** for instance, is associated with being slow.

British researchers John Doyle and Paul Bottomley conducted several studies to demonstrate that typeface styles enhance advertising messages. In one study, they created two brands of chocolate truffles (the candies were the same) and called them either Temptation or Indulgence.[6] Study participants were simply asked to choose between two candy boxes with different names and fonts: for example, between Temptation (Salem font) and *Indulgence* (Signet font) or between *Temptation* (Signet font) and Indulgence (Salem font).

Which would you choose?

Compared to when the boxes were labeled with the Salem font, three times as many people chose a box of chocolates with the Signet font, with no difference based upon the name. Signet appeared to be an appropriate font to link with a high-class chocolate candy, whereas Salem was not—showing that it's all about the wrapping.

It isn't just the design or superficial characteristics of a product that influence us; the context in which the product is presented can also convert us from lookers to buyers. In 2002 Daniel Kahneman won a Nobel Prize for his work establishing that decision-making is biased by contextual information. We can predict the decision most people will make based on how the information is framed, such as whether outcomes are presented as gains or losses.[7] People are more prone to avoid losses than to seek gains, so an advertisement that promotes a product as preventing a health problem is likely to be more effective than one that presents the product as improving health. It could be the same product with the same purpose, but people perceive them differently.

The main barrier we face in resisting marketing efforts is our consistent lack of insight into how much we can be influenced, as well as our inability to recognize when and in which ways we are being influenced. We cannot defend ourselves if we don't know that marketing strategies are leading us to choose something that will harm us.

Obviously, businesses need to market their products. Most people will agree that advertising that uses explicit arguments and provides information and reasons to buy a product is perfectly legitimate and should be encouraged. But marketing that exploits the architecture of our brains and thus leads us to consume foods that can make us sick is very dangerous. For example, displaying candies, chips, and soda at the cash register increases our odds of buying them (and then consuming them), because our ability to resist them is likely to be low at the moment we are forced to encounter them. Much of today's strategic marketing pushes us to make poor choices by confronting us when we are unprepared to make a thoughtful choice.

Advertisers' jobs are to convince consumers why we cannot live without their products, and they invest heavily to do so. Historically, marketers have always tried to analyze shoppers' choices in order to devise the most promising means of promoting their products. Back in the 1950s a behavioral scientist named Mason Haire realized that consumers lack insight into their own preferences. At the time, Nestlé developed Nescafé instant coffee, but consumers said they didn't like the taste. Yet in blind taste tests, consumers could not distinguish Nescafé from home-brewed Maxwell House.

Obviously, taste was not the issue. Haire came up with a method known as a "projective technique" to assess consumer motives indirectly.[8]

To understand more about consumers' negative responses to instant coffee, Haire created two of the same shopping lists, but one included Nescafé while the other had Maxwell House. He asked a hundred women to characterize the personality of the shoppers who used these lists.

The Maxwell House shopper was described as a good housewife, while the Nescafé instant coffee shopper was described as lazy, sloppy, and inefficient. These attitudes had not previously been apparent, and not only explained the negative reaction but also subsequently informed the company as to how it could position the product to increase its acceptability. Here, advertisers learned that they had to conquer stereotypes that people could not articulate.

In contrast, today, by using technology like eye tracking and insights on decision-making processes from the fields of behavioral economics, psychology, and neurophysiology, advertising efforts have shifted from persuasion to manipulation. We can be swayed without ever realizing what has happened. When it comes to food, many experiments have demonstrated how irrational, inconsistent, and oblivious to marketing ruses people can be.[9]

Although the impact of improving advertising effectiveness for processed foods and beverages may influence sales by only a few percentage points, small increases can translate into huge profits for large companies—and increases in extra calories that expand our waistlines. As companies adopt more effective marketing strategies, our risk for obesity increases.

Making Decisions

Although traditional economic philosophy assumes that people will make decisions that will help them achieve the greatest level of well-being and happiness, not only do people routinely make bad decisions, but the choices they make are often inconsistent with what they really want. And what people "really" want seems to change with how the choices are presented. As Nobelist Daniel Kahneman demonstrated, order and framing influence what we select. The following experiments provide some examples showing how easily people can change with simple alterations in one or two elements of a choice scenario.

Professors Klaus Wertenbroch and Ravi Dhar recruited 114 students to participate in a study on preferences for sweets.[10] In a pretest they found that students valued M&M's candy because of the pleasure it brings and glue sticks for their usefulness. Because economists generally think price is a good indicator of value, the professors asked the students what they would be willing to pay for the glue stick and M&M's. The average of the answers was $1.27 for the glue stick but only 83 cents for the M&M's. Nevertheless, in the experiment Wertenbroch and Dhar labeled the M&M's and the glue stick with the same price, $1.25, and then asked each student to choose one. Half the students chose the M&M's, which makes sense if the items were perceived as being of equal value. If they had ignored the price tag and chosen what they thought was the real value, we would have expected more to choose the glue stick.

But in the next version of the experiment, instead of asking the students to select either the glue stick or the M&M's, they gave the students both, and then they asked the students to give one back. Now 85 percent chose to keep the M&M's! The lesson—once we touch, hold, or own something that gives us pleasure, we are less likely to give it up. (Economists also call this the endowment effect.)

Another experiment demonstrated our attraction to instant gratification, especially when the present situation is contrasted with future events. Ninety women were asked to choose a snack to eat right away, either yogurt or a chocolate chip cookie.[11]

In the first setup, with the simple choice, 57 percent chose the chocolate chip cookie. The next group's setup was slightly different. These participants had to make the same choice, but they were also told that they would be coming back in a week to repeat the same experiment with the same choice. After the entire procedure was explained, 83 percent chose the cookie. A third group was also given the same choice but told that when they came back the next week they would only be offered the yogurt. This time, 90 percent chose the chocolate chip cookie. In contrast, when a fourth group was told that they would be offered only the cookie when they came back, the percentage of those who chose the cookie to eat right away dropped substantially—to 43 percent.

Not everyone changes his mind when the context for decisions change. In this case it appears that the yogurt choosers were easier to influence. Thinking about yogurt in the future led to more cookies today (and vice versa). Many people are more likely to choose a smaller immediate reward (like tempting food) rather than forgo it for a more valuable or larger reward in the future (like weight loss). This may also be one of the reasons why it is so hard for us to stay on diets, eating more today and telling ourselves we will make better choices in the future. Marketers exploit this bias all the time.

Not only are marketers clever about getting consumers to purchase products by offering special incentives, but they can manipulate people such that they might change their purchasing patterns or even make choices that are the opposite of previously stated preferences. Several elements, like price, appearance, taste, and quantity figure, strongly in people's choices. When one of these elements varies, the change may be powerful enough to cancel out the influence of any one of the others.

Loyalty programs are extremely successful in influencing repeated business with a particular company. One study showed that the impact of being offered a free coffee after ten are purchased was that people bought coffee more often and sooner than they would have without the incentive. As people got closer to reaching the ten purchases, they accelerated their buying and purchased more coffee in a shorter period of time. This phenomenon has been dubbed the "goal-gradient" hypothesis. It was first noted in a study showing that rats seemed to work harder as they got closer to obtaining an anticipated reward.[12]

Another marketing technique exploits the assumption that something that costs more is better and will be more enjoyable. In one experiment people were asked to choose between a chocolate heart and a chocolate shaped like a cockroach, which they could have for free. Although beforehand, the majority said they would enjoy eating the heart-shaped chocolate more, most participants chose the chocolate cockroach after seeing it labeled with a $2 price tag while the chocolate heart was valued at 50 cents.[13]

Similarly, in another experiment, Professor Christopher Hsee of the University of Chicago's Booth School of Business did a pretest and found that most students did not think pistachio ice cream was better than vanilla. He then recruited ninety-six students to investigate whether using a token—which has no inherent value but can be traded for something of value—could be used to influence people's choices. The first group of students could choose to work either six minutes to earn a gallon of vanilla ice cream or seven minutes to earn a gallon of pistachio. Only 25 percent of students went for the pistachio. In contrast, when the tasks were valued at sixty points (for six minutes) or a hundred points (seven minutes) and the second group of students could redeem sixty points for a gallon of vanilla and a hundred points for pistachio, more than 50 percent went for the pistachio.

In this case, the abstract incentive of points and the higher valuation of pistachio appeared to change many consumers' preferences. How often do people recognize when their behaviors are merely a response to similar marketing ploys?

When you think about it, we have probably all been convinced that some products are more valuable than they are, and we have probably all bought and consumed something based upon a name, a wrapper, or a special price or discount. There are no constraints on the techniques that advertisers can use, as long as promotions are not patently fraudulent or overtly deceptive.

Atmospherics

The concept of atmospherics, which are the contextual factors associated with the retail environment, was first introduced in the early 1970s by Philip Kotler, a strategic marketing guru who is now a Distinguished Professor of International Marketing at Northwestern University. Kotler noticed that retail environments could produce emotional effects that enhance the probability that a customer will buy. Factors like lighting, crowding, layout, scent, and music all influence buying decisions. Although all these factors are either in plain sight or can be noticed by consumers, typically most people are unaware of the way atmospherics influence their choices.[14]

It might surprise you to learn that music can affect our consumption of beverages. In a study conducted by Western Kentucky University's

Dr. Ronald Milliman, researchers compared the effects of slow and fast music on the behavior of restaurant customers. They found that people lingered at restaurants longer when slow background music was piped in. Patrons spent about the same amount of money on food as those listening to fast music but ordered more drinks from the bar, spending 41 percent more on alcohol.[15]

Customers in wine shops have been shown to be influenced by music as well; in one study, patrons were more likely to buy French wines when French music played and more likely to purchase German wines when German music was played. In another study, patrons spent more money on wine when classical music was played.[16]

In an experiment by Professor Adrian North, previously of Heriot-Watt University in Edinburgh, restaurant customers treated to a soundtrack of classical music racked up bigger bills than customers listening to popular music. The classical music listeners were also more likely to order appetizers, coffee, and dessert.[17] If asked, I'm sure none of these customers would say that music had anything to do with whether they ordered a cappuccino or tiramisu. But atmospherics certainly affected their food consumption.

Priming

Think of a typical family sitcom—teenagers want to borrow the family car, but they just don't come right out and ask their parents for it. First, they are unusually helpful and courteous, giving the parents a lot of compliments and saying a lot of nice things. They want their folks to be in a good mood, because if they aren't, the parents will definitely say no when the kids pop the question.

The teens are using the principles of priming. Priming refers to an incidental activation of memories or associations that make a person more disposed to act in a particular way. A priming stimulus at one time will influence how people respond to a related stimulus at a subsequent time, typically soon after the initial priming stimulus. Presumably, if the parents are cheered and in a positive mood from the good behavior of their teenagers, they will be more likely to say yes when asked for permission to borrow the car.

Priming is pervasive in our environment, but it only works when we are not aware of it.[18] If the parents knew the kids were only being nice just to get them to loan the car, they might overcompensate and be more likely to say no.

Many cues in the environment prime us to think about food. Although food advertising presumably is intended to make us buy a particular brand and type of food, people who are exposed to tempting food cues, regardless of the brand, typically react by feeling hungry. Dr. Jason Halford at the University of Liverpool has studied the subject of priming in children extensively. His conclusion: not only does viewing ads lead children to eat greater quantities of food, but overweight children are more sensitive to and recognize a greater number of ads than thinner children.[19]

In a recent study, Dr. Jennifer Harris of Yale's Rudd Center invited 118 children and 98 adults to watch television with food advertising.[20] The children were divided into two groups. The experimental group saw the equivalent of a Saturday morning cartoon program with four thirty-second commercials promoting high-sugar cereal, waffle sticks and syrup, fruit roll-ups, and potato chips, while the comparison group saw the cartoon with four commercials advertising games and entertainment products. The children were each given a bowl of goldfish crackers (150 grams) to snack on while they watched. After they finished watching, the amount of goldfish remaining was weighed. The kids who saw the cartoons with food commercials ate 45 percent more goldfish than the other group, even though goldfish crackers were not advertised.

A similar result was shown for the 98 adults who were asked to watch a sixteen-minute episode of the improvisational comedy show *Whose Line Is It Anyway?* with four minutes of eleven commercials embedded. Everyone saw the same seven commercials for nonfood items, but one group saw an additional four commercials for fast food, candy, and soda; another group saw commercials advertising healthy food: a granola bar, orange juice, oatmeal, and an instant breakfast beverage; and the third group saw four nonfood commercials. Afterward, the adults were asked to participate in a taste test, and the researchers weighed the remaining food to calculate how much they ate. The adults seeing the four junk food commercials ate the most, and those seeing the healthy food commercials ate the least.[21]

Why would seeing unhealthy rather than healthy food prime us to eat more? Shouldn't any food make us hungry? Apparently not. Seeing foods with high sugar and fat—also called "palatable" foods—whets our appetite more than seeing fruits and vegetables. This is probably the consequence of a hardwired evolutionary drive to favor instant energy and concentrated calories.

No Defense Against Priming

Eye-tracking experiments also prove that we are influenced by advertisements we do not intentionally look at. Several studies show that people reading a magazine or looking at a website cannot accurately recall the ads placed in the sidebars. Yet when asked to select items to buy from a list after being exposed to sidebar ads, subjects were more likely to choose items that were in the ads.[22] These studies explain why many companies are dashing to post their advertisements in the sidebars on websites.

Apparently, we can also be primed to consume more by subliminal images—ones that we cannot consciously perceive—and they don't have to be pictures of food. Kent Berridge and Terry Robinson, professors of psychology and neuroscience at the University of Michigan, invited subjects to their laboratory to participate in an energy drink taste test.[23] Beforehand, the participants watched a video with embedded subliminal images lasting sixteen milliseconds. (A typical movie has twenty-four frames per second, so sixteen milliseconds is shorter than a single frame. We typically have to see at least two or more frames to consciously notice the image.) The first group was shown a sixteen-millisecond image of a person smiling, the second group was shown a person with a neutral expression, and the third group was shown a person frowning. Afterward they were offered an energy drink. Individuals shown the smiling person consumed more of an energy drink, and rated it more favorably than the other groups, whereas those shown subliminal pictures of an individual frowning drank the least and rated the beverage lowest. A negative mood may lead us to be more critical, effortful, and cautious, and to use our analytic cognitive resources.

So why does subliminal exposure to a smiling face make someone consume more than seeing a neutral or negative expression? A smile does not just lull us into complacency; it is an indication of happiness. Psychologists have proposed that happiness sensitizes people toward rewards; in other words, a smile might make us react a little more strongly to food.[24] When we are in a positive mood, we react more quickly and resort to automatic, heuristic-based (think shortcut) processing. Restaurateurs know that people order more when they are in a good mood. Maybe that's why Ronald McDonald is always smiling, as are nearly all mascots that advertise products.

In our everyday world, then, with all kinds of stimuli surrounding us—some that are positive, some that are negative—what determines which of the primes will influence us? And with food stimuli all around, why is it that all of us are not eating all the time?

Priming does not work the same way on everyone. All the experiments just described affected a substantial portion of the participants, but not all of them. We know why primes work in most people, but it is not clear why some individuals are less sensitive to primes than others.[25]

In studies looking at how two different primes influence behavior, researchers discovered that when primes are consistent with overall goals, they enhance behavior; but when they conflict with goals, they undermine behavior. So if people are on a diet and would like to control their weight, all the environmental cues promoting food will interfere with their goal to eat less.

Social psychologists James Shah and Arie Kruglanski showed repeatedly that when individuals were subliminally exposed to conflicting goals, their performance on a variety of tasks was undermined, and they were totally unaware that an external prime had influenced them.[26] If the prime is irrelevant, it has no effect.

Branding, Conditioning, and Pavlov's Dogs

Today, the primary way the food industry uses conditioning as a strategy to sell us products is through branding. Branding is a comprehensive approach that coordinates a variety of elements to achieve a consistent, memorable, overall look and feel for a company, service, or product. Typically, that means that products have a standard logo and color; a unique typeface; and a clear, concise, and compelling message. Think of Colonel Sanders's face on a bucket of KFC chicken or the green and yellow colors of Subway's name on its sandwich wrapping paper, napkins, and menu boards.

Advertisers spend a great deal of time and money to make sure that the brand works: they create mock designs and logos and conduct focus groups to see how people react to them. Once they have a brand that grabs our attention and makes us think positive thoughts, they develop a strategy to disseminate that brand image. To do so, they take great pains to increase exposure to the brand, so it is burned into the consumer's brain and becomes the brand of choice.

A popular technique to promote brands using the principles of conditioning is through celebrity endorsement, which is used in about 20 percent of TV commercials. Because celebrities generate positive feelings, pairing them with specific products generates positive feelings toward the products.[27] Think of the cachet that Bill Cosby brought to Jell-O products, imbuing them with a wholesome family friendliness. When Pepsi gave Beyoncé a $50 million contract in 2013, the company obviously hoped her fans would consider the soda as alluring as the singer. Celebrities automatically attract attention because they are familiar and appealing. If the celebrity has something in common with the product being endorsed, the ads are even more effective.

When we think of conditioning, many of us recall Pavlov's classic experiment in which he rang a bell before feeding his dogs. Subsequently the dogs would salivate just upon hearing the bell. Classical conditioning is a form of associative learning, which guides not just animals but also human behaviors and judgments. When two things are paired together, we learn that they are associated. If we see one, we typically also think of the other. And moreover, when there is a close association between two things, we automatically tend to transfer the qualities of one to the other, whether or not the qualities actually apply.

The power of conditioning that comes from pairing different things together has been exploited by the advertising industry since the 1920s. The credit for applying these principles to advertising goes to John Watson, a psychology professor hired by the J. Walter Thompson advertising agency.[28] Watson noticed that customers couldn't distinguish between different brands of a product and that they typically made decisions based upon the image of the product rather than the product itself. With this insight, one of the first commercial campaigns Watson developed was for Pond's Cold Cream. A letter from the Queen of Romania requesting supplies of cold cream was turned into an advertisement and a testimonial. Sales increased dramatically, as people began to associate royalty and high quality with the cream.

Although this approach may seem quaint and relatively harmless, what is so insidious about the use of conditioning principles in advertising is just how little awareness people have of how these techniques influence their behaviors. Questioning buyers as to their reasons for purchase is unlikely to yield an explanation because the mechanism for the association is usually below their radar. It is only in the past thirty years or so that careful experiments have determined how advertising influences individuals in ways they are unable to recognize.

Mere Exposure Conditioning and Product Placements

Although conditioning effects are strong, the impact of simply seeing a product also influences the likelihood that a consumer will choose it. In the jargon of psychology, this has been called "mere exposure conditioning" in contrast to "affective conditioning," in which a positive (or negative) stimulus is paired with the product.[29] Mere exposure is simply seeing or perceiving something without it being paired with another stimulus.

Repeatedly seeing an ad for a soft drink, for example, increases our preference for that beverage. We don't have to be aware that we saw it. In fact, the effect of mere exposure is stronger when we don't even remember that we saw that particular drink. Once we consciously perceive something, then we have the opportunity to evaluate it and attach meaning. But if we see it without paying attention, it becomes part of a familiar background. If there is nothing negative about the drink, our brain evaluates it as safe, and when we are later exposed to that drink with an array of others, we are automatically more likely to choose it instead of one that we have never seen before. This is one reason why the large food and beverage companies try to make their advertising ubiquitous.

Another surprising finding is that being exposed to the same objects repeatedly generates a more positive general mood compared to being exposed to multiple objects. Although we are excited by and attracted to novelty, we also tend to like seeing the same things over and over. Repetition provides a familiar comfort.

Robert Zajonc, the Stanford University professor who first identified the phenomenon of mere exposure conditioning, considered this to be of important adaptive value. Developing preferences for objects that have no negative attributes allows us to automatically distinguish objects and habitats that are safe and should guide us into making positive and long-lasting social attachments.[30]

Another increasingly popular conditioning technique is product placement, mentioned in the previous chapter, an application of mere exposure conditioning. Product placement works best when it is well below our awareness. It has been compared to subliminal advertising because the product is casually included in the film props.[31]

British researchers Susan Auty and Charlie Lewis looked at the impact of product placement of Pepsi in the movie *Home Alone*.[32] They showed one group of children a short clip of the family eating pizza, milk, and drinking Pepsi, while another group saw a clip of similar length but with the star eating macaroni and cheese and drinking only milk.

After the screening, the children were invited to help themselves to a drink before they participated in an interview. The experimenters surreptitiously recorded what they chose. On the table were an equal number of small cans of Coke and Pepsi. Mindful that in Britain Coke outsells Pepsi three to one, the researchers thought that if there were no effect of the product placement, more children would choose Coke. Indeed, among the control group (which didn't see the scene with the product placement), 58 percent chose Coke and 42 percent chose Pepsi. But in the group that saw the scene with the Pepsi product placement, the choices were almost reversed: 62 percent of the children chose Pepsi (38 percent chose Coke).

Over the past few decades, product placements in movies and television have grown enormously. Some blockbuster movies resemble nothing but a string of product placements in search of a story. Not only do they increase familiarity by mere exposure, but they offer double value by pairing the products with celebrities. This is why Oreo cookies were recently integrated into an episode of *Modern Family*.

Conditioning is very hard to unlearn. Multiple studies have been done to see how difficult it is to extinguish associations. If we see Bill Cosby with Jell-O in a few commercials, we may link the two together for months and maybe years to come.[33]

Our brain's anatomy developed slowly over hundreds of thousands of years. And it is only in the past few centuries that we have been able to create artificial environments, where a person doesn't have to hunt for food and can find it with little effort. The brain has not evolved as quickly as our environment has, and it still processes inputs and information as if we were living in an era with no media or other mass communications. Our brain doesn't automatically make adjustments for advertisements, persuasive media, or other background noise.

Modern uses of conditioning are intended to suppress or override the thinking part of our brains and shift our decisions and preferences to choose specific brands. We all know that is what advertisers try to do, yet somehow we don't really believe that it works on us. Until we start looking at real examples of how conditioning works, it just doesn't seem plausible that we can be influenced.

The success of the beverage industry is a case study in how conditioning has made the spread of sugar-sweetened sodas a global phenomenon. The use of conditioning principles in marketing has resulted in sales of expensive sugar water to impoverished millions who would be healthier if they spent their money on more nutritious drinks or more nutritious foods for themselves and their families. The greatest success has been with Coca-Cola, whose strategy for more than a century has been to get the familiar red-and-white logo firmly imprinted in people's minds everywhere in the world.

On a trip to South Africa I visited a township where people live in shacks made of tin. Residents usually do not have running water in their homes and rely on a communal well and toilet. Many children are small, undernourished, and stunted. Yet it wasn't uncommon to see the locals drinking Coca-Cola, even though in South Africa, ounce for ounce, Coca-Cola is more expensive than milk.

On Robben Island, a national monument where Nelson Mandela was incarcerated for decades, the only billboard that can be seen from the prison is sponsored by Coca-Cola. In South Africa Coca-Cola has become the most popular beverage and the largest employer. In fact, Coca-Cola is the largest employer in all of Africa. Many small townships have their welcome sign sponsored by Coca-Cola.

Ron Irwin, a brand consultant and writer based in Cape Town, has written:

> Coke [is] the ultimate American product, manages to assimilate itself into utterly foreign cultures by utilizing local advertising campaigns that brilliantly link its products to people's aspirations and passions. Throughout the late nineties the South African advertising agency of Sonnenberg Murphy Leo Burnett (SMLB) helped promote the drink to the townships and villages through emotively linking Coke with Africa's great obsession: soccer. It also introduced a locally famous commercial, shot in Morocco (ironically one of the few countries in the world yet to enjoy Coke), that likens drinking your first Coke to your first kiss. Lately, SMLB has linked Coke to the African concept of *seriti* (community respect) by airing commercials that show an African boy become a man of stature in his township by selling Coke.[34]

The most effective advertising makes strong associations between products and our deepest desires, associations that belie the long-term consequences of consuming unhealthy food products. Instead, for the brief moment we consume the product we can feel as if our desires have been realized.

Can Conditioning and Priming Be Used to Reduce Consumption?

At the same time that the principles of conditioning were being applied to marketing in the early part of the twentieth century, scientists were trying to use conditioning to help people eat less.[35] As early as

1924, aversive conditioning was used to help people lose weight. One researcher asked subjects to drink vinegar, which was accompanied by a clicking noise. By pairing the clicking noise with drinking a caustic vinegar solution, the hope was that the revulsion from drinking the vinegar would transfer to other foods. The approach failed except for one volunteer, who successfully rejected orange juice when it was offered with the clicking noise.

In a few obesity treatment trials in the 1950s, experimenters gave electric shocks to subjects when they viewed tempting (unhealthy) foods, when they reached for the foods, or while they repeatedly said the word "overeating." None of the approaches worked.[36]

In another aversive conditioning trial, bad smells were paired with favorite foods.[37] For thirty minutes, three times a week for four weeks and then twice a week for five weeks, six subjects were told to handle, smell, and imagine tasting, chewing, and swallowing their favorite foods, and then they were exposed to the smell of skunk oil and other disgusting and noxious smells. After nearly a year, five out of the six lost an average of fourteen pounds, but the sixth subject gained fourteen pounds and reported that the odors never had any effect on her. Most of the subjects reported that the conditioning seemed to last only two to three months. In the end, success was attributed more to the relationships developed between the clinicians and the subjects than to the odor conditioning.

Another approach similar to aversive conditioning is called covert sensitization. In this therapy, subjects are asked to relax and then are told vivid narratives in which they approach forbidden foods and become nauseated and vomit. Several studies tested this technique, but the success was rather modest, with subjects losing an average of just five pounds.[38]

Other conditioning approaches have followed the line of research developed by B. F. Skinner. In this type of therapy people who successfully lose weight are rewarded with approval and tokens or cash (also called token economies). Other experiments used punishment, so that when the subjects failed to lose weight, they also lost personal possessions like clothes and money. These latter approaches were tried among persons institutionalized for mental illness. They were not successful in the long term, although they did have positive results in the short term.[39]

The main problem with eating is that it is a reinforcing activity. Eating is its own reward. If we were able to make eating less pleasurable, as a species we would probably not survive.

Rewarding people financially for losing weight has also been tried repeatedly, but so far no studies have been able to show sustained results.[40] Today, the most effective behavioral treatments for obesity typically include a combination of nutrition education, social support, and reducing food cues; but in general, even the success of these approaches is modest and short-lived.[41]

By contrast, priming may have more potential to help people decrease their consumption because of the way it triggers our brains and can support existing goals. In one experiment, European researchers Esther Papies and Petra Hamstra measured how many free samples of meatballs customers ate when a sign on a shop's door announced that a recipe that was "good for a slim figure" was available at the counter. The number of free meatballs eaten was also measured on days when the sign was not on the door.[42]

Customers concerned about their weight ate fewer meatballs when the sign was on the door than when it wasn't. The sign had no influence on customers who were unconcerned about their weight. Of those apparently influenced by the sign, 80 percent said they didn't see it. This was a short-term study, so we don't know whether such signs would make a difference in the long run. However, the study does suggest that priming could help support people who want to control their consumption.

Although conditioning techniques do not appear to work as an effective therapy to decrease eating, scientists have tried to understand why conditioning is so effective at increasing eating. In 1956 Dr. Albert Stunkard showed that obese individuals could not reliably recognize when their stomachs were empty and thus did not really know when they were physiologically hungry.[43] In 1968 Dr. Stanley Schachter tried to show that obese people were more sensitive to external conditioning cues than people of normal weight.

In one experiment Schachter altered two clocks so that one ran at half-speed while the other ran at twice the normal speed.[44] He invited forty-six obese and normal individuals to the lab at 5 p.m., and in the first five minutes he removed their watches with the excuse that the watches would interfere with the polygraph machine used to measure their heart rates. He then had them wait for thirty minutes; for one group the clock showed it was 5:20, while for the other group the clock showed 6:05. At that time he came in with a box of crackers and invited the subjects to help themselves while they completed a personality inventory. He gave them ten minutes to complete the task and then determined how many crackers they ate. The obese subjects whose clocks showed 6:05 ate twice as many crackers as the obese subjects whose clocks read 5:20. Time conditioned their perception of hunger.

Unexpectedly, the normal-weight subjects ate twice as many crackers at 5:20 as at 6:05. Several of the normal-weight subjects turned down the crackers at 6:05, saying, "No thanks, I don't want to spoil my dinner."

In fact, both groups were conditioned to time, but the obese subjects did not restrain themselves at 6:05, whereas the normal-weight people did. If the normal-weight people typically ate regular meals, they were probably hungry at 5:20 and realized they still had some time until dinner, while the obese people relied on the clock to tell them how hungry they were.

A very different explanation for heightened responsiveness to external cues among the obese was advanced in 1983 by C. Peter Herman, Marion P. Olmsted, and Janet Polivy from the University of Toronto.[45] They compared how 338 obese and normal-weight individuals responded when offered dessert in four different ways at a high-class French restaurant. For the first method, the waitress simply handed out a dessert menu, saying nothing. The second method allowed the diners simply to see the dessert. The third method used social influence: the waitress stated, "I recommend the cake (or pie). That's what I'd have." The last method combined seeing the dessert with social influence: here, the waitress showed two desserts and recommended one.

The obese diners were no more likely than normal-weight participants to order dessert when they got the dessert menu, but were 67 percent more likely to order when they saw the dessert or when the waitress recommended one. It was also hypothesized that perhaps obese individuals are more compliant, that they responded more to the pressing request of the waitress.

Other studies have shown that obese individuals are more likely to model the behavior of others.[46] People who have become obese may also become more sensitive to food cues.

We Are All Vulnerable

The primary job of marketers is to figure out what factors get us in the buying mood. Yet being vulnerable to marketing and to the suggestions or entreaties of others is not always bad. Human capacity and proclivity to be flexible, to continually learn, to be willing to experiment and try new things, and to allow ourselves to be touched emotionally have led to much of the positive advancements of modern civilization. However, these human assets can also become weaknesses when they are exploited for purposes that neglect our well-being.

Have you noticed that sales clerks and cashiers are increasingly responding in an upbeat manner, smiling, looking you in the eye, addressing you by your name, and forever asking if there is anything else they can do for you? Even if we know such behaviors may be artificially scripted, like a teenager using sweet talk to prime us so we will agree to lend the car, the goal is also for the salespeople to make us like them and to positively lift our mood. We may not believe it really influences our choices, what we buy, or how much we eat. But it does. (Or they wouldn't be doing it.)

Food marketing is sophisticated, and most of us don't realize when we are being collared. We might be patting ourselves on that back, happy that we found a great new beverage or cracker or other snack food that we love. But behind the scenes, the marketers have been carefully searching us out and studying how to seduce us. They know we are on our own, and that makes it easier for them to have their way with us. The only proof of our having been manipulated is the extra weight around our middles and a nagging feeling that it's time to eat.

PART III

An Alternate Vision

8

A Plea for Change:
We Are All in This Together

Today, the whole world is facing a health crisis not unlike the one humanity faced in the nineteenth century, when industrialization and urbanization led to the increased transmission of infectious diseases, which were the major causes of death. Government action stopped the infectious disease epidemics then, and I believe government actions will be necessary to stop obesity and related chronic diseases now, using the same public health principles that address environmental risks rather than individual behaviors.

In the early 1800s, typical English urban households deposited all their trash and waste, including excrement, on the land adjoining their dwellings and shops. The garbage accumulated on sidewalks and in alleys, often overflowing onto the city streets, until hired scavengers or dustbin men carted it away. Large drains were built for storm water to prevent flooding, but all kinds of debris flowed through these channels, clogging them with feces, animal carcasses, and other refuse. Waste frequently pooled in the streets and backed up into people's cellars and homes. Conditions were even worse in poor neighborhoods, where people did not have proper houses or easy access to water, which had to be obtained from local pumps.[1]

In crowded cities like London, epidemics of infectious diseases like cholera and typhoid flourished and were the leading causes of death. One-third of children under the age of five did not survive, and few lived past the age of forty.[2]

No one understood the exact mechanism by which these diseases were spreading. The dominant belief was that the decaying filth on the ground contaminated the air, which in turn infected people through invisible toxic fumes called miasma.[3] Even though the science was flawed, a solution soon emerged: a British bureaucrat named Edwin Chadwick suggested that removing waste from densely populated urban areas would curb epidemics like cholera. (In case you think that Chadwick's motive was pure, he proposed this because he did not want to spend the public's money on providing food to the hungry, arguing that hunger should inspire people to work harder. But that's another story.)

Chadwick's suggestion to fight filth was met with great opposition. Although some preferred to spend public money to feed the poor rather than build sewage pipes, the loudest opponents didn't want to spend anything, and argued that the expense associated with waste removal was too large. Others said there was no proof that removing waste would actually work. Why incur such an expense if there is no assurance of benefits? Still others worried about the scavengers who made their living from carting away refuse and excrement from the streets: what would happen to their livelihoods?

In an 1849 letter published in the *Times* of London, an outraged citizen declared,

> We prefer to take our chance with cholera and the rest than be bullied into health. There is nothing a man hates so much as being cleansed against his will, or having his floors swept, his walls whitewashed, his pet dung heaps cleared away, or his thatch forced to give way to slate, all at the command of a sort of sanitary bombaliff. It is a positive fact that many have died of a good washing.

Despite these objections, several forces—including self-interested industrialists, fishermen, and farmers—ultimately pushed through sanitary measures that would remove waste and provide clean water. The sanitary movement spawned public health departments and an extensive infrastructure to enforce regulations promoting hygienic conditions in homes, factories, and communities. The result was the virtual disappearance of cholera and typhoid, a reduction in a host of waterborne infectious diseases, and the assurance that nearly all babies born healthy would survive to adulthood.

Public health is the field of medicine that shouts, "We are all in this together!" Public health policies are intended to level the playing field so that we can all live in conditions in which we can be healthy. Public health is what makes sure that our environment doesn't harm us—from the design of cars to the conditions at the workplace. But public health has been falling down on the job when it comes to chronic diseases.

It's time to play catch-up.

Hardwired cognitive limitations make it nearly impossible for most of us to consistently resist overeating (or to spontaneously engage in physical activity), so ending the obesity epidemic will require changing the food and activity environments or changing ourselves. It is unlikely that human nature is going to change anytime soon, which is why I firmly believe that the best way to tackle the obesity epidemic is by creating a more balanced environment in which individuals can automatically make healthy decisions about when, what, and how much to eat (or exercise). The quickest and most efficient way to do that is through new public health regulations.

Our lives depend on regulations that protect us from pollution, dangerous building and marketing practices, charlatans, and hucksters. In all industries, in all worksites, and for all consumer goods, we have accepted the role of government to discourage practices that increase the risk of unhealthy outcomes, be it unintended injury or long-term disabling disease. We no longer tolerate needless exposures to toxins, unnecessary risks of injury on the job, or the marketing of harmful or defective products without substantial warnings or oversight.

Yet calls for change and more regulation always encounter resistance, especially among those who are profiting massively from the current conditions. The beneficiaries of the current situation argue that their right to sell whatever they want, however they want, is a matter of personal liberty—that it is up to individuals to make better choices if they really care about their health.

Yet these kinds of arguments do not fly in other areas, like the auto industry. Today seat belts and air bags are not optional features; auto-makers must install them and ensure their cars meet safety standards. Would anyone seriously defend automakers who sold cars that didn't meet safety standards by claiming it as a matter of personal liberty?

The defenders of the status quo count on the fact that most people are ignorant of how they are being influenced and believe that their choices are completely independent. Furthermore, many cannot see behind or beyond the current conditions, and assume these conditions are natural, normal, and/or reflect the common will. Many cannot see the hidden forces that undermine individual goals.

Yet there are ample historical precedents of success in changing societal perspectives on human behavior and regulating business prac-tices that were previously considered immutable. The Sanitary Rev-olution, initiated in England in 1848, heralded the onset of changes of such an enormous magnitude that it dwarfs everything proposed herein. From the early to the late nineteenth century, perspectives on poverty and starvation changed dramatically, and societies went from having virtually no laws addressing environmental conditions to having a host of regulations governing water and sanitation, housing, food, worksites, and air quality.

In the early 1800s, England had "poor laws" that required local towns to provide medical care and medicine to people who did not have the means to pay for it (similar to federal mandates to provide emer-gency care at hospitals receiving federal funds). But medical officers often diagnosed "hunger" as the source of debilitation and prescribed food as the remedy. Many of the British, including Edwin Chadwick, who served as secretary of the Poor Law Commission and is the person most strongly linked with the Sanitary Revolution, called the practice of prescribing food instead of medicine "mutton medicine," and con-sidered it completely unacceptable.[4]

Chadwick's major objection was that public subsidies of the basic necessities would encourage malingering and bankrupt local jurisdic-tions that were already feeling the financial pinch of having to provide living accommodations for the poor in workhouses. He believed that hunger should inspire people to work harder. As a consequence, he became the prime architect of new poor laws that not only banned "mutton medicine" but also purposefully worsened the conditions in workhouses to discourage the poor from using them.[5]

Furthermore, Chadwick could not believe that the food allowances given by workhouses were so inadequate that people were dying from hunger.[6] He thought that as long as people were truly hungry and had any possessions, they could always exchange them for food or take advantage of the workhouse safety net, and thus avoid starvation. (Today's belief that people who want to avoid obesity really could be successful if they tried hard enough echoes the nineteenth-century sentiment that anyone who was hungry should have been able to find a way to survive with the meager assistance available to them.)

At the time there was no convincing scientific evidence that malnutrition could be debilitating, or that it could increase susceptibility to other diseases and make it difficult for people to work, so it was easy to spin stories about the poor being lazy or of dubious character that were congruent with favored political philosophies and religious beliefs. Yet because there were such high death rates among the working poor, which left entire families destitute, Chadwick latched on to the idea that the major cause of death in the 1830s was filth rather than hunger. He thought the government would ultimately save more money and avoid promoting malingering if it did something about disease-causing filth and contaminated air rather than increase the poor's food rations or wages.

The absence of a sanitation system was indeed highly conducive to epidemics of infectious diseases.[7] In the early 1800s, no one knew about bacteria; germ theory was not confirmed until the late 1860s. Nevertheless, Chadwick's suggestion to remove wastes from densely populated urban areas was exactly what was needed to curb epidemics like cholera.

These vast, transformative changes in public health in Britain and subsequently adopted in the United States were not merely the gift of a central government that, in its munificence, passed enlightened legislation. In fact, in many cases, changes in sanitation at the local level were forced by lawsuits and injunctions or by the pressures from industrialists who needed pure water for their factories. In other cases, changes were implemented at the local level to support local needs and priorities, and were often the result of the cooperation, competence, and foresight of elected members and appointed officials of local governments.[8]

Sewerage systems were introduced in some British towns after private parties sued localities to halt the pollution of rivers. These actions were won by appealing to English common law rather than public health laws. Successful lawsuits often resulted in a writ of sequestration, which either forced the town to allocate funds to provide a remedy or allowed the winning party to build the necessary sewerage works at the town's expense.[9]

The force of law was substantial because failure to provide the necessary funds could lead to the seizure of the personal property and real estate of the mayor, aldermen, and burgesses of the borough.[10] In most of the nineteenth century debtors were jailed, so being held liable spelled ruination.

Another prominent driving force of technological innovations in sanitary systems was industrialists, especially the proprietors of textile works, who needed pure, soft water in the manufacturing process of yarns and fabrics. The need for soft water was tied to the livelihoods and prosperity of the towns and in many cases led to the municipalization of the local waterworks. In this way, the community ended up supporting the high costs of clean water that was largely used by industry. Indeed, many of those on local boards who made these decisions were stockholders and/or had financial interests in the waterworks.

The cost of re-engineering a city or town that had been established for centuries was unprecedented and often equaled or exceeded the net worth of the entire jurisdiction. However, in England, infrastructure improvements were financed by government bonds, sometimes with a payback period of sixty years.[11] In the United States, given that the country was relatively young, with growing towns and cities, there was perhaps less need for re-engineering and more for construction that incorporated the new sanitary principles.

Originally, sewers were built as unconnected drains intended to affect only a small surface area, not to service an entire city.[12] The challenge was to join the pipes and get all the waste to flow steadily to a destination away from the city where it could be recycled and purified. Because no one had any experience with how to build a sewerage system—how wide the pipes should be, how steep they should be laid, and how deep—the development of such systems was essentially a series of experiments. Designs were continually revised and upgraded when the pipes broke, clogged, or failed to operate as planned. The right answer was not immediately discovered, and it took decades to figure out how to create systems that worked efficiently and effectively.

Local authorities frequently resisted sanitary reforms. They did not want to sacrifice local autonomy or waste the taxpayers' dollars on matters that were considered a concern of individuals. Many officials were afraid of taking the wrong steps because they were bewildered by the technical requirements and legal complexities. They had no assurance that the sewerage systems proposed would be sound or would improve the current conditions. Determining the best methods for sewerage systems was quite contentious, with multiple legal challenges in England.

One of the largest disagreements in design had to do with the size of the sewer pipes. Chadwick, who was deeply involved in the creation of sanitation systems, wanted narrow, thin-walled pipes in which sewage could flow quickly; narrow pipes were also less expensive. Charges of corruption and/or incompetence were made by Chadwick and a handful of engineers, particularly when sewer system designs chosen for adoption were more costly than what they had proposed. However, for Chadwick's design to work, citizens had to be mindful of the materials they dumped, as large objects, hair, grease, and grit would clog the pipes. Chadwick wanted a large-scale education campaign to train the public to use the new systems properly.

Most engineers, however, wanted more expensive, wider pipes and insisted that designers had to allow for accident and error. They thought it foolish to consider the frequent breakdown of narrow pipes avoidable, if it wasn't avoided. In addition, larger pipes could also handle rainwater and other detritus that flowed into sewers. Thomas Page, an engineer, noted, "As the population cannot be hastily fitted for the sewerage, the sewerage must be fitted for the population." He thought it unrealistic to expect people to adhere to the meticulous standards necessary to prevent narrow pipes from blocking up. Ultimately, the wider pipes did prove more effective.

The Sanitary Revolution quickly expanded beyond sewage disposal and clean water provision. One of the first measures undertaken to enforce new sanitary codes in England was the appointment of sanitary police by local towns and cities. The sanitary police were inspectors of nuisances. Their very presence and mission constituted an assault on private property rights, while elevating the protection of the common good.

The decisions about which nuisances to tackle and which to ignore were sometimes arbitrary. Sanitary police could handle accumulation of filth, bad drains, smoke, unsound or overcrowded dwellings, insufficient privies or water closets, unclean workplaces, and a range of other unhealthy conditions. For the most part, nuisances were summarily addressed and legal action was avoided. The stigma and humiliation associated with violating sanitary standards made it less likely for people to be outraged enough to assert and defend their rights to keep their private property in whatever condition they wanted.[13]

The Sanitary Revolution spurred a complete transformation and growth of government, creating the field of urban planning as well as departments of public works, transportation, and parks. Interestingly, in the United States, urban parks were initially created as a means to designate areas where dumping would be prohibited. Subsequently, parks were promoted as places where people could go to recreate, relax, and breathe fresh air.[14]

Although our understanding of disease and human behaviors has significantly advanced since the 1800s, today we are at a similar crossroads. Just as Chadwick and the British Boards of Health faced epidemics of infectious diseases, we are facing unprecedented epidemics of obesity and chronic diseases, and there is a cacophony of voices with conflicting ideas about how to address the problem.

My analysis of what we need to do builds on the public health principles that identify the conditions in which people live as the source of both health and disease. Thomas Page's words of two centuries ago are apt for today: because the population cannot stay fit in the current high-risk environment, we must change the environment to fit people's needs.

To protect our population, we have all kinds of standards that we expect everyone to adhere to when life and limb are at stake. Think of the extensive building codes and regulatory process associated with constructing a house. We have rules governing the types of bolts and screws, the allowable depth, width, and height of the steps in a flight of stairs, as well as the distance between the vertical bars of a stairway guardrail. All these regulations are specifically designed for safety—to prevent buildings from crumbling and people from tripping or falling.

If we can regulate the design of features that protect people from injury, why can't we regulate the malleable factors that lead to chronic disease?

Public health has an important—but admittedly limited—role in stopping the obesity epidemic. It's not the role of public health to force you to eat healthier food or compel you to exercise. However, I believe it is the role of public health to make it easier for us to obtain a healthy diet and to be physically active by minimizing the risk factors that undermine and overwhelm us. I'm not splitting hairs: there is a big difference between regulating people's behavior directly and regulating the environment in which we live. It is not appropriate, for example, for the government's public health department to stop you from eating a candy bar every day if that's what you want to do. But it is appropriate for the government to protect you from marketing practices that force you to confront a candy bar every day.

Our approach to pornography is instructive. We don't ban it, but we restrict its availability. It is not on every street corner, at every cash register, or in vending machines. If it were, it would be impossible to ignore. If we had to see pornography everywhere we went, no doubt our ability to think about anything other than sex would be challenged. Food can be a little like pornography.

There are two ways of thinking about how much regulation we want in our lives. The current approach with respect to the food environment is "You're on your own"—there is a minimal amount of interference in the way food outlets operate, except with respect to hygiene.

The burden is on consumers to figure out our nutritional needs by ourselves, but the deck is stacked against us.

At the opposite end of the spectrum, "We are all in this together," public health departments could establish benchmarks and standards that would require businesses to ensure that the food they serve will not increase people's risk for disease, at least not without the customer's full awareness and consent. New regulations could enhance the food environment so that it would favor consumer health.

"We are all in this together" is how we currently handle water, another commodity that everyone needs to survive. Nearly all the water available to the American public is potable. If it isn't, it is clearly labeled so. We have established rigorous systems in which we test the water supplying most localities on a regular, if not daily, basis to make sure there are no contaminants that could increase the risk of cancer or lead to potentially deadly infectious diseases, like cholera or *E. coli*. Rich or poor, everyone gets the same water quality. Although the system is not perfect—there are instances of groundwater contamination that must be mitigated, as well as many Americans who have to get water from their own wells (usually in rural areas)—most people use municipal water from the tap, either plain or filtered, and do not suffer any ill health from its consumption.

In contrast, in countries where most available water is not potable, anyone who wants safe water to drink has to take arduous steps to make it so—boiling, filtering, and safely storing it. In such societies, rates of infectious disease and childhood mortality are much higher than they are in the United States, partly because for too many people it is too burdensome to take all these steps. Even having a few people who fail to comply with sanitary standards can spread disease to many.

Think how onerous it would be if we did not have a system of safe public water and there were hundreds of unregulated companies selling water, each claiming their product was superior or tastier. How could people be confident that they were not going to get water that would make them sick? After all, water quality testing is not something most laypeople can easily do. What would we do without a trustworthy independent group that could certify the water as safe?

We have long passed the time when anyone would consider it reasonable for the government to merely issue guidance for "Healthy Water Standards" listing all the most common carcinogens, toxins, viruses, bacteria, and parasites, and the maximum tolerable amount we could consume per week. Imagine the absurdity of allowing companies to sell water that had contaminants in concentrations such that it would be easy for consumers to be exposed to amounts greater than recommended by the Healthy Water Standards. Too many people would not be able to make wise choices in a marketplace with all manner of water qualities being sold, if the impurities on the product label were listed in parts per billion or milligrams per deciliter and people had to compare these amounts with the recommended standards on their own initiative.

Yet this is the situation in the modern food environment. The burden for avoiding unhealthy foods and assembling a healthy diet is entirely on the individual. The requirement for calculating calories and essential nutrients for an optimal diet is beyond the capacity of most, and it is just as demanding, if not more, than if we all had to figure out individually which water in which quantity was safe to drink.

For a healthy diet we need to regulate both the quality and the quantity of the food we eat. But the glut of food in America is a primary factor limiting our ability to do so, because it promotes intense competition in the food industry and aggressive marketing. America produces nearly twice the calories that people need—about 3,800 calories per person per day.[15] In contrast, Japan does not produce as many excess calories (only 2,558 per person a day) and does not have a substantial obesity problem.[16]

The excess availability and consumption of calories are now significant contributors to climate change. The production, processing, and transport of foods lead to carbon emissions that contribute to global warming. About 40 percent of all food in America is thrown away, and 97 percent of food waste ends up in landfills, where it decomposes to form methane gas, which has a global warming potential twenty-five times that of carbon dioxide.[17] Food is estimated to contribute more than seven tons of carbon emissions per household per year, and about half of that is attributable to meat and dairy consumption. Furthermore, it is estimated that merely eating less (e.g., reducing average consumption from 2,500 to 2,200 calories per day) could substantially reduce household carbon emissions and save the average American household $850 per year.[18]

The largest environmental strain from food stems from meat and dairy products, for which the production and consumption contribute to 18 percent of all greenhouse gases.[19] Animal protein production requires eleven times as much fossil fuel as vegetable proteins and a hundred times more water.[20] Although the US Department of Agriculture's 2010 Dietary Guidelines for Americans recommends no more than 1.8 ounces of red meat per day, Americans consume 37 percent more than that.[21]

Ironically, humans get no physiological benefit from eating too much meat as compared to other foods. Our bodies can only absorb and use a limited amount of protein—we cannot store it the way we do fat, and so we simply excrete whatever we don't use. We are literally flushing more than half of the protein we consume down the toilet.

Although the goal of improving health is sufficient to justify public action, the monster storms, the rising oceans, the droughts, and all the unusual weather changes we have been experiencing over the past few years should provide an incentive beyond stopping obesity to rethink how we regulate the food environment. The suggestions in the next chapter squarely address how we should target the environment to support individuals who would choose health over heft.

9

A Safer Food Environment

Have you ever wondered why bars from New York to Los Angeles serve beer in twelve-ounce servings, wine in five-ounce servings, and liquor in 1.5-ounce shots? It's because beer, wine, and liquor all contain different concentrations of alcohol, so the standardized serving of each contains 0.6 ounce of pure alcohol. Standardized serving sizes ensure that a drink is a drink is a drink: 0.6 ounce of alcohol, no more, no less, no matter what you choose to imbibe.

Compare that to food, where serving sizes are all over the map. A double cheeseburger at McDonald's has 440 calories and a medium fries has 380. At Carl's Jr., a Super Star Cheeseburger has 940 calories and a medium fries has 430. At Denny's, a cheeseburger and fries is 1,400 calories. And at Chili's, the burger-and-fries platters range from 1,310 calories for the Oldtimer to 2,290 calories for the burger with ancho chili BBQ. Even with calorie labels on menus, you'd have to be pretty good at math, algebra, and geometry to figure out how to divide up your food in order to eat just 640 calories, the amount that is recommended by the Institute of Medicine for a single meal for the average person trying to maintain a normal weight. The IOM assumes adults eat three meals and one snack to obtain the recommended average of 2,000 calories per day.

Although calorie-labeling on menus was intended to help people make better choices in the same way a speedometer helps people estimate and control their driving speed, it hasn't been very successful.[1] Without a speedometer, people cannot precisely estimate how fast they are traveling. Their only clue might be based upon how quickly the scenery flies by. Drivers are trained to regularly check the speedometer. Road signs let them know when they can drive at which speeds and when they need to stop. But there are no signposts that define the optimal calories to choose or stop signs that indicate when we have consumed enough. It isn't patently clear to many people how to respond to the calorie counts on menus.

Every restaurant serves different portion sizes: some are large, some giant, and others gargantuan. This leaves many of us confused and prone to eating far too much. How much easier would it be to control our intake if we knew that a cheeseburger had 400 calories whether we purchased it at McDonald's, Burger King, or Denny's? Or that lunch was going to contain just 640 calories, regardless of what we ordered?

Why can't restaurants be held responsible for designing and serving meals that contain what we need? If people eat too much at one meal, they usually don't eat less at the next to compensate. Similarly, if we don't get enough of something at one meal, like fruits and vegetables, we don't usually make it up by eating more of those foods later. This means that when restaurants serve us too much food with too many calories and too few essential nutrients, they put us at risk for chronic diseases.

Right now, as a society we accept this risk, and we don't expect restaurants to be responsible for taking care of us. However, this is something we need to seriously reconsider, because it is too difficult for most people to figure out how to compensate for meals with too many calories and too few nutrients that protect us from disease.

Just as policies like standardized serving sizes evolved to support the moderate consumption of alcohol, we need commonsense regulations that will moderate our consumption of food. Alcohol regulation provides an excellent model for food because of the inherent similarities: consuming too much alcohol—just like consuming too much food—leads to chronic disease. In the case of alcohol, it's cirrhosis of the liver, hypertension, and a variety of cancers. In the case of eating too much of the wrong kinds of food, it's diabetes, hypertension, heart disease, stroke, and a variety of cancers. (Binge drinking also leads to injury and aggression, but there is no parallel to food in that regard.)

Alcohol control policies have a proven track record of keeping the public safe—or at least safer—from harm. Although they have not eliminated alcohol-related problems or alcoholism, such policies have been highly effective in controlling alcohol's harms. Over the past three decades, deaths from alcohol-related traffic crashes have declined by 60 percent. Alcoholic liver cirrhosis declined by 48.3 percent between 1970 and 2005.[2] Compare this to the incidence of obesity and diet-related chronic diseases, which have been skyrocketing.

We are beginning to recognize that people are limited in their ability to control how much they eat. We have already recognized that many people have limitations when it comes to behaviors like smoking, drinking, and substance use. Although eating food is not the same as drinking alcohol or taking illegal drugs, the evolution of our understanding of people's ability to control how much they consume of these substances is quite instructive. It is only because we changed our view of alcohol that our society developed public health responses that have reduced alcohol-related illnesses and deaths.

The Transition to Alcohol Control

Two hundred years ago, excessive alcohol use was a substantially bigger problem than it is today. William Rorabaugh, author of *The Alcoholic Republic*, wrote that in its earliest beginnings, America was known as a nation of drunkards.[3] Historian Harry Levine, who has written extensively about the changing view of alcohol, notes that for most of the seventeenth and eighteenth centuries, the prevailing belief was that people drank because they wanted to and could stop at any time.[4] The concept of addiction was not part of the common vocabulary. Alcohol was not considered addictive, and habitual drunkenness was not thought to constitute a disease. Alcohol was the beverage of choice in the Colonial period in part because people didn't have access to potable water or couldn't trust the local water supply.

During the Colonial period, most families brewed their own alcohol and produced their own wine because it was too expensive to import. Fermented apple juice, or applejack, was a staple, with an ethanol content similar to that of beer. Alcohol was served to all, even to children.

Spirits became commonly available in America before the Revolutionary War. Slave labor on Caribbean sugarcane plantations made it possible to cheaply produce and sell molasses, the key ingredient of rum. Almost every town had its own distillery to meet increasing demand, and the tavern was the primary social institution. Employers gave workers allotments of rum in lieu of wages. Every man, woman, and child was estimated to have consumed more than 3.5 gallons of hard liquor each year. Alcohol consumption appeared to peak in 1830 at roughly triple the consumption today.[5] Even though lots of people were tipsy all the time, drunkenness was not considered a significant problem, and drinking was a natural, normal choice made for pleasure. Social control was maintained by community relationships.

After the Revolutionary War ended, British traders reduced imports of rum and molasses to America because of higher import taxes. By the early 1800s, the slack had been easily taken up with the expansion of new distilling technology: the perpetual still, which increased the yield of distillation.[6] Corn crops were difficult to ship, so settlers transformed them into abundant supplies of whiskey. Drinking continued to be highly prevalent throughout the American continent.

The general attitude was that drinking alcoholic beverages was healthful, while water was fit only for livestock. Strong drink was frequently prescribed by physicians, even for babies with colic, and was believed to cure colds, fevers, headaches, depression, and snakebites.[7] Spirits were part of the democratic process, and candidates usually courted voters with free drinks.

At some point around the turn of the nineteenth century, people's views toward alcohol changed dramatically. Why this happened is still a matter of speculation—perhaps the growing urbanization led people to have more frequent and unpleasant confrontations with drunks. Perhaps the change was inspired by the religious concerns that drinking constituted sin and gluttony. Or the advance of medical science and identification of cirrhosis may have spurred it. The growing practice of autopsy documented a clear link among excessive alcohol consumption, organ damage, and death.

Dr. Benjamin Rush, a renowned physician of the late eighteenth and early nineteenth centuries, is believed to be the person who developed the idea of addiction. He characterized frequent bouts of drunkenness as a "disease of the will." Compulsive drinking became recognized as commonplace, the cause of ruined health and early death. People who consistently drank too much were unable to earn a living or provide for their families.

The concept of drunkards being physically and mentally unable to refrain from drink became increasingly accepted. However, the source of the addiction was initially considered to be alcohol itself rather than a defect in the person. People were largely sympathetic to drunkards, who were viewed as victims. "Demon rum" was named the perpetrator. Efforts to protect these victims and their families focused on restricting the sale of alcohol; for example, no sales on Sundays, no sales from unlicensed vendors, and no sales to children.[8] In 1849, Wisconsin passed a statute that required tavern owners to post a bond supporting those who became widows and orphans because of a patron's drinking.[9]

Yet the biggest reduction in alcohol consumption occurred between 1830 and 1840, when several things happened along with restrictions on the sale of alcohol: the rapid growth of steamboat transportation in the early 1800s made it possible to ship corn long distances cheaply, so farmers were less motivated to distill it into whiskey; incentives to limit drinking on the job, like reductions in insurance rates, became available; and groups of businessmen agreed to subsidize alcohol-free taverns, so people could socialize without being pressured to drink.

It was only in the late nineteenth and early twentieth centuries, after a myriad of new regulations limited the sale of alcohol and prompted a substantial decline in drinking, that activists began to focus on what are now known as the "externalities" of alcohol use—how inebriated drinkers hurt others, not just themselves and their families. With advancing technology—the building of the railroads, the invention of cars, and the mechanization of factories—liquor became associated with train crashes and industrial accidents that injured innocent bystanders. Drunkards were no longer viewed sympathetically; they were considered social menaces. Inner discipline and individual responsibility began to be considered as a fundamental requirement for societal well-being.

After 1840 the basic regulations that limited the sale of alcohol to particular places and people, and at specific times, along with the evolving norms that reduced drinking in the workplace, kept overall consumption at a low level. Nevertheless, the Temperance Movement kept expanding and was able to get the majority of US states to prohibit the sale of alcohol within their borders. By 1920, when the Volstead Act prohibited alcohol sales nationwide, thirty states were already dry.

The American experience with Prohibition was a clear demonstration of how regulations can go too far. The total ban on alcohol led to black markets, corruption, and gang warfare, which is very similar to what we are experiencing today with regard to illegal drugs. Prohibition ended in 1933, but a substantial portfolio of regulations remained, including "partial" prohibition, which made it illegal for anyone under age eighteen to purchase alcohol. By 1986, every state had expanded "partial" prohibition to those under twenty-one, and as a consequence the deaths of thousands of young adults and teens by alcohol-related car crashes were averted.[10]

Campaigns against excess alcohol use continue in the United States, and multiple organizations are dedicated to alcohol control. It is because we are vigilant that the amount of alcohol consumption has remained substantially lower in the United States than it was in 1820. When regulations are relaxed, as they were in the 1970s, alcohol use rises (see Figure 5).

Alcohol Control as a Model for Obesity Control

Eating too much food leads to being overweight and obese, but this is generally regarded as something every individual has the capacity to control. Yet we no longer think this is the case for a subgroup of people who drink too much alcohol, namely alcoholics. We consider the source of alcohol addiction to be located in the person, not in the product, as was thought in the nineteenth century. Today, we view addiction to alcohol as a disease that is largely genetic and not necessarily the consequence of character flaws. We understand that many individuals are highly vulnerable to alcohol, and that for them staying sober is an eternal struggle that requires unending support.

Although we believe that only a small percentage of individuals are

Annual per Capita Alcohol Consumption[1-3]

Gallons of ethanol

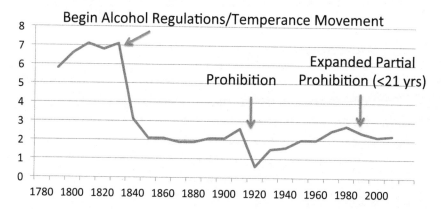

FIGURE 5. *US Annual per Capita Alcohol Consumption.*

1. Hall W. What are the policy lessons of National Alcohol Prohibition in the United States, 1920–1933? *Addiction.* Jul 2010;105(7):1164–1173.

2. Levine HG, Reinarman C. From prohibition to regulation: lessons from alcohol policy for drug policy. *Milbank Q.* 1991;69(3):461–494.

3. LaVallee RA, Yi HY. Apparent per capita alcohol consumption: national, state, and regional trends, 1977–2010. http://pubs.niaaa.nih.gov/publications/Surveillance95/CONS10.htm. Wash, DC: NIAAA, USDHHS;2012.

vulnerable to alcohol addiction, we do recognize that alcohol can cause harm and destroy self-control among people who are not otherwise alcoholics. Everyone is susceptible to becoming drunk if they imbibe too much. Indeed, the majority of alcohol-related injuries and other problems occur among people who are not alcoholics. For example, two out of three people arrested each year for driving while intoxicated are first-time offenders.[11] For this reason, our society has retained broad measures that restrict the sale and consumption of alcohol for everyone, not just the most vulnerable.

Nearly everyone can become addicted to substances like heroin. And most of us would become addicted to tobacco if we smoked it early and often enough in life. We generally locate the source of addiction to tobacco and heroin in the substance rather than in the person.

Is it fair to compare potentially addicting substances like alcohol, tobacco, and heroin with food? The confessions in the beginning of

Chapter 1 about how difficult it is to control a ravenous appetite sound very much like what alcoholics might say about drinking or what drug addicts say about their favored substances. Is it possible that people who have trouble controlling how much they eat are addicted to food?

Addiction vs. the Imperatives of Our DNA

Technically, the term "addiction" refers to dependence on a substance or a practice one does not need for survival. The dependence is usually characterized by physiological, and sometimes life-threatening, withdrawal symptoms when an addicted person tries to stop using the substance. Given the first part of the definition, food would *not* qualify as an addictive substance because we must have it for survival. Notwithstanding that, the criteria for dependence would make us all addicts because we would all suffer physiological "withdrawal" symptoms signifying hunger if we stopped eating.

Scientists like Dr. Nora Volkow, Director of the National Institute on Drug Abuse, have also shown that the neural pathways that are responsible for addiction to drugs are the same ones that are involved in the desire to eat.[12] Some researchers use the term "addiction" loosely and consider any persistent substance use or compulsive or repetitive behavior that brings short-term pleasure an addiction if there are long-term negative consequences that interfere with a person's well-being and functioning.

Still, the issue remains as to whether the concepts of willpower and self-control are actually relevant when it comes to eating behaviors. Is the source of obesity and overeating the mutable characteristics of individuals, or is it inherent in the food itself and the physiological effects it has on individuals?

We are all endowed with the drive and desire to eat, especially when tempting food is at hand. Just as self-control is limited among individuals who feel they need substances like tobacco, alcohol, or other drugs, the degree to which most of us can refrain from eating may be limited. If weight is a measure of our ability to control how much we eat, it is pretty clear that most of us fail.

None of us can use willpower to stop our hearts from beating, although some have learned to slow their pulse through meditation. Most of us can control our breathing for brief periods of time; we can slow it down or speed it up, but sustaining such control for more than an hour or so is extraordinarily demanding. If our heart stops beating or we stop breathing for more than a few minutes, we will die. If we stop eating, we can survive quite a bit longer, but not more than a couple of weeks, depending upon whether we drink water. Thus, it is for good reason that fasting, or any kind of dieting, is significantly more difficult than eating.

Most people cannot routinely control how much they eat in the face of excess availability of food. Replacing the popular misconception that people can always control their diets with a more realistic picture of human limitations is the most important initial step we can take to stem obesity. Once we accept that most of us need help to control our dietary intake when too much food is available, we will feel justified in taking actions to protect ourselves.

Many of the solutions our society adopted to limit the consumption of alcohol are entirely appropriate to help people moderate their food intake. Just as alcohol control policies work by limiting when, where, and how much alcohol is served, similar regulations could very likely offer substantial support to individuals who want to control their weight. The following suggestions will catapult us toward a solution to the obesity epidemic. One of the most powerful would be having standardized portion sizes.

Standardized Portion Sizes

As mentioned earlier, restaurants, unlike bars, have no standard serving guidelines, which means there is no common yardstick for us to judge the number of calories we are consuming when we go out to eat. This may be the most important cause of the clear association between eating food prepared away from home and unwanted weight gain.[13]

"Unit bias," a term coined by scientists Andrew Geier, Paul Rozin, and Gheorghe Doros from the University of Pennsylvania, refers to the idea that people judge how much to eat based on what they are served. If we are served one apple, the entire apple is the unit, and we will typically eat the whole thing. If the unit is a half cup of applesauce or a cup of rice, that is the amount we think is appropriate to consume.[14]

Geier and his colleagues documented that people served themselves more when the unit presented was larger, and less when it was smaller. In their experiments, people ate more M&M's when a quarter-cup scoop was in the serving bowl than when a tablespoon was; they helped themselves to fewer Philadelphia-style soft pretzels when they were cut in half than when they were displayed whole. Yet people are usually just as satisfied when they are served a smaller amount.[15]

Having standardized portions will not only establish the appropriate amount to eat, but will also make portions uniform across all food establishments. Standardized portion sizes have already been determined by the USDA and the FDA. The FDA's system is the basis for the labeling on packaged processed foods. Labeling was mandated by the FDA as part of the 1990 Nutrition Labeling and Education Act. Both the USDA and FDA initially based serving sizes on how much people typically ate in a single meal during 1977–1978—before the obesity epidemic accelerated. However, the FDA adjusted some of its sizes based on food consumption data from 1985–1988, which is why some of its portion sizes are larger than those of the USDA.[16]

When New York City's Mayor Michael Bloomberg floated the idea of capping the servings of sugar-sweetened beverages to sixteen ounces, a common refrain from his critics was that this type of policy would interfere with a person's free choice. At the other extreme, some thought the sixteen-ounce cap on soda was ridiculous. People would just order more than one soda, so it would likely have no impact on the obesity epidemic. In fact, the "standardized" portion size of soda is eight ounces, so the regulation, had it been approved, would still have New Yorkers consuming double what people drank thirty years ago.

Moreover, an eight-ounce size is more in line with the 2009 recommendations of the American Heart Association on daily added sugar intake: about six teaspoons is the maximum added sugar recommended for women, the amount in one eight-ounce cup of soda. For men, 150 calories is considered the maximum, or about twelve ounces of soda.[17]

Bloomberg's proposal to ban serving sizes of soda larger than sixteen ounces was overturned, primarily because it had many loopholes. It applied only to sodas rather than all high-calorie drinks, and it covered only a subset of food outlets, excluding convenience stores like

7-Eleven, which is known for serving the Big Gulp, a thirty-two-ounce serving of soda, and the Super Big Gulp, at forty-four ounces. A comprehensive system of standardized portions would overcome these legal concerns because it would apply to all eating-out establishments and all food products prepared and sold for immediate consumption.

The scientific support for standardized portions is extremely robust: people invariably eat more when they are served more, and they typically do not feel any less satisfied when they are served smaller amounts.[18] Efforts made to train people to control mindless eating and to pay attention to portion sizes generally fail in the long term.[19] Cornell University professor Brian Wansink, author of *Mindless Eating,* says that even when he challenges his students not to eat too much from big bowls, they nevertheless do. Wansink's solution to mindless eating is to use small bowls—a different method for ensuring smaller portions.

Because eating is typically an automatic behavior, the quantity that people eat depends on the quantity they are served. Therefore, if all restaurants serve customers food using standardized portions (based on the national Dietary Guidelines for Americans), we could very likely make a real dent in the number of us who gain unwanted pounds.

The primary requirement of a standardized portion system would be that all foods *must* be available in single portions. But this would not necessarily preclude restaurants from offering the same dishes in larger sizes. Practically speaking, some foods, like a whole fish, cannot easily be divided into a single portion without ruining the presentation. Items that are larger would simply have to be presented with the number of serving units they contain and priced proportionally. For example, many restaurants that offer "family-size portions" would need to state that the serving contains three or four portions, or however many servings it actually has. Given that a single serving of meat is three ounces, a twelve-ounce steak would have to be described as containing four portions.

Standardized portions would serve as a benchmark that would make it much simpler for people to figure out how much to eat. They would also serve as a guide to make adjustments for individual differences. A triathlete might ask for two portions, someone who wanted to lose weight could ask for a half portion, and most people who ordered one portion could be reasonably confident that it would be the right amount.

When foods that are associated with chronic diseases are served in portions that exceed a single serving, there should be a notice that such consumption may increase one's risk of chronic diseases. True consumer freedom is having relevant and accessible information, with the consequences spelled out loud and clear at the time people make their selections. People would still have the right to order and consume as much as they want.

There is no doubt that most restaurants would vehemently protest, no matter how logical or beneficial the new regulations are. Standardized portion sizes would likely have to be implemented over the objections of the food industry.

Restrictions on Impulse Marketing

Another regulation that could help people moderate their food intake would be the restriction of impulse marketing strategies, like displays of candy, chips, and sodas at the cash register that invite us to spontaneously grab sweets and other snacks on our way out the door. Impulse marketing is intended to disrupt cognitive decision-making and encourage impulse purchases based on emotion, contextual cues, and instant gratification. Because our self-control tends to wane on any shopping trip due to all the decisions and trade-offs we need to make, many of us are highly vulnerable to impulse marketing strategies when we shop.

A number of regulations are already in place to protect people from the impulse marketing of alcohol. For example, some states have limits on how alcohol can be displayed and sold.[20] Many states don't allow the sale of alcohol except in specific state-run stores. In California, selling beer from iced barrels or from temporary displays placed within five feet of the front door or the cash register in outlets also selling gas is prohibited, presumably to discourage impulsive purchases that lead to drinking and driving.

A parallel policy for reducing impulsive choices in a supermarket or restaurant would be to limit what products can be displayed in salient locations. For example, the end aisle displays in supermarkets account for 30 percent of sales, and people are two to five times more likely to buy products when they are displayed in these locations than when they are displayed elsewhere.[21] A regulation that restricts what can be displayed at the end aisle areas or at the cash register could help people reduce unhealthy impulsive choices.

During experiments testing self-control, some children were able to resist marshmallows by keeping them out of sight or covering their eyes. Using the same principle of "out of sight, out of mind," moving candy and other junk foods to less salient locations in retail outlets would help people avoid them. Foods that are high in sugar and fat might be restricted to locations such as the back of the store, the bottom shelf, above eye level, behind the counter, or at locations other than the end aisles or at eye level. Such foods might even require clerk assistance. But these policies would still allow people who really want to buy these foods to do so.

Limiting impulse marketing like displaying candy at the cash register will likely affect hundreds of thousands of businesses that sell only snacks. A national assessment found that candy, sweetened beverages, salty snacks, and/or sweetened baked goods were available in 41 percent of all retail outlet stores, usually within arm's reach of the cash register queue. This included 96 percent of pharmacies; 94 percent of gas stations; 55 percent of hardware stores, automobile sales, and repair outlets; 29 percent of bookstores; 22 percent of furniture stores; and 16 percent of apparel stores. Candy was offered for free in 22 percent of these outlets.

Although we might be able to resist buying chocolate at the hardware store, we cannot prevent the craving that the sight of sugary or savory foods ignites. We may not be aware of or even able to prevent the excessive eating that may subsequently occur once we are stimulated or primed. It also may be very hard to refuse the free candy at the bank or the hair salon when we are preoccupied with other thoughts. Food that increases the risk of chronic diseases should not be sold or distributed in retail outlets other than those fully dedicated to food. If we really want to eat, we will go to a food outlet.

Impulse marketing works not just by placing candy at the cash register, but also by making such items salient among a crowded food-scape and reducing the effort people might otherwise make to search for a better option. The placement of items on a menu (e.g., first on the menu board, upper-right corner of the menu) can influence our choices. A couple of controlled studies have shown that the order in which food appears on a menu influences what people buy.[22] Because customers quickly scan a menu, they tend to choose items listed either first or last on a list, as these items are more salient. Even at a salad bar, people are more likely to select items that are at the edges rather than in the middle.[23] Ease, convenience, and salience often trump in-dividual preferences.

Earlier I described how "combo" meals are often preferred because they reduce the effort people have to make in choosing what to eat and because of price manipulations that highlight potential savings.[24] One regulatory option would be to restrict the sale of meals as "combos" or "value meals" if they contain any food that is considered "low nutri-ent" or that has too much fat, sugar, salt, or calories. This restriction wouldn't prohibit people from buying whatever food they want, but it would prevent people from automatically getting something that could harm them just because they made a choice without thinking carefully. Regulations that help people make deliberate choices rather than au-tomatic ones are common in many other settings where people have to make important decisions.

Our society caters to impulse buying, and in doing so it fosters it. Anything that triggers an emotional response and makes it easy to act quickly on the emotion should be considered impulse marketing. It has been shown that restrictions on hours and days of operation are effec-tive in controlling drinking and other alcohol-related problems. Typi-cally bars close at 2 a.m.—but not everywhere. When closing times of bars and other alcohol outlets are relaxed, alcohol-related problems tend to increase.[25]

Limiting hours of operation for food outlets could also have a ben-eficial effect. It has only been in the past thirty years that large num-bers of supermarkets, convenience stores, and even restaurants are routinely open for twenty-four hours per day. Having food available all the time allows people to wait until the last minute and allows fleeting moods to govern people's choices. The food suddenly desired might have just been featured on TV. A craving could be triggered by a billboard or a smell. And more likely than not, impulse buying and eating lead to choosing foods that are higher in sugar and fat.[26] When people are more thoughtful about choices, they are less likely to choose unhealthy items.[27] Restricting the hours of food outlet operation would require people to make a greater effort to plan their shopping, and could reduce the frequency of impulse buying.

Most localities want to discourage drinking and driving. To that end, nearly all prohibit the sale of alcohol through drive-through windows. After New Mexico banned drive-through alcohol outlets in 1998, sales of alcohol decreased and rates of alcohol-related fatalities dropped substantially.[28] The city of New Orleans, however, still has drive-through daiquiri shops and among the highest rates of alcohol-related traffic fatalities in the nation.

Just as limiting drive-through alcohol sales reduced alcohol sales and drinking, limiting the use of drive-through windows for food sales would likely reduce impulsive eating behaviors and would require people to do more planning to obtain food. Outright bans may not be acceptable, but reduced hours for the drive-through windows would certainly help curtail impulsive eating behaviors—e.g., windows open only during peak hours, such as 12 to 1 p.m. or 5–7 p.m. This would reduce the likelihood that people might add an extra meal to their intake just because they passed a drive-through that is open at 3 in the afternoon or 10 at night. If they were really hungry they could park, and go inside or walk up to the window to order.

Counter-Advertising

A lot of attention is being paid to media advertising that targets children; indeed, some claim that this one component of marketing is the largest driver of childhood obesity.[29] Although I agree that targeting children with junk food advertisements is a heinous practice because children lack the capacity to respond critically, I still think it is better to create counter-advertising than to ban such advertising. Furthermore, our society is dedicated to the protection of free speech, and I expect it will be a long time before we are ready to be more stringent on regulating commercial speech—even though, legally, commercial speech is not protected.

From 1968 to 1970, the Fairness Doctrine allowed the placement of anti-tobacco advertising to counter tobacco advertising. One of the most effective ads shown during that time was called "Like Father, Like Son," which pictured a young child mimicking whatever his father did. The opportunity to be better role models gave parents a good reason to quit smoking. With strong anti-tobacco ads, tobacco sales fell by 15 percent—without any increase in tobacco taxes and before there was widespread institution of clean air laws.[30]

Thus, counter-advertising will likely be a promising avenue for countering the promotions of low-nutrient foods. Not only could counter-ads frequently remind us in a strong and convincing way of how unhealthy some foods really are or point out how advertisements manipulate us, they could also function as primes to help us resist junk food and extra-large portions.

Currently there are hardly any counter-ads that discourage people from eating unhealthy foods. Instead, the emphasis is on promoting fruits and vegetables, which has not been shown to reduce weight.[31] For people to lose weight by adding fruits and vegetables to their diets, they would have to give up other foods, which apparently most do not.

Where counter-advertising has been used, it has often been successful in influencing behaviors. People typically pay more attention to negative messages, which is why they are invariably used in political campaigns.[32] When messages include warnings, they can help people avoid foods and consume less.[33]

A limited number of campaigns have been directed against food products. The British Heart Foundation launched a campaign against "crisps" (potato chips), and New York City has launched a campaign against sugar-sweetened beverages.

No formal evaluation has yet been published about the impact of these campaigns. Yet early results from New York City are promising. Dr. Tom Farley, the city's Commissioner of Health and Mental Hygiene, reports that soda consumption there is beginning to decrease.

However, both the British and New York City campaigns were handicapped in that neither had the capacity to directly label these products, thereby allowing people to see the negative information about the product at the point of purchase.

I think that standardizing portion sizes, limiting impulse marketing, and running counter-advertising are the three policies that could make the biggest difference for the most people in the shortest amount of time, if they were adopted. However, there are at least six other interventions that build on our historic experience with alcohol control and are well worth examining. Let me briefly review these below.

1. Density Restrictions

Most states limit the number of outlets that can be licensed to sell alcohol. Why not do the same to limit the number of outlets that primarily sell food that is associated with chronic diseases, like doughnut shops, candy stores, and ice cream parlors? How many of these do we really need? Does it make sense for every office building to have junk food vending machines on every floor? Isn't it plausible that having candy and sodas on every corner and in every building causes people to consume more of these unhealthy foods? Having fewer junk food outlets will likely reduce the frequency with which we consume such foods.

2. Pricing

Increasing alcohol taxes has been shown to reduce drinking, and restrictions on alcohol price promotions are also common. Most US states and localities prohibit "specials," like "all you can drink" nights and "ladies drink free" nights. These policies reduce alcohol use and other alcohol-related problems.[34] Similarly, increasing the price of foods most strongly associated with the risk of obesity and other chronic diseases could lead to reductions in consumption. Restrictions on "all you can eat" buffets and prohibitions on price reductions for junk food, like "ten for $10" or "two for the price of one" should be considered.

3. Warning Labels

Until now, in the United States, the warning labels for alcohol and tobacco have been limited to words. However, in Canada, graphic images showing the harms of tobacco are displayed on cigarette packages. Such images are effective in discouraging smoking and helping people quit.[35]

Why not use graphic warnings for foods that increase our risks of chronic diseases? How many mothers would pack children's lunch bags with bologna sandwiches if the package had a symbol indicating that frequent consumption of bologna is associated with an increased risk of cancer? (It is.) We could create symbols that let consumers know which foods increase the risk of heart disease (e.g., foods high in sugar and high in saturated fat) and other chronic diseases (e.g., salty foods increase the risk of hypertension and stroke), and make sure vivid, graphic warnings are on the package and easily visible right at the point of purchase.

4. Workplace Interventions

Drinking on the job is prohibited everywhere, even though that wasn't always the case. Businesses can establish policies that protect their workers as well as support healthy behaviors during the workday. They could offer walking and exercise breaks for sedentary workers, and establish policies that would reduce the consumption of food—especially junk food available in vending machines, the company cafeteria, at meetings, and in shared workspaces.

5. Server Training (Responsible Beverage Service)

Many localities require anyone who serves or sells alcohol to undergo a server-training program to learn how to protect both the business and consumers and how to adhere to alcohol laws including checking for legal proof of age.[36] Server training may potentially be relevant to obesity prevention if additional regulations that govern sales of foods are adopted and workers need to understand their role in enforcing the regulations or recommending items most likely to support a healthy diet.

6. Age Limits

Raising the drinking age to twenty-one has been a very effective policy, saving tens of thousands of lives.[37] Efforts are already under way to restrict the sale of unhealthy foods to children in school settings. Although prohibitions on the sale of these foods to children outside school might not be politically or socially acceptable, labels on foods that are not allowed in school can help parents identify what to avoid in the supermarket, empowering them to control their children's intake of junk food. Such age-based labels could be very powerful in changing norms concerning children's routine consumption of low-nutrient foods.

Moving Forward

Societies have been very serious about alcohol control for centuries and have developed a large portfolio of regulations that have kept alcohol-related problems under control. But alcohol policies, especially those seen to infringe on business (such as restrictions on outlet density or excise taxes, which might be an inconvenience or burden to moderate drinkers), have been subject to a great deal of controversy. Yet over time, many of these measures have become widely accepted and have been shown to be effective in curbing alcohol-related problems.

Even though alcohol is an addictive substance and it is legal, its accessibility and salience in our society have been kept under control; it has not been allowed to proliferate the way food has. Moreover, the long-term consequences and costs to society of overeating are now considerably higher than the consequences of immoderate alcohol consumption. While some of the laws that are acceptable and feasible for alcohol control may seem overreaching for obesity control at present, I believe this is only because comparing the alcohol environment to the food environment constitutes a new way of thinking.

Innovations for regulating the food environment will likely have to start at the local level, with courageous leaders who are not beholden to special interests. Our towns and cities will likely lead the way by passing model ordinances and demonstrating that regulating the food environment will not be the end of the world but instead will provide a measurable benefit to local constituents.

Some localities are already trying to implement policies that regulate the food environment. In 2010, the City Council in Watsonville,

California, passed regulations that define a "healthy" restaurant. All new restaurants have to adhere to new standards regulating the food that is offered in order to obtain a business permit.[38] In South Los Angeles, activists successfully pushed for a ban on new fast food outlets.

Some of the other policies mentioned, like standardizing portion sizes, could be adopted fairly quickly and may actually have a positive impact on profits if outlets sell smaller quantities of food at the same price or higher. Other policies, like prohibiting bookstores and hardware stores from selling junk food, will undoubtedly reduce the profits of those businesses. Policies like density limits might be the most difficult to pass, but they could eventually be achieved by not issuing new licenses once an outlet closes.

Our society has implemented multiple laws and regulations to protect individuals. Efforts to control tobacco use, like raising the taxes on cigarettes, only affect smokers. Regulations that require people to wear seat belts in cars or helmets when they drive a motorcycle mostly benefit the wearers. Yet any regulation that prevents people from becoming sick and injured has a secondary benefit to families and society by reducing the burden of health-care costs and disabilities. Therefore, society has a strong rationale for intervening on the factors that lead to obesity.

As the prevalence of obesity grows, and with it the costs of dealing with its associated health problems, the need for society to take stronger action is becoming increasingly apparent. Just as regulating alcohol accessibility has been effective in reducing problem drinking, regulating food accessibility is a promising way to control the obesity epidemic. No single policy will be a panacea. Like alcohol control policies, policies that address obesity need to be multipronged, incorporating a mix of approaches that include restrictions on access to problem foods, reductions of impulse marketing, point-of-purchase warnings, and portion control. Alcohol control policies represent a middle ground in the regulation of a substance that is healthful when consumed moderately and harmful when consumed to excess. In the face of the emerging challenge of obesity, alcohol control policies are important models to follow.[39]

10

The Supermarket of the Future

Whenever I ask my husband what he wants me to make for dinner, he says, "You decide. Whatever you want to make. Just make something and tell me to eat it."

He has a very demanding job. He gets up before the crack of dawn, drives to work, puts in at least ten hours (or more), and when he comes home he is mentally exhausted and doesn't want to have to make any more decisions. He also knows that he usually likes whatever I prepare.

Sometimes he does the same thing in restaurants. When he can't decide what to order and he narrows it down to a couple of choices, he asks the waiter, which one do you like? And then he orders what the waiter likes!

Most of the time he takes the leftovers from dinner for lunch the next day. That way, he is not at the mercy of nearby lunch trucks, and he doesn't have to take the extra time out of his day to go to a restaurant. But he also doesn't have to waste his mental energy figuring out what to order.

All of this means that the burden of figuring out what my family should eat falls on me. I'm the one who has to spend a significant part of my limited mental capacity on meal planning. Some people solve this problem by having the same food based on the day of the week— Monday is spaghetti, Tuesday is chicken, Wednesday is hamburgers, etc. Even though I can see the wisdom of such a routine, I hate to have the same thing over and over. But I also find it challenging to find a variety of recipes that are easy to prepare, tasty, healthy—and will be liked by everyone in the family.

If I haven't planned it ahead of time, I might not have the ingredients for a meal that I would otherwise like to prepare. Sometimes I am too fatigued to come up with something that could make use of whatever is in the house. When this happens, we might just splurge and go out to eat. But that also means we end up with food that usually has too many calories, salt, sugar, and fat.

I doubt that we are the only family that finds putting food on the table every day a bit taxing, especially if we care about flavor, freshness, and health. Right now, the design of most supermarkets and restaurants makes it difficult for families to meet the Dietary Guidelines for Americans. But it doesn't have to be this way. Supermarkets and restaurants could be redesigned to help us meet these standards.

Because most people don't grow their own food, these two types of food outlets are the most logical places to change to help people moderate their intake of food. As described in Part II of this book, the design and management of restaurants and grocery stores are among the primary factors that lead people to make poor dietary choices. But even though we know how these places lead people to make poor food choices, we have less evidence about how they could be changed to help people make healthier choices.

We devote an inordinate amount of effort and resources to studying how to improve the quality of health care and to promoting adherence to medical treatment regimens for people with diabetes and heart disease. But we spend precious little on making sure these same people eat a healthy diet that won't exacerbate their medical conditions. It's time we focus on the factors that lead people to consume foods that lead to chronic diseases in the first place.

Even though we may not believe that people have a limited capacity to eat wisely in the current environment, Americans might accept this if there was strong evidence that designing and managing food outlets differently would make it easier for people to change their own behaviors. Americans place great faith in science and usually believe the results of carefully done studies. For this reason, establishing scientific laboratories in real-world food outlets is vital. We need these laboratories to identify, deconstruct, and make transparent the elements of the food environment that lead to unhealthy food choices, as well as to create outlets that help us make us healthier choices automatically.

Most of the time when people eat away from home, they choose foods of a quality worse than what they would prepare at home: foods that are more likely to increase their risk of getting chronic diseases. The reasons behind this are twofold: first, lower-quality food is predominantly what's available and salient; second, in the restaurant setting, people's choices are more likely to be impulsive and thus to favor high-calorie, low-nutrient foods that increase the risk of chronic diseases.[1]

And when people eat too much (or too little) of a particular food or nutrient at one meal, they don't naturally compensate by eating less (or more) at another meal. If people ate out only occasionally, the poor quality of restaurant meals would not be a problem, but most Americans eat away from home routinely.

About one-third of Americans' daily calories come from food purchased for consumption outside the home, yet we eat out less than one of every three meals.[2] The average American eats commercially prepared food about three times per week. Nearly 20 percent of males and 10 percent of females eat commercially prepared foods six or more times each week, while 56 percent of Americans eat out two or more times per week and fewer than 24 percent eat out less than once a week. The more people eat out, the more likely they are to be overweight.[3]

Although most Americans hold the government responsible for making sure that the water we drink is safe and the air we breathe is clean, until recently, we have had no expectations that the government will ensure that restaurant food will not contribute to diseases like diabetes, heart disease, or cancer.

This is beginning to change. For example, following Denmark's lead in banning trans fats, a type of oil known to increase the risk of heart disease, New York City banned them. This was followed by bans in California and in a variety of localities like Philadelphia, Seattle, and Puerto Rico. Similar bans are being considered by dozens of other jurisdictions. This ban has been broadly accepted—and no one has yet demanded that it be rescinded.

Another food regulation policy being pursued on a national basis is salt reduction. Substantial efforts are under way to persuade food companies to voluntarily decrease the amount of salt they put into food because consuming too much salt increases the risk of hypertension and stroke, among the most common causes of death.

Restaurants are now regulated primarily on criteria related to hygiene and the prevention of food-borne infectious diseases. Typically inspectors from the health department check the kitchens of all restaurants to ensure that they are following hygienic procedures with respect to food preparation, storage, and service. These regulations are lengthy and rigorous, yet restaurants all over the country have found it possible to comply, even when it means they have to add ventilation systems, plumbing, and expensive cold-storage equipment.

In Los Angeles, sanitarians, also called environmental health specialists, have a checklist of more than one hundred items they inspect in every restaurant. They measure the temperature of storage and preparation of "potentially hazardous foods," like meats, cut fruit, and even garlic in oil mixtures. They look for signs of rodents and cockroaches, check that the shellfish have tags showing the date of purchase, make sure wiping cloths are clean and that food preparers wear hairnets, and they even check the toilets to make sure they are clean and equipped. Our health departments devote considerable effort to preventing food-borne infectious diseases, but they do next to nothing to prevent diet-related chronic diseases, which are far more prevalent and cost considerably more of our health dollars.[4]

The magnitude of the risk from a poor diet is not well appreciated. For example, the increased risk of getting lung cancer from exposure to secondhand smoke as the result of living with a smoker is estimated to be between 13 percent and 47 percent, which is about the same increased risk we face of getting colon cancer by eating red meat every day.[5] We have regulations that ban smoking in restaurants, but not a single warning to help people reduce their consumption of red meat, much less reduce the gargantuan portion sizes that steakhouses and BBQ restaurants typically serve.

Obesity doubles the risk of premature mortality. Compare this to the risks we face from chemicals and toxins in air and water, which are usually banned or carefully monitored when they increase the risk of cancer by just one case per one hundred thousand individuals.

A primary reason that we have not been more aggressive in regulating what restaurants offer is that we assume what people choose to eat is a result of their conscious decisions. No one is forced to go to a restaurant. We also believe that customers in a restaurant are free to choose the foods they want.

Herein lies a misconception about individual agency and capacity. Many people eat out not because they want to but because they have to. Business meetings are often conducted over meals in restaurants, and failing to participate would be a detriment to one's ability to compete professionally. Social gatherings occur in restaurants, and failing to attend would isolate people from family and friends. Many people must use restaurants when they travel for business, and many have other justifiable reasons why they cannot prepare their own food at home. Some simply lack cooking skills.

But even this is beside the point. People should be able to eat out without putting their health on the line. They should not automatically be served foods that increase their risk of chronic diseases. Most important, as we have seen, people's food choices are often influenced in ways they cannot easily recognize or resist, and in a restaurant those choices are constrained to what is available.

The political changes necessary to foster the Sanitary Revolution of the nineteenth century required a common belief that filth was bad. Passing alcohol control policies required understanding the harms from drinking and the foolish behavior people are capable of while under the influence. And advances in safe working conditions and legislation guaranteeing equal access and reasonable accommodations for the disabled required a sense of fairness and justice.

Once we recognize that restaurants and supermarkets create conditions that interfere with health, we may be more likely to act collectively to change those conditions.

It's Time to Regulate "Away from Home" Foods

Just as we regulate restaurants to prevent food-borne diseases and require food to be obtained from an approved source, prepared in an inspected kitchen, and stored and served in a hygienic manner, we should establish standards that will prevent chronic diseases, or at least not increase the risk for them. At a recent national conference on "Performance Standards on Away from Home Foods," sponsored by the National Institutes of Health, a group of experts and advocates from academia and the food industry developed a series of recommendations to help restaurants offer healthier meals and adopt business practices that would lead to healthier choices and lower calorie consumption. These standards could be implemented first through voluntary approaches; then with a government health-labeling and certification program; and potentially, after evaluation, through enforceable regulations. Development and application of these standards might shift both industry offerings and consumer choices, and ultimately improve public health. The group developed guidelines for healthier meals as well as principles for the operation of restaurants that would help customers moderate their intake.

The healthy meals had two major requirements: not to exceed seven hundred calories for adults (six hundred for children) and to include 1.5 cups of fruits and/or vegetables (at least 0.5 for children). Seven hundred calories is about one-third of the daily caloric requirement of Americans. (See Appendix.) There is an emphasis on fruits and vegetables because these are typically deficient in the average American diet.

For those of us who don't routinely eat healthy meals, think of how hard it is to make up for missing fruits and vegetables. Adults are supposed to consume about 4.5 cups of fruits and vegetables every day. If we don't get any fruits or vegetables at breakfast or lunch, that means we would have to eat all 4.5 cups at dinner. If we miss a whole day of fruits and vegetables, imagine how hard it would be to eat nine cups the next day. And if we tried to catch up after missing them for two days, we would probably get an upset stomach from eating thirteen cups of fruits and vegetables all at once.

Having food available in portions that are appropriate for the majority of individuals does not preclude the minority, who may eat once or twice a day or need more calories at each meal, from ordering additional items to augment their caloric intake.

In addition to defining the minimum characteristics of a healthy meal, the group developed a list of thirty criteria that would support healthy choices when dining out. To be certified as compliant, restaurants would have to offer at least three healthier meals, or 10 percent of the menu options, whichever is greater, and would have to adopt some of the guidelines on the list to help people moderate their intake. Some examples include not automatically putting free bread or chips on a table, not providing free soft drink refills, making whole grains and skim milk available, and limiting the serving sizes of soft drinks and desserts. (See Appendix.)

Evaluating Changes in Restaurant Standards

Although the benefits of discouraging restaurants from serving too much food may seem intuitively obvious, in reality, changes do not always work the way they are intended. People may not compensate for eating too much, but they may compensate if they think they are eating too little. Rigorously assessing the impact of changes is necessary to ensure that a bad situation is at least not being made worse. To do that, we need experimental laboratories in working restaurants.

The "Restaurant of the Future" in Wageningen, Holland, is a consumer behavior laboratory built into a restaurant.[6] Developed and supported mainly by industry—including companies specializing in food preparation, software development, and the manufacture of professional kitchens—the restaurant features taste-testing laboratories and video cameras to observe consumer behavior, and it has the capacity to alter elements like lighting, music, and the presentation of food. The purpose of the restaurant is to help the food industry identify the most effective ways to package and launch new consumer products, not necessarily to improve health.

When I visited in March 2011, the managers were experimenting with the concept of food carbon footprints and sustainability. As I walked

around the food displays—arranged in a manner that was a cross between a cafeteria and a convenience store, with stations for hot food
and refrigerated cases of sandwiches, salads, yogurts, and cheeses—I
saw small signs in front of most items with an indicator pointing to
a spot on a color spectrum from green to yellow to red. A placard explained that green signified a low carbon footprint, meaning the food
was produced locally (for example, apples) and used less energy, causing smaller amounts of pollution; red meant it was imported (bananas
and oranges) and contributed more to global warming because of the
energy it took to import. The color scale indicated not only the distance
the raw ingredients traveled to get to the restaurant, but also the time
and energy it took to grow, process, and prepare it, with local raw fruits
and vegetables having a lower carbon footprint than cooked foods and
meats. The question being studied (and still not published at the time
of this writing) was whether these cues would encourage consumers to
choose more sustainable products.

Although I am not confident that the signs will help customers eat
more sustainably, I know that unless such research is done, we will
never know. Without consumer research, we will also never be able to
figure out the best ways to change our restaurants and supermarkets
so that people will be able to make healthier choices in ways that don't
overwhelm us, drain our brains, force us to be obsessive-compulsive,
or just generally drive us crazy.

There have been no studies that link marketing practices with
diet, so we cannot be sure how changes in restaurants will affect
consumers' diets over the long term. But we could do these studies,
which would likely be very helpful in understanding exactly which
policy regulations would be most useful in controlling obesity. Drawing upon Holland's Restaurant of the Future, we should create laboratories not only in restaurants, but in supermarkets as well. My
dream is to create a Supermarket of the Future, a food store devoted
exclusively to understanding the ways and means of improving the
American diet.

When asked why he robbed banks, Willie Sutton replied, "Because
that's where the money is." The supermarket is where we get most
of the food we eat and is the venue in which we would most rapidly

identify practical and scalable solutions that may ultimately make all of us healthier. To solve the obesity epidemic, the National Institutes of Health should devote just a fraction of its nearly $30 billion research budget to this. If any other organizations, foundations, or "angels" want to accelerate progress in chronic disease control, I urge them to consider funding supermarket-based consumer research, because it will be the quickest way to get there.

The Supermarket of the Future

How could a supermarket be redesigned to help people make better choices? Once people bring food into their homes, they will most likely eat it. Therefore, helping people to make better choices at the grocery store is one key to a healthier diet.

The Supermarket of the Future could employ many of the current marketing strategies used to promote junk food, but instead apply them toward helping people choose foods that promote health. Researchers and developers would start by using the checkout scanners to figure out the best way to design the Supermarket of the Future. The food industry currently mines its scanner data to evaluate how store placement and other promotional strategies influence profits. (This is how the industry knows that the ends of aisles are choice locations from which to sell goods, for example.) By tracking what sells from which locations, we can begin to make changes that would maximize healthy choices and limit approaches that undermine a healthy diet.

Before we do that, we should start by quantifying just how much the current design of supermarkets increases our risk of diet-related chronic diseases. Although we know impulse marketing strategies increase the sales of candy bars, chips, and sodas, we don't know the magnitude of their impact on diet. Do they increase the risk of a poor diet by a few percentage points, or is their contribution on the order of doubling or tripling the excess calories consumed? If we followed a group of shoppers we could see the chain of causation—from store to home to diet to disease. By tracking purchases and then having individuals report what they eat, and by offering regular medical exams, we could directly see, for example, the extent to which discounts on soda and candy lead to a complication from diabetes. Once we know what store factors are the most problematic, we can change them.

How different would the Supermarket of the Future be from the standard supermarkets we shop at every day? Right now, the ingredients needed for a balanced meal are scattered all over the store. Why not organize the store by meal, so there is a section for breakfast, one for a cold meal (like lunch), and one for a hot meal (like dinner)? Having all the elements for a balanced meal in one place would aid customers in choosing all the items needed for a healthy diet, especially because it would mean we would see the same healthy foods in multiple places. After all, one of the most common strategies for selling chips and soda is to place them in several locations in the store. If we miss them at the entrance, in the third aisle, or on the special display, we can pick them up at the cash register. If we did the same thing for fruits and vegetables, I suspect more people would be eating bananas, broccoli, and melons.

Sure, it would be a bit inconvenient if the food products we are used to seeing in a certain part of the supermarket suddenly end up in a new spot. But after shopping at the Supermarket of the Future (which would be much smaller than a traditional supermarket) we would quickly get the lay of the land. Many of us would be delighted to avoid foods full of sugar, fat, and empty calories. Just imagine a store that doesn't assault you with chips, soda, and cakes on eye-level shelves and on every end aisle display!

(Of course, junk food would still be available. You just might have to go to aisle two and look on the bottom shelf for your favorite candies and chips.)

To promote eating at home, the Supermarket of the Future could also feature routine cooking demonstrations and tastings that would show consumers how to prepare healthy foods like whole grains and legumes. A few upscale stores like Williams-Sonoma already do this occasionally, but these stores cater to only the most well-heeled consumers. Why shouldn't all of us have the benefit of seeing easy ways to prepare delicious and wholesome foods on a daily basis?

Cooking demonstrations might be one of the Supermarket of the Future's most attractive highlights; consider the popularity of the Food

Channel and the nearly universal appreciation of free samples. Imagine multiple demonstration areas where you could see five different ways to prepare seasonal vegetables, as well as stations where you could taste foods you have never before prepared or tried.

University of Southern California professors Peter Clarke and Susan Evans found that low-income families who relied on food pantries and were most vulnerable to obesity were not getting enough fresh fruits and vegetables. They arranged for unsold produce to go to these food pantries rather than in the trash. When the food pantry had a shipment of cabbages or broccoli, families could get bags of it—as much as they could carry home. But they quickly tired of eating it, and ended up throwing it out after a day or two.

Clarke and Evans investigated why this healthy food was being discarded. It turned out that most families knew only one or two ways to prepare the vegetables, like boiling or frying; this can make those veggies bland and unappealing. To address this problem, they provided dozens of recipes that helped the pantry users learn new ways to prepare foods. As we saw earlier, variety is critical to whet the appetite. The recipes were personalized and printed in a booklet with the family's picture on the cover. As a result, the families ended up consuming more of the vegetables and wasting less.[7]

If supermarkets provided cooking demonstrations, samples, and recipes, many more families would likely expand the variety of fruits and vegetables and whole grains they would eat, which could lead to substantial improvements in the American diet across all social classes.

Of course, to be sustainable the Supermarket of the Future has to be profitable—or at least to break even. If such a store keeps people healthy and doesn't lose money, then it is a no-brainer for the government, health insurance companies, and large employers to sponsor the enterprise. There appears to be a widespread belief in the food industry that the only way a supermarket can be profitable is by selling foods that increase our risk of chronic disease. I believe, however, that there is a good chance that healthier supermarkets would also be very successful.

For example, Whole Foods' business model is built on the premise that it offers its customers healthier foods. As a consequence, it has become a highly profitable company. But a new kind of supermarket model could go well beyond what Whole Foods offers and provide more support for consumers to choose a healthy diet without the higher cost.

We need supermarkets that link meal planning, purchasing, and consumption so that people can optimize their nutrition. Having a functioning, practical supermarket-based consumer laboratory that studies how people decide on food purchases could be a critical scientific endeavor that could make an enormous difference in population health.

A hybrid supermarket/consumer behavior laboratory would have two main goals: first, to identify marketing techniques that can help people choose foods for a healthy diet; and second, to determine whether promoting healthy foods and discouraging the consumption of discretionary calories can be economically sustainable and/or profitable. By documenting the arrangements and presentation of foods and keeping track of the nutrient value of the purchases made through cash register receipts, it will be possible to track not only how changing store factors might influence diet, but also how profits can be maximized without sacrificing health.

What Will the Supermarket of the Future Look Like?

I believe the best size for a Supermarket of the Future would be relatively small, less than ten thousand square feet, and considerably smaller than the fifty thousand square feet of today's average supermarket. The Supermarket of the Future will carry a limited number of items, a fraction of the 40,000–50,000 items that major supermarkets typically carry. The arrangement of displays and shelf space will be considerably different from those of traditional markets.

Because most Americans need to cut down on salt by nearly 50 percent, a supermarket that promotes a healthy and tasty diet should have a special spice and herb section. Here, customers could learn how to flavor foods and make them delicious without adding too much salt. Store employees would encourage customers to taste foods with different flavors. Spices could be provided in small quantities for sampling, as well as in bulk.

Indeed, tasting and sampling would be a primary strategy for introducing new foods. Offering free samples has been successful because it provides the consumer with valuable experiential information and an implicit obligation to return the favor as a result of having been given a taste. Arizona State University Professor Robert Cialdini calls this phenomenon the principle of reciprocity.[8]

The Supermarket of the Future will also carry some foods that are not entirely healthy, like sweets and other desserts, but the relative amount of shelf space devoted to items whose consumption we have to moderate would be sharply curtailed in contrast to that of the typical supermarket. These items won't be displayed as impulse buys at the cash register or at the end of an aisle, but reached only after the shoppers have made all their other purchases.

The experimental supermarket can study how changing prices and promotions affect purchases. Just using words like "sale" and "discount" often leads to buying because people think they are getting a bargain, whether or not they are. Many supermarkets have now adopted "ten for $10" specials, which may not in fact represent a price break but is perceived as a discount. In addition, by tying a quantity to the sales price, the terminology also provides a benchmark against which people might decide how many of an item they should buy and serves the purpose of what behavioral economists call an "anchor."[9] It will be fascinating to see whether these techniques can be effective in promoting healthier choices.

Measuring Economic Impact

Would the Supermarket of the Future be affordable? Would it make a profit, or at least break even? Practically speaking, this is the most important question. To answer this question, it will be critical to keep detailed financial records of the entire process, from conception to implementation. If the store helps improve diet, doesn't lose money, and is sustainable, we could build one in every neighborhood on a nonprofit basis.

Another experiment might investigate how a supermarket would fare if the business model was like that of a health maintenance organization (HMO), in which the food cost for customers was capitated.

For example, for the cost of $50 per person per week, the supermarket would have to provide all the food a person needs to stay healthy, but not more than that. This would help people who don't have the time or energy to figure out how to find the right amount of food for a reasonable price. I know I would love such a service, especially if it came with recipes that were both easy to prepare and flavorful.

For several years I participated in a type of consumer-supported agriculture (CSA) that selected bags of fruits and vegetables from a farmers' market and delivered them to my office on a weekly basis. Each bag was designed to include at least 31.5 cups of fruits and vegetables—the recommended amount the average person should consume in a week. Those bags of groceries formed the basis of my family's diet for the week and helped me figure out what to prepare. If I managed to finish all the bags, I knew my family had gotten enough fruits and vegetables that week. If the leadership of the organization hadn't changed and canceled the program, I would still be using that fabulous service.

The work of helping people achieve a healthy diet is so important that we should open several supermarket-based consumer laboratories simultaneously in many parts of the country. With multiple working laboratories, marketing strategies can take into account regional, cultural, and racial/ethnic differences and preferences while accelerating progress in addressing obesity and diet-related chronic diseases.

What If Promoting a Healthy Diet Is Not Profitable?

Even if selling food that doesn't make people sick turns out to be a losing proposition financially, as a society, we may still want to figure out ways to support these outlets. Compare the need for a healthy diet to our need for clean water, clean air, or even police and fire protection. Do these services make money? No, they are subsidized because they are essential. Without clean air, water, and safe communities, we would be more sick and less productive. Although there is widespread agreement that everyone should have access to healthy food, we also need to protect people from being exposed to too much unhealthy food. Learning how to do that is an effort that I believe society should underwrite.

Certifying Restaurants and Supermarkets

Once we identify the features of restaurants and supermarkets that contribute to healthier choices and healthier diets, we can develop a rating system to grade how well these businesses comply with the standards. In 1998, Los Angeles County introduced a restaurant rating system using the grades A, B, and C to indicate the quality of hygienic practices, and it mandated that the results of kitchen inspections be posted within five feet of the restaurant's entrance.[10] Restaurants fought this regulation, complaining they would lose business if they got less than an A. Because the county supervisors agreed that knowing whether a restaurant met hygienic standards was a critical right-to-know issue, the health department prevailed. Food establishments that score below C (70 percent) twice within a twelve-month period are now subject to closure until all the violations are corrected. A low grade remains posted until the inspector returns to confirm that conditions have improved.

This rating system has changed both restaurant and consumer behavior.[11] Within one year of the program's initiation, restaurants improved their preparation standards, and the number of those performing at an A level (above 90 percent) on the inspection scores increased from about 25 percent to more than 50 percent. Improved scores were generally maintained on subsequent inspections. Restaurants with low grades reported a loss in revenue and customer patronage. Sales at restaurants receiving an A grade rose 5.7 percent, or about $15,000 a year, whereas B-level restaurant sales increased 0.7 percent, and sales at C-level establishments decreased 1 percent. The system also focused efforts on restaurants with lower ratings, which were inspected more frequently than establishments with higher scores. The rate of closures decreased.

In the year after the restaurant rating system was introduced, the number of patients admitted to hospitals in Los Angeles for food-related illnesses dropped by 13 percent.[12] When restaurant ratings are posted or published, consumers become aware of how well outlets meet standards and can avoid outlets with lower ratings.[13] Grades serve as a heuristic—or shortcut—that will help people automatically make a better choice, but they do not prevent anyone from eating what they want.

If the inspection standards included assessing the quality of prepared foods, menus in restaurants, the design of food stores, and their use of promotional strategies, with the goal of limiting the risk of nutrition-related chronic diseases, it would help people choose healthier restaurants and eat a healthier diet. Food-borne infectious diseases are now relatively rare because hygienic standards are rigorous and compulsory. Just think of what similar regulations could do to reduce chronic diseases.

Making Regulation of Restaurants and Supermarkets for Chronic Disease Prevention a Reality

Politically, adding regulations is always difficult because it upsets the status quo. Historically, change is always accompanied by protest, even for such changes that we now consider as common sense, like requiring adherence to sanitary codes. Yet we need to demand that the government initiate a process to move a chronic-disease-prevention agenda forward. This includes building a consensus on feasible standards, developing product labels and marketing practices that allow people to make healthy decisions rapidly and that delay impulse purchases, allowing them only after thoughtful deliberation, creating certification and incentive programs, and instituting evaluation and monitoring protocols.

It would be the government's job to establish a set of minimum performance standards and facilitate compliance among stakeholders, including food industry and nutrition experts. To help disseminate the standards, the adoption of tried-and-true marketing techniques like branding would be useful. A symbol identifying adherence to the performance standards (e.g., like a LEED* standard for a green building) must become widely recognized and easily understood by consumers.

---

* LEED stands for Leadership in Energy and Environmental Design, and was developed by the US Green Building Council to set a benchmark for design, construction, and operation of high-performance green buildings.

In addition, local governments should certify restaurants whose practices conform to the performance standards; provide incentives (e.g., tax credits, fee rebates, marketing) to outlets that meet or exceed performance standards; and sponsor industry learning and dissemination of best practices.

Labeling for away-from-home food could borrow from the clear successes of eco-labeling programs for consumer products.[14] For example, eco-labels provide a simple signal to consumers that products have met environmental, social, and other sustainability standards of verifying agencies. The US federal government has a great deal of experience in developing and managing label programs. The Environmental Protection Agency's Design for the Environment (DfE) logo helps consumers choose household cleaners that meet standards for minimal toxicity, the EPA's Energy Star label identifies energy-efficient electronics and appliances, and the USDA's certified organic label identifies food grown without chemicals or hormones. In each of these cases, eco-labeling and certification by an authoritative agency have contributed to the growth of markets for sustainable products.

Whatever changes are made to foods, food labels, and the food environment, we should evaluate their impact. Surveillance systems can be established to see whether people indeed order healthier options and whether, in the long term, that change has an impact on their diet and health. If evaluations show the changes don't work, then we should go back to the drawing board and try something else.

Would Restaurant and Supermarket Performance Standards Interfere with Individual Choice?

Some may argue that performance standards are a threat to individual freedom and choice. The claim is that constraining how foods are sold will prevent people from getting what they want. Yet the regulations I am proposing are directed at food establishments (not individuals) and don't ban any particular foods. Regulations might make getting unhealthy foods less convenient, but they would not reduce consumers' freedom to eat what they want. Performance standards are intended to change industry behavior and thus the range of choices offered to individuals. Furthermore, the ability to make informed choices would be enhanced rather than diminished by clear, understandable designations of the health risks or benefits.

Ultimately, adopting and enforcing stricter guidelines regulating food outlets will not preclude people from choosing what they prefer. Instead, they will guide food outlets to routinely offer foods that promote long-term health.

Professionalizing the Food Industry

We require all health professionals to attend accredited schools, pass comprehensive exams, and be licensed in order to ensure that they will not perform at a substandard level and potentially put their patients at risk. We monitor their performance, investigate consumer complaints, require continuing education, and often mandate recertification to make sure they stay up-to-date with scientific advances.

We now know that food providers are in many respects also health-care providers. The food we eat can reduce or increase our risk for both infectious and chronic diseases, yet restaurateurs and their employees are not required to have any formal training in nutrition or chronic disease prevention.

Just as other professions have raised their images by undergoing training and professionalization, the food industry should do the same. Food service employees should understand the consequences of eating the food they serve, and take some responsibility for their role in their customers' health. Developing standards and requiring food providers to receive nutrition training are necessary so they can properly prepare, label, serve, and promote foods that won't increase the risk of or exacerbate chronic diseases.

Everyone from the chefs to the busboys should have some basic knowledge and certification to be able to inform customers about the health consequences of the foods they order, and make recommendations that are appropriate.

My husband is not the only person who finds it difficult to choose what to eat for dinner in a restaurant. Often customers ask their waitstaff, "What do you recommend?" and many maître d's make suggestions for their specials. Their recommendations should not be for items that have too much salt, too many calories, or too much sugar. Just as it would be unethical for a doctor to recommend a treatment that carries a worse prognosis over a more favorable one, or for a lawyer to advise a client to make a plea bargain for the harshest sentence, the recommended meal of the day should always be balanced and healthy.

Reframing the way we think about the food industry and the way we promote careers in the food business, from a field that requires no skills and no training to a highly respected profession that has as much responsibility for the health of our nation as the health industry itself, is a critical paradigm shift that I believe is necessary to control obesity.

We won't know the impact of any of these proposed new regulations until they are enacted. Offering healthy meals could backfire if people become more likely to overcompensate by eating poorly afterward, rewarding themselves with foods they should avoid. All innovations should be accompanied by rigorous evaluations to see whether unintended consequences negate any short-term benefits. We may have many false starts and bumps in the road ahead, but the more we keep at it, the more likely we are to succeed.

11

Fit and Fat:
What About Physical Activity?

Although I spend the majority of my professional life studying physical activity, exercise is my Achilles' heel. I know how important it is to my health, yet I find it personally challenging and rarely get the 150 minutes of moderate-to-vigorous activity that is recommended as a weekly minimum. Moderate-to-vigorous physical activity—the intensity of a brisk walk or higher—is necessary to avoid health problems like heart disease, diabetes, colon and breast cancer, osteoporosis, and hypertension.

I am in good company: 95 percent of American adults do not meet the national physical activity guidelines. Although only two out of three are overweight or obese, nearly everyone fails to move enough to get the full health benefits that physical activity confers.

Children and teens are doing only slightly better than adults, in part because of scheduled physical activity at school. Children and teens require more than twice the amount of moderate-to-vigorous physical activity that adults need—sixty minutes a day. But in 2006, just 42 percent of children ages twelve and under met the guidelines of sixty minutes of moderate-to-vigorous physical activity every day. Among teens, fewer than 9 percent did.[1] Moderate-to-vigorous activity is crucial for bone growth and muscular development. Vigorous exercise, like running and playing energetically so that the heart beats faster and breathing is more rapid, may determine whether the calories children consume are used to multiply lean muscle cells and build strong bones.[2] Sedentary behavior, in contrast, will convert excess energy into fat cells.[3]

Currently, the United States has no physical-activity-related entitlements or safety net support systems that children or adults can count on to help them get moving. Instead, it is up to individuals to figure out for themselves how to get enough exercise. Many special tools are available, like smartphone apps, pedometers, accelerometers, and GPS trackers that provide advice and feedback about the duration and intensity of a person's physical activity. Anyone with money can hire a personal trainer, join a gym, or purchase home exercise equipment. And even if money is a barrier, everyone can walk the streets, do jumping jacks in their home, or jog through a public park. Nevertheless, you are on your own when it comes to figuring out an approach to physical activity that fits best with your abilities, budget, and lifestyle.

In my view, that's why so few of us maintain regular physical activity.

Adults need about thirty minutes a day, five days a week. That doesn't seem like much, but somehow I seldom find the time, even though I actually enjoy being active. My family and my job usually get priority over my exercise. When my kids were younger, after being away at work all day I felt I had to spend all the rest of my time caring for them, from getting dinner on the table, to helping with homework, to making sure they bathed and brushed their teeth. And of course, chauffeuring them to their sports activities and making sure that *they* got regular exercise kept *me* pretty sedentary. You would think that now that three of my four sons are adults and don't need me to ferry them around, I would finally have more time for myself. But I still have a teenager at home, and if he needs a ride to school, I find myself driving rather than biking to work, which I keep telling myself I have to do more regularly.

With so many demands between work and family life, I feel guilty about taking time out for myself, even though I should be able to and still have enough time to accomplish most everything else I have to do. I know several people who find a way to do it. In fact, if they don't get their daily exercise they feel cranky and depressed. Fortunately (or unfortunately), up until recently I never got any recognizable signals from my body demanding that I get up and run a few miles. And when I did make the effort to be active, I also didn't notice much improvement in my mood or feeling of well-being.

But now, I feel twinges and mild aching in my hips, legs, and lower back when I sit for too long. After decades at a sedentary job, I expect it is finally catching up with me. Even though I am of normal weight, if I don't get my act together soon it is likely that an overweight person who exercises regularly will be healthier and live longer than I will. Surprisingly, it's very possible to be "fit" and fat at the same time.

Staying Active Can Protect
Against the Harms of Obesity

In fact, exercising and staying fit can mitigate most (but not all) of the harms associated with excessive weight and obesity. The World Health Organization ranks physical inactivity a greater risk to health than excessive weight and obesity.[4] But lack of exercise has less to do with the obesity epidemic than we might think.

In the United States, levels of physical activity appear to have stayed relatively stable since the early 1980s, when rates of obesity accelerated. Although leisure-time physical activity has been increasing slightly, this has been largely balanced by the decline of physical activity at work, as jobs have shifted from manufacturing to the service sector.[5] Overall, we expend on average sixty to one hundred fewer calories per day at work today than we did in 1980.[6] It's not much, at least compared to the 571 extra calories we've been consuming on average every day since then, but it's a gap that is important and should be relatively easy to close.

There is no doubt that increasing physical activity can help people prevent weight gain. And it can also help people lose weight, if they also diet. But it is very hard to lose weight merely by becoming more active. That's because exercise burns a relatively small number of calories. To burn off an extra 500–550 calories, the amount in one typical bakery cupcake or a single Dunkin' Donuts chocolate muffin, the average person would need to walk for an hour and a half (about 5.2 miles) or do an hour of high-impact aerobics.

Yet even among people who do not lose weight, physical activity can stave off diabetes and other chronic diseases.[7] This has led many physicians and health providers to discuss physical activity with patients at every clinic visit.

This is the source of my next confession about my relative inactivity. When I went to the doctor for a checkup a few months ago, a new protocol for preparing patients for a doctor visit led the nursing assistant who took my blood pressure to ask if I exercised thirty minutes a day, five days a week. When I said no, she gave me a lecture about the importance of exercise. The next time I came in, and she asked me again, I just said yes. After all, I really, really do intend to exercise.

Cajoling or haranguing people to exercise no doubt falls on many deaf ears. The reasons are multiple: besides not liking being told what to do, we don't really appreciate the consequences of inactivity because they are so long-term, and we don't see our health and functional capacity slowly slipping away. We are often stuck in a routine: commuting, working, and taking care of family, over and over again. Habits are hard to interrupt.

As far as why we exercise so little, it's important to remember that the history of civilization is the story of the search for labor-saving devices and luxury. The ultimate purpose of most of our endeavors is to make our lives a little easier and more pleasurable. The hierarchies of civilizations have developed so that the people at the top do not labor. Because labor and physical activity are so unappealing, civilizations have developed positions for a wide variety of workers and servants. In the past, slaves were forced to do the most backbreaking and unpleasant of duties.

Most important, we have to recognize that over the past century physical activity has been engineered out of our lives by cars, machines, and technology, and that it is only getting worse with more desk jobs, electronic media, the Internet, and online shopping. Yet if we want optimal health and lower rates of heart disease, diabetes, hypertension, depression, and cancer—diseases from which exercise can protect us—we need to make physical activity part of our daily lives. Because it is so difficult for individuals to exercise on their own initiative, a variety of policy changes could make routine physical activity automatic, and in ways that will either find the time we cannot find ourselves or in other ways we may hardly notice.

Physical Activity for Children

Many of us will agree that children need to be given the opportunity to exercise at school. Although most school districts no longer offer daily PE classes for all students, it makes sense to build PE into the school day so all school-aged youth can get their exercise. I expect that most parents would be grateful if their children came home with sixty minutes of exercise under their belts and just enough energy left to finish their homework and chores before bed. If the school day were lengthened so our kids got the full hour of activity every day, working parents wouldn't have to spend so much on child-care services and would probably worry less about what their kids were doing in the late afternoons.

But even when youth have PE scheduled at school, children seldom spend more than 50 percent of gym class, if that much, getting moderate-to-vigorous physical activity. Instead much of class time is spent getting instructions from the teacher or waiting turns to play or perform. Although the goal of school PE is to be engaged in such activity at least 50 percent of scheduled class time, studies examining the quality of PE class instruction indicate this is rarely achieved.[8] In one study, children actually got more physical activity during lunch than they did during PE class.[9]

Curricula and teacher training programs have been developed to help PE classes provide more moderate-to-vigorous physical activity, but to be successful schools usually have to invest in more equipment. For example, instead of having children in a class of thirty play basketball with five on a team (the majority would have to wait for their turn), providing the class with fifteen balls would allow everyone to practice drills with a partner.

In too many PE classes students have to sit on the bench and watch a few select others be active. The worst are elimination games like dodgeball, where a student who is hit has to stop playing. Those who are the least athletic or fit, and would benefit more from physical activity, are often eliminated first.

Unfortunately, when it comes to children's extracurricular sports in large communities, where the demand for participation exceeds the supply of opportunities, elimination is the standard. Children's sports, like soccer, baseball, basketball, track, and football, can be quite competitive, and winning trophies can be seen as the most important goal. Children who develop better skills become more highly sought after for team sports. At the same time, those who do not excel may be discouraged from continuing to play.

Two of my sons loved soccer and wanted to play on the high school team. But their high school had more than 3,500 students and only one soccer team. Even though they were decent soccer players, neither was skilled enough to make the team, and both were shut out of the physical activity they loved.

Few schools have intramural sports teams that allow those who don't make the varsity teams to participate. There is typically only one gym or field for soccer, football, or baseball, and these are reserved for the talented few. Is it fair that only a limited number of students can use the field every day for practice, while the majority can merely watch?

Even more egregious is when the high-school level of competition is emulated among younger children. One friend told me her eight-year-old son was kicked off a community-based track team that had been advertised as open to any child. The coaches said he was too slow. Is winning trophies and ribbons for eight-year-olds more important than inclusion? Can you imagine how that kind of rejection would make a child never want to even try the sport again?

We have to stop treating sports and vigorous physical activity as something restricted to serious athletes and professionals. Instead, we need to rediscover fun, teamwork, and tolerance.

In 1972 Congress passed Title IX, which says that "no person in the United States shall, on the basis of sex, be excluded from participation in, be denied the benefits of, or be subjected to discrimination under any education program or activity receiving federal financial assistance." This legislation opened up high school and college sports to females, allowing them to benefit from the resources that were directed at sports that previously only males enjoyed.

Today we need new legislation that allows youths in public schools to participate in sports even if they don't make varsity teams. Yes, it makes sense that every high school should have a varsity team, but training should not come at the expense of the majority of students. Students who are not athletically gifted should not be excluded and condemned to sedentary activities.

If *any* student can participate in a school sport, then *every* student who wants to play should be able to. This means that schools with large student bodies and competitive varsity teams should also offer less competitive intramural sports teams. A rotating schedule will allow every team to use limited fields. On days the fields are being used by one team, the other teams can do conditioning exercises and activities elsewhere that will keep them in shape. All students should have access to facilities and coaches who are supported by tax dollars. Children need all the support they can get to stay active.

Physical Activity for Adults

If children need daily exercise in school, isn't it logical that employed adults should engage in daily exercise at work? Especially if our jobs force us to sit for eight hours a day, shouldn't some effort be made to mitigate the risk we find ourselves bearing? After all, employers are required to mitigate risk for other worksite hazards. In eight states, including California, where I work, employers are required to give their workers a ten-minute break every four hours. But if this work is sedentary, shouldn't it be an exercise break?

Once a week I participate in a yoga class at work, but I have to pay for it and do it on my lunch hour. The type of yoga available focuses mainly on stretching and flexibility and doesn't provide enough moderate-to-vigorous physical activity.

If I had ten or twenty minutes set aside in my schedule (on the time clock) and my employer expected me to be active during that time—either in an exercise class, walking up and down the stairs, or dancing in the corridors—I would definitely do it. And I am confident that most of my coworkers would also become more active, especially if our employers showed us they cared by pleading with us to take regular "action" breaks to avoid long-term health problems from steadfastly sticking to our desks.

A study on heart disease in the 1950s, among the earliest of its kind, found that sedentary workers in London like bus drivers and mail sorters had higher rates of heart disease and heart attacks than ambulatory ticket collectors and postal workers.[10] Sitting too long can also lead to the development of low back pain and herniated discs.[11] Musculoskeletal complaints arising from occupational activities cost hundreds of millions of dollars in workers' compensation claims every year.

Recently, some researchers have argued that sitting for prolonged periods can create health risks, even if a person gets exercise at other times.[12] The evidence for this is still inconclusive, but the thinking is that muscular inactivity may lead to metabolic syndrome, a condition marked by high blood pressure, as well as too much sugar and cholesterol in the blood, all of which increase the risk of heart disease and diabetes.[13] Whether or not sitting leads to metabolic syndrome, the evidence that excessive sitting can reduce the lifespan is very strong.[14]

Dr. Toni Yancey, a Professor at the UCLA School of Public Health, left an invaluable legacy called Instant Recess—a ten-minute exercise program that can be used in schools or at the workplace. Where it has been adopted, benefits include improved attitudes, higher productivity among employees, lower injury rates, and lower absenteeism.[15] Yancey claimed that the monetary benefits from decreased workers' compensation payouts and lower absenteeism make this a highly cost-effective approach. You just pop in a DVD, and an instructor on the video models how everyone should move in time with the music. Everyone just copies the leader. With peppy music and silly moves, it can be a lot of fun.

The Instant Recess concept is extremely promising, and may one day be a standard part of our work environments and other professional settings and meetings—if we advocate for it.

Graduating from high school or college shouldn't end routine physical activity. Continuing PE on a modified basis in the workplace will surely help our population stay in better shape. Policies that help everyone stay active and reduce the harms from sedentary jobs would show we are all in this together.

Modifying Urban Design

Although office workers would benefit from worksite exercise programs, not everyone works in an office. Another approach to encouraging more physical activity is to change the design of our neighborhoods and cities so we can be active when we leave home to do errands or go to work, by walking, bicycling, or even taking mass transit.

Over the past six decades the car has come to dominate our cities and suburbs. During this time, old methods of mass transportation, including streetcars and trolleys, were mostly eliminated, and our roads were widened and developed to accommodate an increasing number of cars.

By studying the physical activity patterns of people who live in different cities and neighborhoods, we have recognized that in areas that are walkable, where destinations can be reached on foot and people live fairly close together, more people walk and enjoy better health.[16] Moreover, if parking spots are scarce and mass transit is plentiful, people are more likely to use mass transit, and as a result to walk to or from their destinations.

The populations of countries that have invested in mass transit tend to be more active. Japan, for example, has done an outstanding job of managing its national transportation system. The Japanese have not only made mass transit convenient; they have also made car ownership expensive and parking less convenient than using city trains and buses. Japan's bullet trains and subways get people where they need to go quickly and reliably. Another important reason why the Japanese are slimmer than Americans may be their higher levels of physical activity. Not only do Japanese eat less, but they also walk considerably more, burning a few hundred more calories a day than the average American.[17] Using mass transit is an automatic way to get exercise.

As a nation, America is way behind other countries in having a reliable mass transit infrastructure, except in a few cities. In 2007–2008, the city of Charlotte, North Carolina, expanded its light rail system. I worked with several RAND researchers to evaluate whether this new system would pay dividends in health among light rail users.[18]

We surveyed individuals living within one mile of the planned light rail line before it opened and then a year later, after it began running. At each time point we asked about their levels of physical activity and their height and weight.

When comparing those who started using the light rail to those who did not, we found that light rail users increased their physical activity and reduced their risk of obesity. The weight of nonusers increased by more than six pounds compared to the light rail users. Although we can't be sure about the magnitude of the effect, because it was based on self-report rather than objectively measured weight, the study does seem to support the potential health benefits of mass transit.

Yet instead of emphasizing mass transit or concentrating our populations in a way that makes mass transit a sensible alternative, America has invested heavily in building roads so homes can be spread out. Our nation now has large areas of sprawling suburbs, such that in many parts of the country one must have a car to go anywhere, even to pick up a quart of milk or a local paper.

In a study I conducted with my colleague Roland Sturm on the impact of urban sprawl, we found that the health of people who live in cities like Atlanta, where the average person drives four to five miles to a supermarket, is much worse than among those who are otherwise similar but live in cities like Pittsburgh or San Antonio, where it is much easier to walk to a local grocery store. For every thousand residents, Atlanta's citizens chalk up ninety-six more health problems than residents of Pittsburgh or San Antonio. That number is roughly equivalent to giving the residents of Atlanta the health problems of people four years older than they are, as if living in sprawl ages a person by four years.[19] This is one of the reasons why where we live is an important determinant of our health.

Changing urban design so that we can get out of our cars and walk more, however, is a long-term process, necessary not only to improve health but also to address problems like global warming, because transportation accounts for about 27 percent of all greenhouse gas emissions in the United States.[20]

Leisure-Time Physical Activity

If you haven't gotten your dose of physical activity at work or on your way to wherever you go, then you can still catch up in your leisure time. After all, most people still work about forty hours per week, making it theoretically possible to carve out thirty minutes before or after work to get some physical activity. But the reality is, unless there is a draw to be active, few will.

Therefore, it is incumbent on our society to invest in making leisure-time physical activity as attractive, available, and ubiquitous as junk food, so more people will be likely to participate.

What would such a society look like? Over the past ten years I have focused a good portion of my research on studying the use of parks and other open spaces. What I have found is that even when people live right near a beautiful park, they may not use it, especially if there is nothing interesting going on or if they are not aware of its programs or facilities.

How parks are managed varies considerably across America and depends on the resources available through local taxes. Even in the wealthiest communities, a minimal proportion of those resources is usually devoted to marketing park use or encouraging physical activity there.

Consider this: the entertainment industry spends hundreds of millions of dollars to encourage people to watch electronic media and passive entertainment. Is it any wonder people are more likely to watch others be active than to be active themselves?

Neighborhood parks are among the most logical places where we should be promoting physical activity, because most people live within two to five miles of a public park and their wide-open spaces are uniquely designed for moderate-to-vigorous activity like running and playing sports. And there are many other reasons to be outdoors. An important one is to be exposed to sunlight, which creates vitamin D, important for bones and a healthy heart. Insufficient levels of vitamin

D are epidemic in the United States, particularly among the elderly; such deficiency could be cured if people spent more time in the sun.

Although people of all age groups need to be outside and stay active, most park programs are primarily designed for children and teens. There are many children's soccer and basketball leagues, a few for adult men, but almost none for women of all ages or for seniors. In fact, in our research we count the people in neighborhood parks by their age group and, except in Asian communities where a lot of seniors do Tai Chi, we seldom see older adults, and considerably fewer adults than would be expected if all residents used their parks equally. It's as if we intend for people to be less active as they age. If we want to encourage physical activity for everyone, we should be sponsoring sports leagues and programs for all age groups, not just children.

Will such investments pay off?

Brazil is a country where a substantial effort is being made to encourage more physical activity for adults. There is some evidence that the community-wide physical activity promotion programs in São Paulo are leading to reductions in hospitalizations for problems like hypertension.[21] A local campaign called Agita encourages community leaders to creatively stimulate physical activity in any way they can. They have repaired sidewalks, built more running and cycling tracks, scheduled citywide walking events, offered classes in parks, and even promoted walking around a cemetery.

In the United States, garnering support to invest in parks is challenging because local resources are limited. The tug-of-war between "We're all in this together" and "You're on your own" plays out in local politics—with "You're on your own" prevailing in economic downturns. Generally, the public has a favorable view of parks and recreation, but funding them often seems to be considered a luxury, secondary to other services like police and education, rather than an investment in health and well-being. Furthermore, the health benefits from increasing physical activity would be accrued by individuals, their employers, and insurance companies, and not directly by the departments whose budgets would be most affected.

Nevertheless, getting people to be active in the park may not cost a lot of money. I recently completed a study in which we tried to get parks to expand their outreach and marketing to encourage more people to engage in physical activity. We offered a few training sessions and a small incentive of $4,000 to each park that was serving an average of forty thousand people in a one-mile radius. We found that just putting up banners and signs letting people know that something was going on at the park resulted in more people engaging in moderate-to-vigorous activity within the park. The impact was very cost-effective, and we estimated it helped hundreds more people to exercise in parks every week.

Even when municipal funds are limited, there are many businesses, community-based organizations, and faith groups that might be willing to partner with parks to support more physical activity programs and events. In addition, lots of people may be willing to volunteer to run free exercise classes. I was very surprised to find out that nearly all the exercise classes at my local YMCA are taught by volunteers. Why couldn't we organize this type of system in public settings to supplement existing services?

Activating parks will likely yield multiple benefits beyond physical activity. When more people are out, the parks become safer. Neighbors are more likely to meet one another and have the opportunity to interact in a relaxed and fun atmosphere. Such interactions can promote familiarity and tolerance, and can help build what has been called "weak ties"—relationships that support sharing beneficial information without the burden of heavy obligations.[22] For example, many people hear from casual acquaintances about job opportunities, events, programs, or services that might meet their particular needs, but they would not be expected to owe any debt for receiving this information.

Another promising approach to leisure-time physical activity is through novel events and happenings that draw people into the streets, where they can be active. Street fairs, concerts, dances, and *ciclovías*—bicycling events scheduled when streets are closed to automobiles—attract tens of thousands of people to take to the streets and become physically active.

In Bogotá, Colombia, the main streets are closed every Sunday, and two million pedestrians and bicyclists (30 percent of the population) come out to play. Stages are set up in city parks, and aerobics instructors, yoga teachers, and musicians lead people in exercise and dance across more than 120 kilometers of car-free streets.

Wherever *ciclovías* are held in the United States, thousands participate. The main problem is that such events are few and far between, and no city has yet been able to match the weekly *ciclovías* of Bogotá. The demands on police and traffic safety professionals make weekly or even monthly *ciclovías* difficult and expensive. But their success suggests that we must develop cost-effective solutions so they can become a regular feature of city life. And we may find out that over the long run, getting the population active is actually worth whatever it costs to make it happen.

One of the most revealing events demonstrating the role of novelty in increasing physical activity was *The Gates* exhibit in New York City's Central Park during the winter of 2005. The artist Christo draped a series of bright orange banners over twenty-three miles of walkways, creating an amazing and glorious sight. The installation attracted four million visitors to the park, about four times the usual number, and they walked through Central Park in the dead of winter, with snow and ice on the ground.

Did the visitors think they were just going to get some exercise? Probably not. They just wanted to be part of something that was unique and novel. Did they get exercise? Definitely.

Mitigating the Harms of Sitting in All Venues

The entertainment industry dominates leisure time in America, with most people watching television or videos upwards of four hours per day.[23] If we believe that worksites should mitigate the harm from sedentary jobs, shouldn't we expect the entertainment industry to also mitigate the harm it might contribute to? Should there be an exercise break during all spectator events? If a movie makes you sit for two hours, shouldn't there be an intermission midway to allow people to stretch and move? Should television broadcasters build in a ten-minute break with an exercise or Instant Recess video transmission every two hours? Why not?

Certainly, the more reminders we have to exercise and move, the more we are likely to do it. Right now television reminds us to eat and drink several times an hour, even though we have built-in hunger and thirst mechanisms that would no doubt take care of the situation. We really don't need any special reminders to eat. But we do need reminders and cues to exercise, because we have no inherent internal signals that stimulate physical activity.

Physical Activity in Finland

Finland is one of the few Western countries where physical activity has been increasing substantially over the past thirty years. This is despite its extreme weather conditions, with only six hours of daylight in the winter and temperatures below freezing for five months of the year. In Helsinki, it rains or snows about 175 days a year—almost every other day. Yet somehow, its citizens are very active and often commute to work and school by foot or bike, and engage in sports and exercise frequently in their leisure time—all year round.

Finland's success is partly attributable to the deliberate steps taken by the central government since the 1970s, when it developed a National Sports Council that had some clout with respect to policy and resources.[24] In 1980 the government mandated that every municipality elect a Sports Board to oversee the planning of physical activity services and maintenance of sports facilities. In 1981 there was a mandate to hire a manager to develop services for people with disabilities to engage in physical activity.

Almost twenty years before Michelle Obama launched "Let's Move" to prevent childhood obesity in the United States, Finland initiated a "Finland on the Move" campaign on behalf of all its citizens to support local physical activity projects with seed money.[25] Rather than focus only on children, the government also developed "Fit for Life" in 1999, a program targeting adults over age forty, and subsequently expanded this to target seniors as well.

Furthermore, a lot of attention is paid to the construction and maintenance of sports facilities there. There is one physical activity site for every 176 Finns, and these are used by 90 percent of the population. There is one public swimming pool for every eighteen thousand citizens, and they are used by 70 percent of the population. Few Finns report barriers to exercise, like distance or lack of money.

In my studies of park use, where we surveyed residents who lived within a half mile of their neighborhood park in Albuquerque; Philadelphia; Los Angeles; Chapel Hill, North Carolina; and Columbus, Ohio, the percentage who *never* visit it ran between 40 percent and 60 percent.[26] In general, about half our citizens don't know what programs or facilities are available in our local parks.[27]

The way to increase leisure-time physical activity in America is, in large part, to help people take advantage of opportunities and facilities that already exist in their local communities and by developing and promoting "happenings" like the *Gates* exhibit along with interesting programs and events on a regular basis.

In general, we should not expect everyone to spontaneously exercise on their own, as if the conditions they live in had no influence. Instead, we should dedicate more resources to change the conditions that keep us sedentary.

12

In the Meantime:
What Individuals Can Do

Until all the necessary impulse control policies are in place and all the grocery stores and restaurants stop encouraging customers to buy food that increases their risks of chronic diseases, individuals still have to face the onslaught of foods and food cues that lead them to eat too much. Not only was Rome not built in a day, but it took a hundred years before we had solid alcohol control laws and more than fifty years before we started making progress on tobacco control. It is certainly going to take time to create a groundswell of support for widespread regulation of food sales and harmful marketing practices. So what can we do in the meantime?

Here is my advice:

1) Don't go out to eat.
2) Don't go into supermarkets.
3) Stop watching TV.
4) Spend your leisure time in a park.

Right!

This is highly unlikely to work for any but the most fanatical. Not everybody wants to make avoiding the food environment a centerpiece of his or her life. Not everybody has the inclination to cook every night. Not everybody lives near a supermarket with delivery service.

Dieting has been the mainstay of our approach to obesity for decades, though its general failure for the majority of people should make us question its efficacy. Many dieting behaviors that are believed to protect us from eating too much don't hold up to scrutiny. For those who have already tried dieting without success, I would not recommend going that route again. There are many reasons why dieting fails, and often it makes some people even fatter.

The Problem with Dieting

One difficulty we might face when trying to reduce food intake is trying to limit our thoughts about food. It may seem like a good idea when we go on a diet to avoid thinking about food, because when we start thinking about food, we typically end up going to the refrigerator or the store to get something to eat. As sensible as it seems to try not to think about food, this is a very big mistake. The moment we try to forget about food, it seems that it's all we can think of. This phenomenon has been dubbed the "ironic process of mental control" by researcher and professor Daniel Wegner of Harvard University, who has devoted quite some time to understanding why, when we are asked not to think of a polar bear, that's exactly what we think of.[1] If only someone hadn't told us *not* to think of a polar bear, the image would never have crossed our minds.

Wegner noted that people have deficiencies in their ability to control their mental activities, and our conscious thoughts are often the opposite of what we really want. Again, the dual system of effortful and automatic processing comes into play. It takes a lot of effort not to think about something because we have to distract ourselves. But our automatic processing system constantly checks our consciousness to determine if we have achieved our goal.

We are wired to be hard on ourselves, to notice mistakes, so we can strive for perfection. Studies of brainwaves indicate that a specific release of "event-related brain potential" occurs when we make mistakes.

It occurs only one-tenth of a second after the onset of electric activity of the muscle that is about to make the mistake—indicating its automaticity and our inability to stop ourselves from checking for errors. When our goal is to avoid or ignore something, our monitoring system is looking for the exact thing we are trying to forget, which makes forgetting impossible.

Being on a diet increases our sensitivity to food cues. Some begin to notice foods they otherwise would have ignored. Thus dieters become "restrained" eaters, and resisting food may become increasingly difficult to the point where they are more likely to lose self-control than if they had not been trying to diet.

Can Eating Slowly Help Reduce How Much We Eat?

One typical piece of advice about dieting is to take smaller bites and eat more slowly. Eating more slowly is supposed to enhance the taste and enjoyment of food and increase the ability to feel full, which may otherwise be delayed until one has already eaten too much. Some believe that eating slowly will help obese people feel satisfied with smaller amounts of food.

This advice was examined in a laboratory setting by Dr. Theresa Spiegel and her colleagues in 1993.[2] She invited nine obese women and nine lean women to participate and told them the purpose of the study was to observe their reactions to the taste of food to be provided in a lunch meal under different conditions. The researchers hooked up electrodes to the chewing muscles of the women's cheeks so they could precisely count the chews and measure the speed of eating.

The food the women were given consisted of tuna or turkey rolled in a piece of bread and sliced like sushi rolls into pieces weighing five, ten, or fifteen grams. They were also given bite-size pieces of bagels and cream cheese. The five-gram pieces were relatively small bites, but the fifteen-gram pieces were a big mouthful. Ten grams was considered the most comfortable size to put in the mouth. Each person was given a plate of twenty pieces, a cup, and a pitcher of water. The women were instructed to eat and drink as much as they wanted; but whenever they took any food, they were instructed to put the whole piece in their mouth at once. This way the scientists could differentiate between big and little bites. The scientists then analyzed the rate of chewing, the time between bites, and the total amount of food consumed.

First, they found no differences between the eating behaviors of lean and obese participants. Obese participants did not eat faster than lean ones. The larger the size of the bite, the faster the subjects ate. If the subjects ate the smaller pieces, they just took longer to eat. Regardless of whether the eating pattern included large or small bites, or whether the women took a longer or shorter time to complete the meal, the participants ended up eating the same amount of food. There were large differences among people with respect to how quickly they ate, but the speed of eating was not related to the total amount consumed. Although this was a small study, it did not appear that slow eating and little bites will likely be helpful in reducing the total amount consumed.

Will Using Smaller Plates Help?

Another bit of advice we often hear is to use smaller plates so that we will be more likely to put less food on our plates and thus eat less. Once again, this seemingly commonsense advice did not hold up to rigorous scrutiny.[3] To understand more about the potential role of plate size, Dr. Barbara Rolls, the Penn State researcher whose experiments on food variety and portion size were described earlier, invited participants to her lab to eat lunch once a week. Each week, she served the same foods but varied the size of the plate. Just as with the pizza example in Chapter 4, the largest plate had more than double the surface area of the smallest plate. The participants were asked to help themselves either to one main course or to a buffet with five different food choices. The foods were weighed before they ate and the remaining amount was weighed when they finished, so it was possible to determine the quantity eaten.

It turned out that the size of the meal consumed did not differ regardless of the size of the plate. The participants' ratings of hunger and satiety did not differ by the size of the plate either. When the participants had only one main course to choose from, three-fourths of them didn't even notice there had been a difference in the size of the plate. However, when the participants had to go back and forth to the buffet table to get food, most of them did notice the difference in the plate sizes.

In a follow-up study, participants were given a set amount of food. The researchers then gave them plates seventeen, twenty-two, or twenty-five centimeters in diameter (about 6.5, 8.5, or 10 inches). In this condition, again, the size of the plate had no effect on how much they ate.

Will Hundred-Calorie Packs Help?

Portion size appears to be more important than plate size in determining how much people eat. When portion sizes are reduced, people eat less. Because of this the food industry has developed products like hundred-calorie packs. These are typically limited portions of snack foods—like chocolate chip cookies, crackers, chips, or other foods that have high levels of calories per gram. It makes sense that if we are served less, we will eat less. However, one study suggests that small snack bags might have a perverse effect and encourage people to eat more.

Researchers invited people to a laboratory with the cover story that they wanted participants to watch television and rate some TV advertisements.[4] They told the participants they wanted to simulate the same conditions as in a typical home, so they left snacks in the room, telling them to feel free to help themselves, because a lot of people snack when they watch TV.

For all the groups, the researchers measured how many chips they ate while watching and rating the TV advertisements. For half the participants, they provided five small bags of potato chips (forty-five grams); for the other half, they provided one big bag of potato chips, weighing two hundred grams. They also divided each of these groups in half. One group got no other instructions, but the second group was first primed to be concerned about their body image. Before being asked to watch the advertisements, they weighed the second group of participants, measured their waists, and had them look at themselves in the mirror.

The results were unexpected. The group that was in the room with the small bags ended up eating more than the group with the single big bag. This was mainly because the people offered the small bags were more likely to open one, while just a small number opened the big bag. Of the individuals who opened any bag, the group that ate the least were those primed to worry about their body image and who had access to the big bag.

It seems that when the participants were reminded about their weight, they were more likely to monitor themselves and limit what they consumed. In contrast, the group with the small bags may have felt that having the chips already measured out for them ensured that they would not be eating too much.

An alternative explanation is that the participants may have been inhibited about opening the big bag because there was only one available and they were "guests" in a strange setting, whereas they were less inhibited about opening one of five bags available.

It may work the same at home. If you have only one bag of chips, you might save it for a special occasion; but if you have several small bags, you might be more likely to have one every day.

Alternatives to Dieting

If we want to control what and how much we eat, applying insights on human behavior from psychology and behavioral economics could potentially be more helpful than trying to diet. Instead of focusing on avoiding food, we might be more successful by paying attention to the food environment. Here's what I suggest:

1. Look at the current food environment and purveyors of processed foods with suspicion. One of the strongest human drives is the desire to be treated fairly and not to be duped or taken advantage of. We don't like to think we are getting a raw deal. So try to remember that food branding, celebrity endorsements, and elegant packaging are simply tricks to get you to buy a product. The value of the product remains unchanged regardless of what is on the wrapper. If we start viewing the worst offenders in the food and beverage industries with disdain, their efforts will fail to persuade us to buy their products. We will have inoculated ourselves against companies that sell us junk foods and that advertise and market those foods relentlessly. The best thing about this approach is that we won't have to use up any of our willpower or limited cognitive capacity to reject these unhealthy foods—we will say no automatically, as we do when faced with anything suspicious.

2. Take a stand on food. Most people, including me, love to eat sweet foods and crunchy, salty snacks. But it's possible to learn to dislike them on principle, which will make resisting them a lot easier. The trick is seeing beyond the food and appreciating how the process of creating, processing, packaging, and marketing it creates a spiral of problems for many people and for the planet.

By way of example, I have learned to dislike sugar-sweetened beverages. As a youth, my favorite beverage was a root beer float, but now I won't drink any soda except soda water. Basically, I have conditioned myself to associate sodas with poor health and social harms like poverty and even global warming. (Yes, you can help reduce global warming by consuming less!) Sodas and other bottled drinks as well as processed foods waste a lot of materials, create a lot of trash, and generally waste the money of people who are sucked into the illusion that the drink is more than the drink or the snack is more than the snack. By focusing on the bad qualities of foods that should be avoided—the horrible chemicals and preservatives in them, the negative consequences of consuming them—it is possible to learn to dislike them. Once you dislike something, it is much, much easier to refuse.

3. Cut your food budget. Instead of going on a diet, try saving money. If you buy less, you will usually end up eating less. If you are not losing weight doing what you are doing now, you are probably buying (and eating) too much food. Think of weight loss as money in the bank. The first thing to save on is snacking. Just don't eat between meals. (Or if you must, limit yourself to a fruit or vegetable that costs less than fifty cents.) Whatever you would have ordinarily spent on a snack, whether it is an energy bar or a cappuccino, take that money and put it in a special wallet. Don't spend it on any other food. If you have already cut out snacks but are still having trouble losing weight, then you need to eat smaller meals. Buy less bread. Skip the pasta. Save money on the amount of meat or cheese you buy. Any person who wants to lose weight but is spending more on food as a result is missing a key concept of weight loss: eating less should translate into spending less.

4. Share whenever possible. Most of us are attracted to food and tend to eat everything on our plate. Even so, we can restrain ourselves if we think of higher social obligations. Consider hunger strikes: people are able to starve themselves because they are thinking of a goal that is larger than themselves. Of course, most of us will never be that extreme, but we are all quite capable of being generous, charitable, and willing to sacrifice for the sake of others. Many parents, for example, will forgo things they like in order to provide more for their children or aid to those in need. If you see something tempting or are dining in a restaurant that serves particularly large portions, share your meal with your companions or save a good amount for the other people in your life who might like it as much as or more than you. If you go out to eat, put at least half of your entrée in a "to go" box—give it to someone else or think of the benefits that a compost pile will derive from your contribution. In general, thinking about others is a good way to take your mind off your own problems.

5. Structure your meals and eating habits—control your personal food environment. If you develop stable routines, it will be easier to avoid eating too much. The standard advice to eat three meals a day at the same time and same place can help you avoid all the extra calories from snacking and grazing, a common challenge for weight control. Plan your meals ahead of time for the entire week so that you don't get in the position where nothing is available and you have to go out. Last-minute restaurant or supermarket runs often lead to impulse buying and impulse eating. Enjoy the planning, anticipation, and creation of delicious meals. Eating only what you need doesn't mean food will not be enjoyable. Rather, eating will be more enjoyable because you won't feel any guilt or dismay that you are compromising your health.

6. Forget about dieting. Just get active, especially if your main concern is your lifespan. You will probably live longer by getting fit rather than getting thin. Give up as many motorized trips as possible. Instead, walk, skate, cycle, and use the stairs. Walk or bike through every park and neighborhood in your city. Join or start a walking club, a soccer team, a basketball league, or a regular dance event in your local park. Advocate for *ciclovías* in your city. Put all the energy you have previously devoted to food into physical activity—increasing your own as well as others'.

7. Don't give up on collective action. As long as we allow companies to exploit our neurophysiology, it's not going to be easy for us to control our eating behaviors. If it were easy, I wouldn't have to write this book, and you wouldn't have to read it. We are a species that functions socially. Just as one of the mechanisms for overeating is through imitation of others to achieve social harmony and cohesion, we have to find the common factors in our eating behaviors and work together to address the true causes of our dietary problems. We have to worry less about the corporate imperatives of the food and beverage industries and instead focus on developing regulations that are good for our health. The collective health of our nation must be our ultimate goal.

You Can Act for the Collective (and Your Own) Good

As much as I would hope that people would be able to transcend the food environment on their own, not everyone will be able to trick their brain and ignore tempting foods. Instead, it will be collective action that will change business as usual. We can make simple changes in our environment that will protect people from obesity.

Just as advocates for people with disabilities passed the Americans with Disabilities Act, which has transformed every community, one curb cut at a time, you can foster the changes in the food environment that will protect people from obesity. Many people are already deeply involved in this work. Changes depend on individuals who either take the bull by its horns and do it themselves or who goad their elected officials to pass necessary legislation to promote our health.

Here are a few things individuals can try:

Write letters to the editor, blog, tweet, and contact your elected officials. Share the idea that the environment has to be changed to work for people rather than against them. The more people hear about this perspective, the more rapidly a movement for a safer food environment will take off. Don Gaede, a physician in Fresno, sent me the following letter that he had published in his local paper, the *Fresno Bee*:

Dear Editor,

I was waiting in line at the pharmacy to pick up my prescription when my eyes settled on the large rack of candy bars, conveniently located within easy reach. For a moment, I was tempted to indulge.

Then my emotion changed to annoyance: Why is this pharmacy trying to entice me and all their other customers to eat junk food? I began taking note of the checkout lanes in other stores. Almost every one of them, whether they're selling groceries or crafts or hardware, puts high calorie snacks in their checkout lines.

With nearly two thirds of Americans overweight or obese, and childhood obesity tripling within a generation, the last thing we need is enticingly placed junk food everywhere we shop. These "impulse buys" obviously help the businesses' bottom lines, but this profit comes at the expense of people's health.

We don't need a new law to fix this problem. What we do need is for businesses to voluntarily get rid of junk food near checkout lines. Many school districts are changing their policies about selling sugary sodas in schools. Now let's start moving those Reeses Pieces to the backs of the stores.

—*Don H. Gaede, MD*

The more people complain about the conditions that undermine us, the more likely things will change.

Start a restaurant certification program that makes healthier meals available. Ask your favorite food outlets to prepare healthier five-hundred- and seven-hundred-calorie meals and encourage your friends and coworkers to dine there and order these meals. Ask your workplace or health-care plan to partner together to provide free PR for all restaurants that offer these healthier meals. Figure out how to make it worthwhile for restaurants to meet the needs of consumers like you, such as holding school fundraisers at these locations.

Ask your supermarket to make candy-free cash register checkout lanes available. Write to the CEO, talk to the store manager, and ask your friends to do the same. If there is more than one supermarket in town, let them know that you and your friends will only be shopping at the one that doesn't undermine you or your family. Do the same with the hardware stores, bookstores, and everywhere you notice unwanted candy displays. And then start tackling the end aisle displays and floor displays.

Ask your workplace to adopt practices and policies that reduce snacking and increase physical activity. Get your coworkers to sign a request to remove the soda and snack machines, or request they be moved to a less salient location, like a closet in the basement. Lead an "Instant Recess" during your ten-minute breaks.

Contact your elected officials. Another option is to focus your efforts on elected officials and government employees who make and enforce the rules that govern the food environment in your town, city, or state. Ask them to:

- Hold forums with the health department, and start a public discussion on the kinds of factors that lead people to eat too much, from ubiquitous food marketing to the junk food in many retail outlets.

- Discuss instituting standardized portions.
- Discuss adding licensure requirements to mandate that any restaurant serving meals *must* offer options that won't increase the risk of chronic diseases in order to get their operating permits.
- Plan on requiring licenses for all places that sell food—whether it is through vending machines or candy at the cash register.
- Then ask the health department to cap the number of licenses it issues for vending machines and for outlets that exclusively sell sodas and junk food.

Be creative. Even if you cannot accomplish anything on the above list, if you can convince others that environmental barriers are the main forces that need to be addressed to control obesity, you will have moved us much closer to a solution. It is all about framing the problem and generating the political will to act. With more than 150 million Americans who are overweight or obese, how can people continue to doubt that at least some of us, if not most, are vulnerable to a food environment that is filled with temptations?

You Are Not Alone

Although what a single individual might be able to accomplish is limited, according to the well-known anthropologist Margaret Mead, "Never doubt that a small group of thoughtful, committed citizens can change the world. Indeed, it is the only thing that ever has." Together, a group of similarly minded people could work to change the food landscape across our communities, cities, states, and the country.

Just twenty-two years ago, the Americans with Disabilities Act was signed into law after a relatively small group of committed activists persuaded Congress to pass it. In many ways, this legislation was more groundbreaking than the changes mandated by the Sanitary Revolution because of the way it reframed how we view people with disabilities. In his book *No Pity: People with Disabilities Forging a New Civil Rights Movement,* Joseph Shapiro summarized the forces that led to the ADA's passage.[5] He noted that disabled people did not want to be pitied but wanted to be considered as equals to nondisabled citizens. Thus, the ADA squarely established that people with disabilities are "people" first—and, as such, are entitled to the same rights and benefits as people without disabilities.

Disability rights activist Mark Johnson said, "Black people fought for the right to ride in the front of the bus. We're fighting for the right to get on the bus." Until 1990, many wheelchair-bound individuals who were otherwise fully capable of working full-time could not work at all because they were unable to get to or into an office building. Having buses with wheelchair lifts and buildings with ramps were key demands of disability activists, who fought for the disabled to become fully functioning and employable members of society. They no longer wanted to be shut in, isolated, and dependent on subsidies or charity. Even with disabilities, most are able to work with appropriate support.

Judy Herman, a wheelchair-bound disability activist, said, "Disability only becomes a tragedy for me when society fails to provide the things we need to lead our lives—job opportunities or barrier-free buildings."

One of the tenets of the disability rights movement was that people with disabilities, even the most severe disabilities, like quadriplegia, still have lives worth living. Even being disabled, they can contribute to society and enjoy life as much as able-bodied individuals.

Just as reframing our expectations was critical to helping the disabled become part of mainstream America, we must reframe our view of obesity. We can no longer consider obesity the consequence of an individual's deliberate and thoughtful choices. Just as we think of infectious diseases as the result of exposure to bacteria, viruses, parasites, or fungi, and cancers the consequence of exposure to carcinogens, obesity is primarily the result of exposure to an obesogenic environment. If people were not exposed to an environment with too much readily available food, fewer would be overweight or obese.

Hand in hand with the view that obesity is largely caused by environmental conditions, we must also reevaluate the widely held view that most individuals have the capacity to transcend obesogenic environments and to maintain a normal weight. Yes, some people can do it, but they are the minority. Many who are thin remain so despite this environment, and not because they have a superior ability to resist the temptations of too much food. Actually, I put myself in this category. I believe I am thin, not because I am able to count calories or resist sweets (which I can't), but because I am not frequently exposed to an obesogenic environment. I seldom watch television, eat out, or have easy opportunities to snack. This is not a conscious choice, but an unintended consequence of the demands of my career and family and the physical limits of a twenty-four-hour day. But when I go on vacation and have to eat out every meal for more than one week, I often come home packing a few extra pounds around my waist.

Others who maintain a normal weight are protected by physiological conditions, like early satiety, malabsorption, or an active metabolism. Many are protected by habits—of having a structured life, of eating a routine diet that doesn't have the novelties, variety, and other foods that can lead to obesity. Thirty to forty years ago, most people were able to maintain a normal weight just by going about their routine activities; they weren't faced with too many choices, too many snacks, or extra-large portions. The extra burden of navigating through a plethora of options overwhelms those who are sensitive and pay attention to their surroundings—which is most of us.

We must finally accept the fact that most people cannot limit their intake without significant support, without controls on the environmental sources of food, and without constraints on the ubiquitous cues that make us feel hungry when we do not need to eat. Just as the physical environment constitutes a barrier for people with disabilities, the food environment is the primary barrier to achieving a normal weight for most Americans.

Another lesson from the disability rights movement is that the leaders were able to finesse the issue of cost to eliminate barriers. Initially, the cost of mandating curb cuts, building ramps, renovating bathrooms, and the like was estimated to be in the billions of dollars. Significant opposition to the ADA arose from both likely and unlikely quarters. Some religious groups opposed it because it would have required churches to make costly structural changes to ensure access for all. One church estimated it would have had to spend $6,500 for a ramp.[6]

Many in the business community were also against the passage of the ADA. They claimed that the costs of accommodation would make business services and products unaffordable and would spell financial ruin to small businesses in particular. Yet a 1982 Department of Labor study found that most accommodations for the disabled were simple and cheap. For example, the cost of putting blocks under a deck to raise it for a wheelchair user was negligible, and 30 percent of all accommodations cost between $100 and $500—a pittance to allow someone to work full-time. Other changes did cost more—all buildings with more than two stories needed an elevator. Stores would have to widen their aisles to make room for wheelchairs. Phone companies had to hire operators to relay messages from the deaf using new telecommunications devices. Bus companies had to install wheelchair lifts. But the law included a potential break or waiver for businesses if the expense of the accommodation was beyond reasonable.

Surely, when it comes to implementing policies and regulations for obesity control, we will hear the same objections—that change is too expensive and will harm more people than it helps. Yet it is absurd to think that it is too difficult or expensive for a restaurant to figure out the nutritional content of the food it serves. The complaint was accepted without question by our lawmakers when they exempted from menu-labeling laws food outlets that have fewer than twenty locations. After all, packaged foods are already labeled with the nutritional ingredients, and the nutritional ingredients of unprocessed food are listed in free databases published by the USDA.

Moreover, there is ample free software that allows anyone to figure out the nutritional content of any recipe. All it takes is some basic knowledge of arithmetic and algebra. If businesses in the food industry can figure out how to order their supplies, pay wages, fill out their taxes, and meet the demanding requirements of sanitary regulations, surely they can figure out what is in the food they are serving and how much is in each portion. Worse comes to worst, a restaurant can hire a registered dietician to help on a one-time basis.

Nobody would expect restaurants to make changes to their serving sizes overnight, but it should take no more than a day for a restaurant to teach its servers how to use measuring cups and kitchen scales, and less than a year for all types of food outlets to implement standardized portion sizes. It should take no more than a few years to figure out how to redesign supermarkets to help people make better dietary choices—if we make it a national priority.

After all, bigger changes are being made all across the United States to integrate the more than fifty million Americans with disabilities. Cities and towns everywhere are changing the designs of sidewalks and intersections so people in wheelchairs can navigate the streets. All new stores and restaurants and buildings are now wheelchair-accessible, with ramps or elevators so people who cannot walk can patronize the premises. All the bathrooms in these facilities had to be designed to accommodate wheelchairs as well.

Despite many of the provisions of the ADA, it was popular with politicians and passed with few concessions. Why? Because every politician knew someone or had a close friend or family member who was disabled, or was himself suffering from some disability.[7] Tony Coelho, the bill's original House sponsor, had epilepsy. Senator Lowell Weicker, the original Senate sponsor, had a son with Down syndrome. When he lost reelection, Tom Harkin, who had a deaf brother, became the Senate sponsor. Other politicians had close experiences with disabilities. Edward Kennedy's son, Teddy Jr., had lost his leg to cancer. Bob Dole had a paralyzed arm from a World War II injury. Orrin Hatch had a brother-in-law with polio who slept in an iron lung. President George H. W. Bush's son Neil suffered from a learning disability. His son Marvin had much of his colon removed and had to wear an ostomy bag. And his favorite uncle was a quadriplegic.

At the time of the bill's passage there were forty-three million American constituents who were disabled—most of them voters. It would have looked cold and somewhat cruel for a politician to vote against the disabled.

Now there are more than 150 million Americans who are overweight or obese. If everyone could agree that a food environment that encourages consumption of extra-large portions and impulse buys of junk food is as much of a barrier to weight control as a flight of stairs or a curb is to the disabled, we could create an atmosphere that would be conducive to fixing the problem at a common and malleable leverage point.

The analogy with the ADA shouldn't be taken too far. I am not at all suggesting that people who are overweight or obese are disabled. It's just that we are all human—not machines, not automatons. We are a species that is wired to be inquisitive, adventurous, and to take advantage of opportunity. When too much food is available, our DNA has us wired to eat more than we need. Our natural proclivities must be taken into account as we build a society that prides itself on creating conditions that do not increase our risk of disease but do provide us the possibility of achieving our full potential.

A Manifesto Claiming Victimhood? Is There No Role for Personal Responsibility?

Personal responsibility is always the ultimate determinant of people's behavior; even with the best social and environmental conditions, there are some individuals who manage to get into trouble. And of course, given the worst conditions, there will be some with the capacity to triumph—but they will be the exception. Nevertheless, in a free society, it is not the role of government to strictly regulate people's behavior. But if people find it too difficult to achieve their goals or to stay healthy even after repeated attempts, it is a societal role to address the environmental conditions that undermine or interfere with their well-being. If 96 percent of the water is not potable, you can bet that a lot of people will be getting waterborne diseases. If most restaurants, supermarkets, and advertisements primarily encourage the consumption of foods that increase the risk of chronic diseases, we should anticipate that a lot of people will get sick.

Are we victims? Definitions of "victim" include a person who is harmed by or made to suffer from an act, circumstance, agency, or condition; one who suffers injury, loss, or death as a result of a voluntary undertaking (e.g., a victim of your own scheming); one who is tricked, swindled, or taken advantage of (e.g., a victim of misplaced confidence). We are victims of our own DNA, the forceful strategies of marketers, and an affluent society with more than enough to go around. In the end, it doesn't matter whether we blame human nature, the aggressive nature of the food industry, or our wildly successful systems of food production and distribution. People are suffering, and thus need protection.

Going Up Against the Food Industry

There is no doubt that the food industry will fight any regulatory changes tooth and nail. Its advocates will invoke the typical complaints: The government should not interfere in the marketplace. Individuals know best and we don't need any "nannies." Regulation will cause the food industry to lose money, which will prompt layoffs and increase unemployment. The economy will crash and farmers will go broke. Food isn't the problem behind obesity; it is the lack of physical activity.

The food industry will bring all its resources to bear to forestall any action that will protect consumers, as did the tobacco industry in the struggle to regulate tobacco and stop the epidemics of lung disease, cancer, and heart disease that smoking caused.

Nevertheless, public health advocates were able to make a dramatic dent in smoking rates by addressing how, when, and where tobacco is advertised, priced, and sold; thus we should be able to tackle obesity. But more people have to be convinced that food environments are the main concerns. Once we have the correct targets in our crosshairs, there should be no stopping progress. We must move forward to protect our friends and families from exposures that threaten our health and well-being.

I have made many suggestions, though I am the first to admit that there is no existing proof that these new policies will work. But there is also no reason to expect that the obesity epidemic will spontaneously resolve itself. We must try something new.

13

Conclusion

In the hot days of the summer of 1972, the New York City Health Department investigated an unusually high incidence of deaths among toddlers who fell out of tenement windows.[1] Initially mothers and caregivers were blamed for not being alert, not properly supervising children, or simply neglecting naturally curious toddlers and adventurous young children who leaned out of apartment windows or crawled onto fire escape stairwells to cool off.

After an investigation, the Health Department launched a campaign, "Children Can't Fly," and offered free window guards to families in tenement buildings. The next summer, there were no falls from buildings that had the new window guards. Subsequently, despite a protest from landlords, the requirement for these $3 devices was added to the city's health code. One landlord filed suit against the city, claiming the regulation was unconstitutional on the grounds that the new health code shifted the obligation for the care and protection of children from parents to the real estate industry.[2] He lost.

The story of the "Children Can't Fly" campaign is an apt analogy for the problem and the solution to the obesity epidemic. Children are born curious and may wander to an open window even if (or because) we tell them to stay away. All of us were born with the capacity and inclination to eat more than we need. In a world where there is too much food, we have no constraints that limit our natural tendencies to eat what is readily available.

In the case of the open tenement windows, if we simply blamed the families and didn't hold the landlords accountable, children would still be falling to their deaths. And similarly, in the case of obesity, restaurateurs and purveyors of food need to be held responsible for what they serve. The amount of food we eat depends on the conditions in which it is served and sold. If the food industry wasn't selling us so much food that makes us sick, we wouldn't be sick. Together, as a society, we have the power to change the conditions that favor overconsumption—for our own protection and preservation.

The public health experience is that blaming people for their own problems rarely yields any fruitful solutions. Indeed, throughout history, the lack of self-control has been blamed for nearly every poor health behavior and human failure—alcoholism, smoking, sexually transmitted diseases, injuries, and car crashes.

One approach to addressing these societal ills is to focus on individuals and to motivate them to change through either incentives, negative consequences, or education. In contrast, the public health approach usually focuses on the conditions in which people live and seeks to address the upstream forces that lead individuals to behave the way they do. For example, public health approaches to alcoholism, smoking, sexually transmitted diseases, injuries, and car crashes are not to punish, incentivize, or educate people, but rather to regulate alcohol and tobacco availability; give sex partners prophylactic treatment; and make products, cars, and roads safer.

In the nineteenth century, before germ theory was understood and bacteria and viruses were discovered, poor health behaviors, moral turpitude, the lack of discipline, and even belonging to certain racial or ethnic groups (inherited genetic defects) were cited as the causes of diseases like tuberculosis, cholera, and smallpox. Blaming individuals for their own health problems also fit in with prevailing religious views that God was simply meting out consequences for bad behavior. Individual responsibility has often been the default position when we don't really understand what is going on.

Yet the great advances in public health have all occurred when entire societies took monumental steps to change the conditions in which people lived. Regulations that mandated standards for sewerage systems, housing, working conditions, food storage and preparation, and air and water quality were not timid, incremental steps. These regulations were bold leaps whose impacts have extended our lives and reduced untold human miseries suffered by populations a century ago. We no longer have exceptionally high rates of occupational injuries, with workers falling into rendering tanks or becoming ground meat, as muckraker Upton Sinclair described in *The Jungle,* his 1906 book about the meatpacking industry. Nor do we have the level of industrial pollution associated with the London smog that killed between four thousand and twelve thousand people in five days in December 1952 and sickened more than one hundred thousand others. We can thank regulations, rather than the voluntary behavioral improvements of otherwise motivated individuals, for these healthier living conditions.

Our view of the responsibilities of societies and individuals has changed dramatically over the past century. Today, we expect our government to ensure that the air we breathe and the water we drink will not make us sick. We expect the government to make sure that housing and buildings will be constructed according to a rigorous code and won't be defective or crumple in storms. We expect our government to make sure we are treated fairly at work and that conditions in the workplace are safe. We expect the government to ensure that transportation is safe, to protect us from terrorists in the air, and to prevent bridges from collapsing and trains from crashing. Moreover, we demand that the government test the safety of consumer goods and curtail false and misleading advertising.

The government's role in monitoring the risks that individuals cannot easily protect themselves against is continually expanding. Our increasing demands on government are paralleled by our decreasing expectations of what individuals can effectively be responsible for. Everything has become so specialized and sophisticated that it is impossible for a single person to master it all. We expect the government to assume responsibility for what individuals cannot do to protect and promote their own welfare. In general, the populace has mostly welcomed these protections.

It is true that many regulations today seem to be arbitrary or over-the-top, and certainly we don't need any more of those. Yet what now seem like reasonable demands to remove animal carcasses from the streets, and to clean human and animal wastes from the public byways, and not to sell alcohol to children, seemed like arbitrary and unjust impositions in the nineteenth century.

Coming to terms with the host of regulations I have proposed is not going to be easy. I have great sympathy for complaints against a government that seems as if it already has too many onerous and unreasonable regulations now that I am trying to build my dream cottage in the middle of a rural area. I have had to face and comply with what seems like a host of burdensome requirements by the County Department of Building and Safety. The house I am planning is relatively small, with a thirty-by-forty-foot footprint, yet I need to get a zoning clearance, a soils test, a flood permit, a grading and earth removal permit, a permit for a septic tank, a well permit, a water quality permit, a permit for electricity, a building permit, a traffic permit, an integrated waste management permit, and a fire permit. I must hire several licensed professionals—an architect, a structural engineer, a soils engineer—to sign off on my plans. I need twenty-two separate documents, and I have to pay at least twelve different fees, including a traffic mitigation fee, a fire protection fee, a school district fee, an acreage assessment fee, a flood hazard clearance fee, and fees for seven different departments to check and approve my plans. Personnel have to come to the building site at every step along the way to approve the progress. They insist on personally checking that all the construction follows the building code.

I have had to change my plans dramatically and spend way more than I planned because of these building codes, which were presumably created for my benefit. Today, all new buildings in California must be equipped with fire sprinklers. Even though I must include them, I also have to build my house within 150 feet of the public street so a fire truck can reach it in case of emergency. Although I wanted to build the house as far from the road as possible to have more privacy and peace and quiet, approval would have required paving a road strong enough to bear a sixteen-ton fire truck and wide enough for it to turn around. This would have been unaffordable, and it would have also defeated the purpose of moving to a rural area, which was to avoid a lot of asphalt and cement.

Not only are there multiple permits, but the specialists checking all the details of the building process also seem to have obsessive-compulsive disorder. We have had to go back and forth multiple times with multiple departments to specify everything on the plans. We have to state the location of all the valves and pipes and indicate each pipe's diameter. We have to locate a hydrant not less than a hundred feet from the house. We have to specify the depth of the foundation and the height of the electric panel. And the land around the house has to have at least a 2 percent slope away from the house for proper drainage.

What is the public health impact of such rigid, extensive, and meticulously specified building code regulations? A poor-quality house would pose a danger to relatively few people—just my husband, any guests we might have, and me. So much attention to such a small project hardly seems worthwhile (except that it appears that our permit fees are the way government bureaucrats get paid).

Although there are some quirky requirements that appear not to make sense and the extra cost of the permits and inspections is quite burdensome, the truth is that I very much appreciate that the county is checking to make sure my new home will be sound. I have no expertise and would otherwise have to rely on the builder. Having someone else's eyes on the plans increases my confidence that I am making a good investment in a house that will be able to withstand earthquakes, floods, and other problems that may arise.

Compare the massive amount of regulation I face to build a small bungalow with minimal impact to the minimal regulation of food outlets like restaurants and grocery stores and their massive impact on dietary intake. The typical fast food outlet may serve more than 1,500 people every day.[3] A supermarket might serve a few thousand customers every day. As we have seen, the design of restaurants and markets and how they present and promote food strongly influence what people eat. We already have a huge infrastructure of "food police," but they currently focus only on food safety and the prevention of infectious diseases like *E. coli* and salmonella. These "food police" inspect factories, supermarkets, and restaurants and make sure that the food served is prepared and stored hygienically, and that appropriate equipment is available and functioning.

If there is any lapse and anyone gets sick, the public screams, "Why isn't the government doing even more to protect the food supply?" No one is clamoring to eliminate food policing. We do not tolerate leniency when an outlet sells food that threatens the lives of its customers with deadly viruses or bacteria. We demand that the business be shut down immediately.

Our system works fairly well: outbreaks of deadly food-borne diseases are uncommon, and infectious diseases from unclean food are no longer in the top ten causes of death in the United States. In 1900 enteritis and diarrhea were grouped as the third major cause of death, after pneumonia and tuberculosis. Today, an estimated three thousand Americans die annually from a food-borne disease—but that is a drop in the bucket compared to the estimated four hundred thousand who die annually from poor diets and lack of physical activity.[4]

One argument for protecting people from food-borne infectious disease rather than from chronic diseases is that people cannot easily tell whether food is contaminated with viruses and bacteria. Customers may have no way to protect themselves from bacteria, but in theory they should be able to avoid unhealthy foods.

Yet under the current conditions, most people cannot make their short-term choices conform to their long-term goals. Regulating food outlets would make achieving one's optimal weight within reach for the average person. Many people regret the decisions they have made to eat unhealthy foods. They recognize they are making poor choices, but they cannot easily change. Most of us are vulnerable to the positioning, placement, pricing, priming, and conditioning strategies that lead us to eat more than we intend.

Regulation of construction, from the designation of the types of bolts and screws to the allowable height of the building, has become very well accepted, and many, if not most, would consider it an absolute necessity. I have no doubt that regulation of the placement, presentation, and sale of food directly associated with chronic diseases will eventually stop the obesity epidemic and limit diet-related chronic diseases. Moreover, I believe that food outlets that exceed these minimum regulations and take care to serve only food that protects against chronic diseases will eventually become the most exclusive and desirable.

Ironclad scientific proof that a policy will be effective is often demanded before enacting any regulation that might be burdensome. Yet obtaining proof may require implementing a policy. How can one know if something works if it has never been tried? Indeed, many laws and policies are "experimental" and instituted or revoked based upon whether the politicians in power find them to be an advantage or a disadvantage. Given the crisis we are in, we should be willing to try all sensible approaches that help people moderate consumption. If the approach doesn't meet expectations in a reasonable period of time, it can be changed.

The regulations proposed herein are not bans on food, but rather constraints on salience, marketing, convenience, and accessibility.

Many people reading the ideas in this book will worry that I am proposing regulations that tell people what they can and cannot eat or that I am proposing a new cadre of food police to snatch prohibited foods out of people's mouths or force people to exercise. Not at all. What I am advocating is really no different from the principles already being implemented by my County Department of Building and Safety. Just as we have standards that govern construction design, layout, and how raw building materials are used in homes, we also need standards for how foods are prepared and marketed to the public. "Choice architecture" is a term that suggests we should create environments and conditions that are conducive to better health. We should make certain that poor choices are deliberate rather than automatic, and make the consequences of a poor choice transparent. Healthier choices should be the easiest choices.

Because the current epidemic is primarily the result of wide-sweeping changes in the way food is marketed and sold, including the excess availability of high-calorie, low-nutrient foods, too-large portion sizes, and ubiquitous food advertising, we need to work collectively to address these root causes of the problem. Alone, our powers are extremely limited. We would have to remove ourselves from society to avoid its influences.

We can't forget that the food industry's aggressive marketing strategies undermine our health behaviors. Even though the food industry may claim it does not intend to exploit us, many current marketing tactics that are acceptable for items like tennis shoes, picture frames, or flowers should not be employed to push food. We won't become overweight or sick with a chronic disease if we buy too many T-shirts, but we will if we purchase and eat too much food.

As a public health approach, diets are the wrong solution. Diets are only appropriate for select individuals. Diets place the onus on the individual, but we have to focus on and remediate the environment around us. We have to keep reminding ourselves that this new epidemic is not the result of people's irresponsiblity, weakening moral fiber, or inferiority of character; it is the result of excess food availability and salience.

Placing the burden on each individual to avoid supermarkets, restaurants, and convenience stores, not to watch television or visit theaters, to avoid company meetings and common work areas, and to identify routes that do not pass vending machines is unreasonable. The placement of food and food cues where we don't need to eat is similar to yelling "Fire" in a crowded theater. It gets us into action unnecessarily, artificially triggering a chain of events that force us to make a decision—to choose or resist. Making a decision to resist will tax our cognitive reserves, a waste of our precious but limited mental resources.

Increasing the level of government regulation in a country that abhors big government is not going to be easy. Contractors always complain about building code regulations, but people whose homes survive earthquakes and other natural disasters appreciate the fact that the buildings are strong. When buildings and structures are not built according to code, terrible disasters occur. Think of how the canal walls failed in New Orleans after Hurricane Katrina. Tens of thousands of people lost their homes because the contractors had taken shortcuts and did not ensure the canals' structural integrity. And think of the children crushed in collapsed schools in earthquakes in China or the three hundred thousand killed in Haiti by buildings that were constructed without the benefit of strict regulations, inspections, and architectural reviews.

When we finally realize how the current regulatory neglect results in our developing chronic, preventable diseases that make us miserable and shorten our lives, perhaps we will introduce public health policies that will be effective.

Most important, new rules and interventions should be accompanied by evaluations—we need a research agenda that carefully checks whether these policies are working. If the new policies don't work, then we should change them.

These proposed new rules don't ban foods or tell anybody what they should or shouldn't eat. They would only make unhealthy foods a little less accessible and a little less attractive. In a world that protected people against obesity, we would still have plenty of food that satisfies our cravings for variety, novelty, and pleasure. We would dine on fresh fruits and vegetables, whole grains, and eat much smaller quantities of meats, sugars, and saturated fats.

In the future we will want to eat because we feel hungry, rather than having pseudo-feelings of hunger being constantly stimulated by cues on radio, television, billboards, posters, and personal computers. We will enjoy our meals, which will be designed to be tasty and satisfying and to keep us in optimal health. We will be able to spend our mental energies and time in pursuit of happiness, working on our careers, raising our families, participating in civic life, and getting sufficient leisure and recreation to maximize our health and well-being, rather than fretting about dieting or worrying about what to eat.

We won't have to stay home and cook every meal for ourselves because restaurants and fast food outlets will be able to prepare healthy meals that are just what we need. The atmospherics in restaurants and other settings that previously made us buy and eat too much will be replaced by atmospherics that will both keep us in energy balance and keep the food industry in business. In fact, restaurants and food outlets will be able to customize the foods so that they are in the appropriate portion for each of us. An ID card or a driver's license could encode our individual energy requirements so that when our cards are swiped with our orders, the restaurant will know exactly how much to serve us. The grocery store will know our preferences and will present us with a bag of groceries that contains not only the foods that provide the nutrients we need but also the ones we like. If we want to override these selections, we can, but most of the time we will be delighted that we are being served exactly what we need, and we will be satisfied with that.

This idea is not that futuristic. Once restaurants figure out what the nutrient qualities of their food items are, which many already do, it's only a matter of simple math and measuring spoons, cups, rulers, or kitchen scales to determine the right quantity to serve. Expecting that customers will be able to do this themselves, to be given an extra-large portion and then to have to carry their own measuring spoons and cups is unreasonable. We won't be able to carry utensils and keep them clean, nor, as I showed earlier, will we be able to judge appropriate portions without measuring tools.

Instead of pointing fingers at overweight and obese individuals for having self-control problems, let's recognize that, for the most part, they are doing the best that they can given the conditions in which we live. We will look back on this era with astonishment, and wonder how we allowed—without challenge—companies to create the illusion that drinks that are no more than sugar water and other highly processed junk foods are better, classier, more prestigious, and more valuable than nutritious beverages and foods.

We have to make some accommodations in the environment so that we can avoid overconsumption without having to struggle so much. If we can make reasonable accommodations for the disabled, no doubt we can accommodate the tens of millions who want to control their weight.

With any change there will be winners and losers. Although some businesses may adapt and maintain their market share, others may lose profits, and still others may gain if they can offer superior products or alternatives that meet new standards that reduce obesity and chronic diseases.

A society that will keep us healthy will not exist anytime soon unless we take steps to make it so. It will not come easily, but it can happen if we want it to. Between now and then, many incremental steps have to be taken. The good news is that we have the resources to create a healthy, and more than sufficient, food supply. What we lack are leadership, vision, and the general acceptance of the fact that most individuals will not be able to improve their health without the support of society as a whole.

The steps we have to take to control obesity are not earth-shaking or unreasonable. In contrast to other societal reforms, the changes we need may be barely noticeable, especially if phased in gradually. While menu-labeling may seem revolutionary now, in a few years, it will seem archaic and slightly misguided as we find more effective ways to help people choose healthy foods. Similarly, once we institute practices like standardized portion sizes, impulse marketing constraints, counter-advertising, restaurant ratings, and other policies in worksites, schools, and communities, we will soon take them for granted, just as we now take for granted the conditions that have been engineered to make us overweight and obese.

It is neither normal nor natural for us to be confronted multiple times each day with images of and access to unlimited foods, especially candy, cookies, soda, pastries, fries, and chips. The environment is engineered on behalf of a food industry that is so concerned with profits that it will do anything to get us to eat as much as we can. A food industry that cared about us would not be pushing sugar, fat, and salt. It would not manipulate us to eat too much with extra-large portions and processed foods. We need to un-engineer the environment so that it doesn't artificially make us hungry and provide us with too many foods that make us sick.

<hr />

I have hoped to show in this book that being overweight is not an individual problem but rather a consequence of human nature functioning in normal, predictable ways when too much food is available. Ultimately, our personal behaviors depend on local conditions, conditions that we do not design and cannot control as individuals, but that are potentially controllable through public health policies and regulations.

It's a hard truth to accept that, when it comes to eating, the environment may be more powerful than we are as individuals. Nevertheless, we must accept and embrace our limitations. Let's stop being so hard on ourselves. Let us heed the lessons learned from the Sanitary Revolution, from the battles against alcohol-related harms, and from the movement to accommodate Americans with disabilities. These movements have proven the benefits of creating environments in which people can be healthy so they can flourish and achieve their goals. Creating healthy environments is not only the mission of public health; it is also the basic foundation of the United States.

We can tackle the obesity epidemic. We just can't do it alone. Please join me in a new movement that views obesity as a public health crisis—and demands serious public health solutions that will protect us all.

Appendix: Healthier Meal Guidelines for Adults and Children

Healthier Meal Guidelines for Adults and Children*

Adult Meals	Children's Meals
• ≤ 700 calories	• ≤ 600 calories
• ≤ 10% of calories from saturated fat	• ≤ 10% of calories from saturated fat
• < 0.5 g of artificial trans fat per meal	• ≤ 35% of calories from total fat
• ≤ 35% of calories from total sugars	• < 0.5 gram of artificial trans fat per meal
• No sugar-sweetened beverages	• ≤ 35% of calories from total sugars
• ≤ 770 mg sodium	• No sugar-sweetened beverages
• ≥ 1.5 cups of vegetables and/or fruits (this can include no more than 0.5 cup of white potatoes)	• ≤ 770 mg of sodium
• If the meal includes a grain, it should be whole grain rich	• Must include two sources of the following—one of these must be a vegetable or a fruit (not including juice):
	• > 0.5 cup fruit
	• > 0.5 cup nonfried vegetable
	• Contains whole grains
	• Lean protein (lean as defined by USDA, skinless white meat poultry, fish/seafood, beef, pork, tofu, beans, egg); > 2 oz. meat, 1 egg, 1 oz. nuts/seeds/dry beans/peas
	• > 0.5 cup 1% or fat-free milk, or lower-fat dairy

*The criteria for healthier meals and healthier restaurants were developed by working groups associated with the NIMHD-funded conference #R13MD006698 on Performance Standards for Away from Home Meals. The authors are:

Deborah Cohen, MD MPH, *RAND Corporation*
Rajiv Bhatia, MD, MPH, *San Francisco Department of Public Health*
Mary Story, PhD, *University of Minnesota*
Stephen D. Sugarman, JD, *School of Law, UC Berkeley*
Margo Wootan, PhD, *Center for Science in the Public Interest*
Christina D. Economos, PhD, *Tufts University*
Linda Van Horn, PhD, RD, *Feinberg School of Medicine, Northwestern University*
Laurie Whitsel, PhD, *American Heart Association*
Susan Roberts, JD, MS, RD, *Partnership for a Healthier America*
Lisa Powell, PhD, *School of Public Health, University of Illinois at Chicago*
Angela Odoms-Young, PhD, *University of Illinois at Chicago*

Jerome D. Williams, PhD, *Rutgers Business School*
Bechara Choucair, MD, *Chicago Dept of Public Health*
Brian Elbel, PhD, *New York University School of Medicine*
Jennifer Harris, PhD, MBA, *Rudd Center, Yale University*
Manel Kappagoda, JD, *ChangeLab Solutions*
Catherine Champagne, PhD, *Pennington Biomedical Research Center*
Kathleen Shields, *San Antonio Metropolitan Health District*
Lenard Lesser, MD, MSHS, *Palo Alto Medical Foundation Research Institute*
Tracy Fox, MPH, RD *Food, Nutrition & Policy Consultants, LLC*
Nancy Becker, MS RD LD, *Oregon Public Health Institute*

Principles for a Healthier Restaurant

Participating restaurants must meet the following criteria, plus adopt a combination of principles below that add up to 20 points:

- Offer three meals or 10% of items listed on the adult/regular menu (whichever is greater) that meet the Healthier Meal Guidelines
- Offer two children's meals or 25% of the children's menu items (whichever is greater) that meet the children's Healthier Meal Guidelines, if the restaurant has a children's menu

*BEVERAGES**

- Offer container/cup sizes for sugar-sweetened beverages that are no larger than 16 oz. (3 pt)
- Make low- or no-calorie beverages the default with all bundled adult meals (3 pt)
- Do not offer free refills of sugar-sweetened beverages (2 pt)
- Have free water available and listed on the menu (1 pt)
- Make low-fat or fat-free milk the default milk option (1 pt)
- Serve milk (whole, 2%, 1%, or fat-free) as the default option rather than cream or half-and-half with coffee service (1 pt)

FOOD COMPONENTS

- Offer half portions for at least 50% of menu items and indicate on the menu that option is available (3 pt)
- Do not charge extra or prohibit customers from splitting a meal (3 pt)
- Serve nonfried vegetables and/or fruits as the default side dishes with meals (3 pt); or allow customers to substitute a fruit or nonfried vegetable for any side dish for no extra charge, and list option on the menu (2 pt)
- Offer at least three fruit or nonfried vegetable side dishes (2 pt)
- Serve whole-grain-rich options as the default with meals, when grains are offered (3 pt); or offer 25% of the grain products on the menu as whole-grain-rich options (2 pt)
- Three meals that meet the Healthier Meal Guidelines provide at least 7 grams of dietary fiber (2 pt)
- All meals and menu items are free of artificial trans fats or partially hydrogenated oils (2 pt)**
- Offer healthy spreads, such as olive oil, lower-fat margarine, or hummus, with bread in place of butter (1 pt)
- Do not offer free bread, chips, or other starters (e.g., such items must be ordered for an extra charge) (2 pt); or offer only upon request (1 pt)
- 50% of the dessert options are available in half-sized portions or are less than 300 calories (2 pt)
- Offer at least one fish/seafood meal meeting the Healthier Meal Guidelines (1 pt)

---

*Beverages with children's meals are addressed on the following page.
**Remove this criterion if this is legally required in the jurisdiction.

CHILDREN'S MEALS

- Sugar-sweetened beverages are not offered with children's meals (excludes flavored milk) (3 pt); or default beverages with children's meals are water, low-fat or fat-free milk, or 100% juice (2 pt)
- Fruit and/or nonfried vegetable is served as the default side item/s with meals (3 pt)
- Whole-grain-rich options are served as the default with meals, when grains are offered (2 pt)

MARKETING, PROMOTION, AND INFORMATION

- List calories per menu item, as offered for sale, on the menu or menu board (3 pt)
- Meals that meet the Healthier Meal Guidelines are sold at equal price or lower price than equivalent available items (3 pt)
- Train employees to prompt customers to choose nonfried vegetables when ordering (1 pt)
- Train employees to prompt customers to choose low- or no-calorie beverages when ordering (1pt)
- List prominently healthier options and low- and no-calorie beverages on menus, menu boards, or where displayed (1 pt for each approach employed, for a maximum of 3 pt):
  - Depict on the children's menu or section of the menu only options meeting the children's nutrition guidelines
  - Depict at least 50% of the items on the menu as healthier options
  - List healthier options first for each category of the menu
  - List low- or no-calorie beverages before sugar-sweetened beverages on the menu
  - Highlight healthier items on the menu using bold or larger font
  - Place healthier items more prominently (e.g., closer to customers and at eye level) for foods on display
- Promote healthier menu options through advertising, coupons, price promotions, window signs, in-store signage, kiosks, table tents, etc. (1 pt for each approach used, for a maximum of 3 pt)
  - At least half the promotional signage in the restaurant is for healthier items (2 pt)

Definitions

- Healthier options are those that meet the Healthier Meal Guidelines or are a fruit, a nonfried vegetable, whole-grain-rich grain (excluding sweet baked goods), low- or no-calorie beverage, water, or low-fat or fat-free milk.

- Whole-grain-rich—at least 50% of the grain ingredients are whole grain. This can be determined by the product having whole grain as the first ingredient, from the manufacturer, or if the product has a whole grain claim. Examples include brown rice, whole-grain rolls, corn tortillas, whole-grain pasta, oatmeal, and whole-grain cereal.

- Sugar-sweetened beverages include sodas, fruit drinks, sports drinks, iced teas, coffee drinks, and other beverages (excluding low-fat or fat-free milk) that contain added caloric sweeteners, and that have more than 25 calories per cup/container as offered for sale.

- Low- and no-calorie beverages include water and other beverages with no more than 25 calories per cup/container as offered for sale.

Frequently Asked Questions

1. What about personal responsibility? Shouldn't people be able to control themselves better?

Personal responsibility requires insight into the factors that lead to obesity and the capacity to overcome barriers to a healthy diet. Unfortunately, too many people lack both insight and capacity. Our expectations of most people are unrealistic given the conditions of our modern food environment.

Imagine that the roads are poorly lit, full of deep potholes, and there are ditches on each side with no barriers to prevent people from falling in. Most people should be able to navigate these roads if they go slowly, travel in the daylight, and look carefully at what lies ahead. And some may have better vision or faster reflexes that place them at lower risk of a mishap. However, anyone in a hurry or who travels at night and doesn't take the proper precautions will get a flat tire, crash, or both. With broken roads every journey becomes a risk. Wouldn't it be better if the roads were smooth and in good repair, so people could traverse them quickly without having to make a special effort to be careful? By repairing the roads, everyone's risk for a crash will be reduced.

The modern food environment is like a road filled with potholes and ditches. There are food hazards all around us, and only by being very careful, deliberate, or completely avoiding most restaurants and supermarkets are some of us able to protect ourselves. Yet there are plenty of people who don't have the wherewithal to defend themselves from all the food hazards around us. If we had standards for the way food is marketed, fewer people would have problems choosing a healthy diet and most of us wouldn't have to worry all the time about what we are being served. People will have a greater capacity to be responsible in an environment that has fewer hazards and risk factors for diet-related chronic diseases.

2. If the environment is so overwhelming and personal responsibility doesn't count for much, why isn't everybody obese?

Although most people will eat more than they should when presented with more food than they need, that is not the case with everyone. Some people have early satiety, which makes them feel full when eating relatively small amounts. Some people are seldom exposed to the triggers that cause excess eating. Others are insensitive to such triggers because they are preoccupied or depressed or engaging in other unhealthy behaviors like smoking or using drugs, which can limit eating. Some have conditions like malabsorption or diseases that make them lose weight or lose their appetite. Some, as research has shown, can successfully resist temptation and routinely work very hard to carefully choose what and how much they eat, but this group is the minority, as most Americans are overweight or obese. I don't think it is appropriate to think of two-thirds of the population as irresponsible. It doesn't square with everything we know about the American people and their general ethic of hard work.

3. What about corporate responsibility? Why should businesses have to worry about consumer choices?

Responsible businesses should not encourage people to consume more food than their bodies need to stay healthy. Businesses should not be creating conditions that result in harm to individuals. In other sectors, businesses are not allowed to encourage people to take risks without proper warnings or without obtaining signed consent forms. Right now, if a restaurant serves somebody food with an amount of fat, salt, sugar, or calories that could increase his or her risk of chronic diseases, the customer is not usually warned. Nevertheless, rather than merely warning people, a better approach would be for businesses to promote foods that are healthy and don't require caution. Food should be promoted in a manner that makes it less likely for people to increase their risk of chronic diseases. That way, if people do eat poorly, it would be their own choice and not the result of an outside party overly influencing them.

4. Can't you teach people not to eat mindlessly?

We often eat mindlessly because we can; humans have evolved to be able to do this. In fact, our capacity to eat without having to pay attention to the food and to do other things simultaneously should be considered a valuable and important asset. We can pay attention to our surroundings, socialize, and plan for the future while eating automatically. Not only does this save us a lot of time, but it helps us create bonds and positive relationships with others. Trying to teach "mindful" eating as a consistent practice would be an uphill battle and may also have negative unintended consequences, such as interfering with social relationships.

Many weight-loss interventions try to make people more aware of what they are eating, but usually after an initial period of success people fall back into the more natural routine of eating automatically. Besides being boring, being mindful of eating all the time precludes doing other things during meals. Most people do not want to "waste" time by concentrating on every bite and would rather use their brains to ponder other things.

5. How is the obesity epidemic related to global warming?

Too much carbon dioxide (CO_2) in the atmosphere traps heat and warms our planet. Our lifestyles are the direct cause of the release of excess CO_2, from our use of motor vehicles to our watching plasma televisions, which suck up lots of energy. But it isn't obvious to most of us how our everyday actions are linked to global warming. For example, we can't see the immediate impact on climate change of our use of air-conditioning, taking an airplane to go on vacation, or buying a steak dinner.

When we eat too much, our society has to produce more food and burn more fuel for harvesting and transport—all of which increase carbon emissions. An estimated 30–40 percent of all food is wasted, and 97 percent winds up in landfills. Food decomposes to methane, a potent global warming gas twenty-five times more powerful than CO_2.

Serving less would reduce waste, and eating less would reduce carbon emissions. Eating less meat and dairy in particular would have a huge impact because of the methane produced by cattle and dairy herds; meat and dairy products, account for about 18 percent of all greenhouse gases. Giving up meat and dairy one day a week is equivalent to driving 1,160 fewer miles per year.

Everything we do that consumes energy and/or produces waste contributes a little to the warming of the atmosphere. Multiply the energy use of a single person by a few billion people—that is the source of global warming. If we all reduced our behaviors that require energy consumption by just a small percentage, we could stem global warming. We could spend less time indoors (reducing air-conditioning and heating costs), travel more by walking or bicycle (driving our cars less), and eat less red meat and dairy products (reducing methane gas production). As a result, we would also get more exercise, burn more calories, and be less likely to gain weight and develop chronic diseases. Fortunately, taking steps to improve our health will also help protect our planet.

6. Shouldn't people be free to make their own decisions?

People's decisions are constrained by what is available, and people are vulnerable to a wide variety of framing effects, including prominence, position, and pricing. Change any one of these things and people's decisions will change.

Who controls how food is presented? Right now corporate America manipulates all the factors that guide people toward making choices that increase their risks for chronic diseases. The elements that influence people's choices should be made transparent so our decisions can be thoughtful and deliberate rather than the consequence of manipulation.

We accept a host of regulations that were created to protect people, including regulations about hygiene and safety that force restaurants to follow standard procedures in preparing, storing, and serving food. We accept regulations that force architects and contractors to build according to standards that govern construction and safety measures. We accept regulations that limit the sale of alcohol to licensed outlets at certain hours and in standard portions. We accept and appreciate regulations that keep our air and water clean and safe. Many of us depend on regulations that protect workers and specify safe working conditions, minimum wages, and overtime. Regulations are generally intended to protect people from situations where they have a limited capacity to protect themselves. Regulations can also make the consequences of our choices transparent at the time we are making decisions.

While some regulations can go too far and make every task unnecessarily onerous, most regulations that have stood the test of time have made life more predictable and living conditions safer. If we can be confident that our air, water, and shelters are safe, we will have the time and ability to focus our energies on activities beyond the basics of survival. Today we lack sufficient regulations that would help people make safer food choices. Regulations that govern how food is sold and served could protect us from being manipulated and undermined and reduce our exposure to foods that increase the risks of chronic diseases.

Regulations don't stop people from making their own decisions. Setting uniform standards makes it easier for people to make informed choices and protects us from relying on automatic, impulsive choices that compromise our health. People would still have the freedom to choose an unhealthy diet, but they would know that the choice was theirs rather than a consequence of an unregulated environment.

7. Why is regulation a reasonable approach to stop the epidemic?

Regulations have been effective in limiting alcohol-related harm and in reducing tobacco use. The regulations we have in place for alcohol are good models for potentially controlling obesity. Although the alcohol industry might like to see people drinking alcohol all day long in large quantities, most of us accept the legal limitations on alcohol availability and consumption as necessary to prevent too many people from becoming drunk and harming themselves and others. How many people think we should sell alcohol from vending machines, display it at every cash register from bookstores to hardware stores, serve it at meetings at work, allow people to routinely drink on the job, or sell it to children? Limiting the availability of alcohol, drinking on the job, and drinking in public settings has helped reduce drunkenness and alcohol-related harm. By and large most Americans will agree that our restrictions on alcohol are reasonable. Restrictions on nonessential, low-nutrient processed foods and on serving sizes that increase the risk of chronic disease could eventually be considered as acceptable as alcohol regulations, especially if they help people moderate their consumption.

8. Can't we educate people to make better choices?

Lack of education is not the main reason why people eat too much. Most people already know they need to eat less to lose weight, and that they should avoid foods like candy, cake, cookies, and chips. The problem is that people's choices are highly influenced by the environment. Usually people fail to recognize how they are influenced by merely seeing tempting products or by viewing others' behaviors. Lack of insight is a key barrier to making better choices. Unfortunately, because we often lack the capacity to recognize the triggers of our behaviors, it may not be possible to train everybody to overcome environmental barriers to a healthy diet.

9. Doesn't the food industry just give people what they want?

What people "really" want depends on how goods are presented. If hamburgers were marketed as being disproportionately responsible for global warming and for increasing the risk of cancer and heart disease, rather than as mouth-watering, delicious, and satisfying, fewer people would "really" want them. Our tastes and preferences largely depend on culture, availability, and marketing. Our preferences change all the time. Take sushi, for example—it was practically unheard of thirty years ago, and now it is quite popular in the United States.

10. Are people too stupid to make their own choices?

People are not stupid, but they are also not robots that can make wonderful and optimal decisions twenty-four hours a day, especially when they are exhausted, work two jobs, are trying to raise a family and make ends meet. We are not perfect. Everyone has his or her limits. In addition, marketing methods influence people in ways they cannot easily recognize. A society that allows food marketers to push at our limits and undermine us all the time is not helping most of us.

The kinds of regulations I am advocating do not remove individual choice. They increase transparency so that people will be able to make decisions deliberately, not automatically. Regulations can protect people from strategies that influence them without their awareness, like priming and conditioning.

11. Aren't there effective solutions to the obesity epidemic other than creating more regulations?

So far, solutions that leave the problem to individuals to solve by themselves have not worked. Benign neglect is not benign, as the rates of obesity appear to be worsening for some groups. Although obesity rates are stable for others, we have not seen strong evidence that the prevalence is declining in any populations. As a society we have been reluctant to address the malleable forces that lead to obesity because of the common misperception that most individuals have the capacity to control their own consumption, regardless of the conditions of the food environment. Indeed, many groups prefer not to address the problem at all, and take the "You're on your own" approach.

Yet if we care about our population and want everyone to be able to enjoy a healthy life free of chronic diseases, we need to make a normal, healthy weight attainable for the majority. We should not be unrealistic about what most people are capable of when the food environment is constantly tempting us. As long as we allow foods to be promoted and served in a way that routinely puts patrons at risk, most of us will not be able to defend ourselves. Instead, every day will be a struggle and feelings of inadequacy, inferiority, and shame will continue among the overweight and obese. Just as we don't tolerate seeing people go hungry, we should not tolerate conditions that create misery from exposure to chronic disease risk factors, including impulse marketing and excessively large portion sizes.

12. Won't regulation make people less responsible?

Some make the argument that all modern methods, technology, and devices make people lazy and less responsible. Will repairing a road make people drive less safely? Does giving people birth control devices or pills make them more promiscuous? There are always unintended consequences of every change, but we have to judge based upon the results that prevail. Repaired roads probably reduce more crashes than they cause, birth control probably prevents more unintended pregnancies than the absence of birth control, and labor-saving devices probably lead to greater happiness and productivity. While some public health regulations may be excessive, the majority protect people from exposure to conditions that could put them at risk for many negative outcomes.

Regulations that address the food environment could protect people from factors that lead to diet-related chronic diseases, and will help people be more successful in their efforts to reduce the incidence of those diseases and control their weight.

13. Is there anything worse (or better) than living in a nanny state?

Nannies do not deserve the bad rap they have been getting. Although there may be a few bad apples, most nannies are caring and loving and highly skilled at protecting their charges. For example, Mary Poppins was a fun-loving, model nanny, and one of her trademarks was portion control. She recommended just one spoonful of sugar (to help the medicine go down). This amount is unlikely to lead to chronic diseases. Without a nanny, every day, too many people are exposed to servings with sixteen or more spoonfuls of sugar (the amount in a twenty-ounce soda). We might all flourish and be healthier with more nanny wisdom and support. We should no longer consider "nanny" a pejorative term; it should be a badge of honor.

Acknowledgments

For their help and guidance in shaping this book I would like to thank Rachel Sussman, Martha Kaplan, Carl Bromley, Joanne Wyckoff, Anna Shapiro, Sandra Lapham, Jill Luoto, Paul Koegel, Toni Sciarra Poynter, Amy Goldman Koss, Melissa Veronesi, Mark Sorkin, and the YaleWomen LA Writers group, especially Laura Brennan, Monica Nordhaus, Eileen Funke, Lisanne Sartor, Colette Sartor, Hyun Mi Oh, Swati Pandey, Barbara Bogaev, Maria Burton, Ursula Burton, Rachel Resnick, Heather Nolan, Robinne Lee, and Gloria Loya. For their early support and feedback much thanks is owed to Peter Clark, Susan Evans, Lorraine Zecca, Roland Sturm, Margaret Maglione, Bob Brook, and Barry Wilson. I am also grateful for the historical insights offered by Professor Harry Levine. And thanks to my family: my husband, Avi; my sons Abe, Jeremy, Russell, and Max; and my brother and sister, Richard and Wendy, who have all been a source of strength, sustenance, and inspiration.

Parts of Chapter 4, Chapter 9, and Chapter 10 have borrowed conceptually from academic papers with Tom Farley, Lila Rabinovich, and Rajiv Bhatia, respectively.

Notes

Introduction

1. United States Department of Health and Human Services. Dietary Guidelines for Americans, 2005. Washington, DC: USDHHS;2005. Stock Number 001-000-04719-1.

2. Wu HW, Sturm R. What's on the menu? A review of the energy and nutritional content of US chain restaurant menus. *Public Health Nutrition*. May 11, 2012:1–10.

3. USDHHS. Dietary Guidelines for Americans.

4. USDHHS. Physical Activity Guidelines for Americans. www.health.gov /paguidelines/guidelines/default.aspx. 2008.

5. Troiano RP, Berrigan D, Dodd KW, Mâsse LC, Tilert T, McDowell M. Physical activity in the United States measured by accelerometer. *Medicine and Science in Sports and Exercise*. Jan 2008;40(1):181–188.

6. Flegal KM, Carroll MD, Ogden CL, Curtin LR. Prevalence and trends in obesity among US adults, 1999–2008. *JAMA: The Journal of the American Medical Association*. 2010;303(3):235–241. See also Ogden CL, Carroll MD, Kit BK, Flegal KM. Prevalence of obesity and trends in body mass index among US children and adolescents, 1999–2010. *JAMA*. Feb 1 2012;307(5):483–490.

7. Pischon T, Boeing H, Hoffmann K, et al. General and abdominal adiposity and risk of death in Europe. *The New England Journal of Medicine*. 2008;359(20):2105–2120.

8. Sun Q, Ma J, Campos H, et al. A prospective study of trans fatty acids in erythrocytes and risk of coronary heart disease. *Circulation* 2007;115(14):1858–1865.

9. Park Y, Hunter DJ, Spiegelman D, et al. Dietary fiber intake and risk of colorectal cancer: a pooled analysis of prospective cohort studies. *The Journal of the American Medical Association*. 2005;294(22):2849–2857.

10. Schulze MB, Manson JE, Ludwig DS, et al. Sugar-sweetened beverages, weight gain, and incidence of type 2 diabetes in young and middle-aged women. *The Journal of the American Medical Association*. 2004;292(8):927–934.

11. Dall TM, Fulgoni VL, Zhang Y, Reimers KJ, Packard PT, Astwood JD. Potential health benefits and medical cost savings from calorie, sodium, and saturated fat reductions in the American diet. *American Journal Of Health Promotion*. 2009;23(6):412–422.

12. Finkelstein EA, Zuckerman L. *The Fattening of America: How the Economy Makes Us Fat, If It Matters and What to Do About It*. Hoboken, NJ: John Wiley & Sons; 2008.

13. US Census. Graphic Summary of the 1977 US Economic Censuses. www.census.gov/econ/census07/www/historicaldata.html. See also National Restaurant Assn. 2013 Restaurant Industry Pocket Factbook. http://www.restaurant .org/News-Research/Research/Facts-at-a-Glance.

PART I: HUMAN NATURE AND FOOD

Chapter 1: It's Not Your Fault

1. Kaminskas. Calorie Count: Weight Maintenance. http://caloriecount.about. com/cant-control-eat-anymore-q3284. 2008.

2. 3 Fat Chicks on a Diet support forum. www.3fatchicks.com/forum/chicks -control/113625-i-feel-out-control-i-can-not-stop-eating.html. 2007.

3. Hartwell-Walker M. My eating is out of control. http://psychcentral.com /ask-the-therapist/2011/09/04/my-eating-is-out-of-control/. *Psych Central*. 2011.

4. World Health Organization Global Strategy on Diet, Physical Activity, and Health. Obesity and Overweight fact sheet. www.who.int/dietphysicalactivity /media/en/gsfs_obesity.pdf. 2008.

5. Vainio H, Kaaks R, Bianchini F. Weight control and physical activity in cancer prevention: international evaluation of the evidence. *European Journal of Cancer Prevention*. Aug 2002;11 Suppl 2:S94–100.

6. The Surgeon General's call to action to prevent and decrease overweight and obesity. In: US Department of Health and Human Services PHS, Office of the Surgeon General, ed: US Department of Health and Human Services; 2001. See also: Sullivan PW, Morrato EH, Ghushchyan V, Wyatt HR, Hill JO. Obesity, inactivity, and the prevalence of diabetes and diabetes-related cardiovascular co-morbidities in the U.S., 2000–2002. *Diabetes Care*. Jul 2005;28(7):1599–1603. See also: Dietz WH. Health consequences of obesity in youth: childhood predictors of adult disease. *Pediatrics*. 1998;101(3 Pt 2):518–525.

7. Finkelstein EA, Trogdon JG, Cohen JW, Dietz W. Annual medical spending attributable to obesity: payer- and service-specific estimates. *Health Affairs*. 2009;28(5):w822–w831.

8. Mobbs O, Crepin C, Thiery C, Golay A, Van der Linden M. Obesity and the four facets of impulsivity. *Patient Education and Counseling.* Jun 2010;79(3):372–377.

9. Morgan C. Dieting: Confessions of an Emotional Eater. www.catherine-morgan.com/2010/04/30/dieting-confessions-of-an-emotional-eater/. 2010.

10. WedMD. Emotional eating and weight loss. www.webmd.com/diet/emotional-eating. 2012.

11. Young LR, Nestle M. The contribution of expanding portion sizes to the US obesity epidemic. *American Journal of Public Health.* Feb 2002;92(2):246–249. See also: Young LR, Nestle M. Expanding portion sizes in the US marketplace: implications for nutrition counseling. *Journal of the American Dietetic Association.* Feb 2003;103(2):231–234.

Chapter 2: The Limits of Self-Control

1. National Weight Control Registry. NWCR Facts. www.nwcr.ws/Research/default.htm. 2008.

2. The Nurses' Health Study. http://www.channing.harvard.edu/nhs/?page_id=70. 2009.

3. Field AE, Willett WC, Lissner L, Colditz GA. Dietary fat and weight gain among women in the Nurses' Health Study. *Obesity.* Apr 2007;15(4):967–976.

4. Jeffery RW, Kelly KM, Rothman AJ, Sherwood NE, Boutelle KN. The weight loss experience: a descriptive analysis. *Annals of Behavioral Medicine: A Publication of the Society of Behavioral Medicine.* Apr 2004;27(2):100–106.

5. Francis LA, Susman EJ. Self-regulation and rapid weight gain in children from age 3 to 12 years. *Archives of Pediatrics & Adolescent Medicine.* Apr 2009;163(4):297–302.

6. Seeyave DM, Coleman S, Appugliese D, et al. Ability to delay gratification at age 4 years and risk of overweight at age 11 years. *Archives of Pediatrics & Adolescent Medicine.* Apr 2009;163(4):303–308.

7. Birch LL, Fisher JO. Development of eating behaviors among children and adolescents. *Pediatrics.* Mar 1998;101(3 Pt 2):539–549.

8. Anzman SL, Birch LL. Low inhibitory control and restrictive feeding practices predict weight outcomes. *The Journal of Pediatrics.* Nov 2009;155(5):651–656.

9. Friedman NP, Miyake A, Robinson JL, Hewitt JK. Developmental trajectories in toddlers' self-restraint predict individual differences in executive functions 14 years later: a behavioral genetic analysis. *Developmental Psychology.* Sep 2011;47(5):1410–1430.

10. Mischel W, Shoda Y, Rodriguez MI. Delay of gratification in children. *Science.* May 26, 1989;244(4907):933–938.

11. www.youtube.com/watch?v=x3S0xS2hdi4.

12. Casey BJ, Somerville LH, Gotlib IH, et al. Behavioral and neural correlates

of delay of gratification 40 years later. *Proceedings of the National Academy of Sciences of the United States of America.* Sep 6, 2011;108(36):14998–15003.

13. Hofmann W, Baumeister RF, Forster G, Vohs KD. Everyday temptations: an experience sampling study of desire, conflict, and self-control. *Journal of Personality and Social Psychology.* Jun 2012;102(6):1318–1335. See also: Hofmann W, Vohs KD, Baumeister RF. What people desire, feel conflicted about, and try to resist in everyday life. *Psychological Science.* Jun 2012;23(6):582–588.

14. Baumeister RF, Bratslavsky E, Muraven M, Tice DM. Ego depletion: is the active self a limited resource? *Journal of Personality and Social Psychology.* May 1998;74(5):1252–1265.

15. Vohs KD, Heatherton TF. Self-regulatory failure: a resource-depletion approach. *Psychological Science.* May 2000;11(3):249–254.

16. Pietilainen KH, Saarni SE, Kaprio J, Rissanen A. Does dieting make you fat? A twin study. *International Journal of Obesity (London).* Mar 2012;36(3):456–464.

17. Vohs K, Baumeister R. Making choices impairs subsequent self-control: a limited-resource account of decision-making, self-regulation, and active initiative. *Journal of Personality and Social Psychology.* May 2008;94(5):883–898. See also: Schwartz B. *The Paradox of Choice: Why More Is Less.* New York: HarperCollins; 2004.

18. Gailliot MT, Baumeister RF. The physiology of willpower: linking blood glucose to self-control. *Personality and Social Psychology Review.* Nov 2007;11(4):303–327.

19. Masicampo EJ, Baumeister R. Toward a physiology of dual-process reasoning and judgment: lemonade, willpower, and expensive rule-based analysis. *Psychological Science.* Mar 2008;19(3):255–260.

20. Gailliot MT, Baumeister RF, DeWall CN, et al. Self-control relies on glucose as a limited energy source: willpower is more than a metaphor. *Journal of Personality and Social Psychology.* Feb 2007;92(2):325–336.

21. Bellisle F. Effects of diet on behaviour and cognition in children. *British Journal of Nutrition.* Oct 2004;92 Suppl 2:S227–232.

22. Wang J, Novemsky N, Dhar R, Baumeister RF. Trade-offs and depletion in choice. *Journal of Marketing Research.* 2010;47(5):910–919.

23. Bruyneel S, Dewitte S, Vohs KD, Warlop L. Repeated choosing increases susceptibility to affective product features. *International Journal of Research in Marketing.* 2006;23(2):215–225.

24. Spears D. Economic decision-making in poverty depletes behavioral control. http://www.princeton.edu/ceps/workingpapers/213spears.pdf. Accessed December 6, 2011. *CEPS Working Paper.* 2010;213.

25. Stroebe W, Mensink W, Aarts H, Schut H, Kruglanski AW. Why dieters fail: testing the goal conflict model of eating. *Journal of Experimental Social Psychology.* 2008;44(1):26–36. See also: Roefs A, Herman CP, Macleod CM, Smulders FTY, Jansen A. At first sight: how do restrained eaters evaluate high-fat

palatable foods? *Appetite.* 2005;44(1):103–114.

26. Stroebe et al. Why dieters fail. See also: Polivy J, Herman CP, Coelho JS. Caloric restriction in the presence of attractive food cues: external cues, eating, and weight. *Physiology & Behavior.* Aug 6, 2008;94(5):729–733. See also: Jansen A, Oosterlaan J, Merckelbach H, Van den Hout MA. Nonregulation of food intake in restrained, emotional, and external eaters. *Journal of Psychopathology and Behavioral Assessment.* Dec 1988;10(4):345–354. See also: Jansen A, Van den Hout M. On being led into temptation: "counterregulation" of dieters after smelling a "preload." *Addictive Behaviors.* 1991;16(5):247–253. See also: Urbszat D, Herman CP, Polivy J. Eat, drink, and be merry, for tomorrow we diet: effects of anticipated deprivation on food intake in restrained and unrestrained eaters. *Journal of Abnormal Psychology.* May 2002;111(2):396–401.

27. Bryan J, Tiggemann M. The effect of weight-loss dieting on cognitive performance and psychological well-being in overweight women. *Appetite.* Apr 2001;36(2):147–156. See also: Green MW, Rogers PJ. Impairments in working memory associated with spontaneous dieting behaviour. *Psychological Medicine.* Sep 1998;28(5):1063–1070. See also: Kemps E, Tiggemann M. Working memory performance and preoccupying thoughts in female dieters: evidence for a selective central executive impairment. *The British Journal of Clinical Psychology.* Sep 2005;44(Pt) 3:357–366. See also: Vreugdenburg L, Bryan J, Kemps E. The effect of self-initiated weight-loss dieting on working memory: the role of preoccupying cognitions. *Appetite.* Dec 2003;41(3):291–300.

28. Vohs and Heatherton, Self-regulatory failure. See also: Vohs and Baumeister, Making choices. See also: Vohs KD, Baumeister RF. Ego depletion, self-control, and choice. In: Greenberg J, Koole SL, Pyszczynski, T, eds: *Handbook of Experimental Existential Psychology.* New York: Guilford Press; 2004:398–410. See also: Vohs KD, Faber RJ. Spent resources: self-regulatory resource availability affects impulse buying. *Journal of Consumer Research.* Mar 2007;33(4):537–547.

29. Baumeister RF, Muraven M, Tice DM. Ego depletion: a resource model of volition, self-regulation, and controlled processing. *Social Cognition.* 2000;18(2):130–150.

30. Baumeister RF, Vohs KD, Tice DM. The strength model of self-control. *Current Directions in Psychological Science.* Dec 2007;16(6):351–355.

31. Schwartz. *The Paradox of Choice.*

Chapter 3: The Overworked Brain

1. Shah J. The automatic pursuit and management of goals. *Current Directions in Psychological Science.* Feb 2005;14(1):10–13.

2. Bargh J, Chartrand T. The unbearable automaticity of being. *American Psychologist.* 1999;54(7):462–479.

3. Shiv B, Fedorikhin A. Heart and mind in conflict: the interplay of affect

and cognition in consumer decision making. *Journal of Consumer Research.* Dec 1999;26(3):278–292.

4. Ibid.

5. Dijksterhuis A, Smith P, van Baaren R, Wigboldus D. The unconscious consumer: effects of environment on consumer behavior. *Journal of Consumer Psychology.* 2005;15(3):193–202.

6. Bellisle F, Dalix AM. Cognitive restraint can be offset by distraction, leading to increased meal intake in women. *The American Journal of Clinical Nutrition.* Aug 2001;74(2):197–200.

7. Higgs S. Memory and its role in appetite regulation. *Physiology & Behavior.* May 19, 2005;85(1):67–72.

8. Higgs S. Memory for recent eating and its influence on subsequent food intake. *Appetite.* Oct 2002;39(2):159–166. See also: Higgs S, Williamson AC, Attwood AS. Recall of recent lunch and its effect on subsequent snack intake. *Physiology & Behavior.* Jun 9, 2008;94(3):454–462.

9. Banks E, Jorm L, Rogers K, Clements M, Bauman A. Screen-time, obesity, ageing and disability: findings from 91,266 participants in the 45 and Up Study. *Public Health Nutrition.* Jan 2011;14(1):34–43.

10. Robinson TN, Hammer LD, Killen JD, et al. Does television viewing increase obesity and reduce physical activity? Cross-sectional and longitudinal analyses among adolescent girls. *Pediatrics.* Feb 1993;91(2):273–280. See also: French SA, Mitchell NR, Hannan PJ. Decrease in television viewing predicts lower body mass index at 1-year follow-up in adolescents, but not adults. *Journal of Nutrition Education and Behavior.* Sep/Oct 2012;44(5):415–422. See also: Robinson TN. Reducing children's television viewing to prevent obesity: a randomized controlled trial. *JAMA.* Oct 27, 1999;282(16):1561–1567.

11. Wilson T, Brekke N. Mental contamination and mental correction: unwanted influences on judgments and evaluations. *Psychological Bulletin.* Jul 1994;116(1):117–142.

12. Salwen M, Dupagne M. The third-person effect. *Communication Research.* Oct 1999;26(5):523–549. See also: Duck J, Hogg M, Terry D. Social identity and perceptions of media persuasion: are we always less influenced than others? *Journal of Applied Social Psychology.* Sep 1999;29(9):1879–1899.

13. Hall KD, Sacks G, Chandramohan D, et al. Quantification of the effect of energy imbalance on bodyweight. *Lancet.* Aug 27, 2011;378(9793):826–837.

Chapter 4: Eating Is Automatic

1. Bargh J, Chartrand T. The unbearable automaticity of being. *American Psychologist.* 1999;54(7):462–479.

2. Libet B. Voluntary acts and readiness potentials. *Electroencephalography*

and Clinical Neurophysiology. Jan 1992;82(1):85–86. See also: Libet B. How does conscious experience arise? The neural time factor. *Brain Research Bulletin.* 1999;50(5–6):339–340. See also: Libet B. Timing of conscious experience: reply to the 2002 commentaries on Libet's findings. *Consciousness and Cognition.* Sep 2003;12(3):321–331. See also: Libet B, Gleason CA, Wright EW, Pearl DK. Time of conscious intention to act in relation to onset of cerebral activity (readiness-potential): the unconscious initiation of a freely voluntary act. *Brain.* Sep 1983;106(Pt 3):623–642.

3. Baumeister RF, Masicampo EJ, Vohs KD. Do conscious thoughts cause behavior? *Annual Review of Psychology.* 2011;62:331–361. See also: Libet B, Pearl DK, Morledge DE, Gleason CA, Hosobuchi Y, Barbaro NM. Control of the transition from sensory detection to sensory awareness in man by the duration of a thalamic stimulus: the cerebral "time-on" factor. *Brain.* Aug 1991;114 (Pt 4):1731–1757.

4. Berridge KC, Winkielman P. What is an unconscious emotion? (The case for unconscious "liking"). *Cognition and Emotion.* 2003;17(2):181–211. See also: Dijksterhuis A, Aarts H. On wildebeests and humans: the preferential detection of negative stimuli. *Psychological Science.* 2003;14(1):14–18. See also: Dijksterhuis A, Aarts H, Smith PK. The power of the subliminal: on subliminal persuasion and other potential applications. In: Hassin RR, Uleman JS, Bargh, JA, eds. *The New Unconscious.* New York: Oxford University Press; 2005:Ed.

5. Bargh JA. Losing consciousness: automatic influences on consumer judgment, behavior, and motivation. *Journal of Consumer Research* 2002;29(2):280–285.

6. Baumeister, Masicampo, and Vohs. Do conscious thoughts cause behavior?

7. Nijs IMT, Muris P, Euser AS, Franken IHA. Differences in attention to food and food intake between overweight/obese and normal-weight females under conditions of hunger and satiety. *Appetite.* 2009;54(2):243–254.

8. Milosavljevic M, Koch C, Rangel A. Consumers can make decisions in as little as a third of a second. *Judgment and Decision Making.* 2011;6(6):520–530.

9. Ibid.

10. Thomas M, Desai KK, Seenivasan S. How credit card payments increase unhealthy food purchases: visceral regulation of vices. *Journal of Consumer Research.* Jun 2011;38(1):126–139.

11. Volkow ND, Wang GJ, Maynard L, et al. Brain dopamine is associated with eating behaviors in humans. *International Journal of Eating Disorders.* Mar 2003;33(2):136–142.

12. Volkow ND. This is your brain on food. Interview by Kristin Leutwyler-Ozelli. *Scientific American.* Sep 2007;297(3):84–85.

13. Barker RG. Explorations in ecological psychology. *American Psychologist.* 1965;20(1):1–14.

14. Diliberti N, Bordi PL, Conklin MT, Roe LS, Rolls BJ. Increased portion

size leads to increased energy intake in a restaurant meal. *Obesity Research.* Mar 2004;12(3):562–568. See also: Levitsky DA, Youn T. The more food young adults are served, the more they overeat. *Journal of Nutrition.* Oct 2004;134(10):2546–2549. See also: Orlet Fisher J, Rolls BJ, Birch LL. Children's bite size and intake of an entree are greater with large portions than with age-appropriate or self-selected portions. *The American Journal of Clinical Nutrition.* May 2003;77(5):1164–1170. See also: Rolls BJ, Morris EL, Roe LS. Portion size of food affects energy intake in normal-weight and overweight men and women. *The American Journal of Clinical Nutrition.* Dec 2002;76(6):1207–1213. See also: Rolls BJ, Roe LS, Kral TV, Meengs JS, Wall DE. Increasing the portion size of a packaged snack increases energy intake in men and women. *Appetite.* Feb 2004;42(1):63–69.

15. Diliberti, Bordi, Conklin, Roe, and Rolls. Increased portion size.

16. Chandon P, Wansink B. Is food marketing making us fat? a multi-disciplinary review. *Foundations and Trends in Marketing.* 2010;5(3):113–196.

17. Fisher, Rolls, and Birch. Children's bite size and intake.

18. Fisher JO, Liu Y, Birch LL, Rolls BJ. Effects of portion size and energy density on young children's intake at a meal. *The American Journal of Clinical Nutrition.* Jul 2007;86(1):174–179.

19. Levitsky and Youn. The more food young adults are served.

20. Diliberti, Bordi, Conklin, Roe, and Rolls. Increased portion size.

21. Rolls BJ, Roe LS, Meengs JS. The effect of large portion sizes on energy intake is sustained for 11 days. *Obesity.* Jun 2007;15(6):1535–1543.

22. Rolls, Morris, and Roe. Portion size of food affects energy intakes.

23. Young LR, Nestle M. The contribution of expanding portion sizes to the US obesity epidemic. *American Journal of Public Health.* Feb 2002;92(2):246–249.

24. Schwartz J, Byrd-Bredbenner C. Portion distortion: typical portion sizes selected by young adults. *Journal of the American Dietetic Association.* Sep 2006;106(9):1412–1418.

25. Nestle M. Increasing portion sizes in American diets: more calories, more obesity. *Journal of the American Dietetic Association.* Jan 2003;103(1):39–40.

26. Bruemmer B, Krieger J, Saelens BE, Chan N. Energy, saturated fat, and sodium were lower in entrees at chain restaurants at 18 months compared with 6 months following the implementation of mandatory menu labeling regulation in King County, Washington. *Journal of the Academy of Nutrition and Dietetics.* Aug 2012;112(8):1169–1176.

27. Raghubir P, Krishna A. Vital dimensions in volume perception: can the eye fool the stomach? *Journal of Marketing Research.* 1999;36(3):313–326.

28. Yuhas JA, Bolland JE, Bolland TW. The impact of training, food type, gender, and container size on the estimation of food portion sizes. *Journal of the American Dietetic Association.* Oct 1989;89(10):1473–1477. See also: Bolland JE, Yuhas JA, Bolland TW. Estimation of food portion sizes: effectiveness of training. *Journal of the American Dietetic Association.* Jul 1988;88(7):817–821.

29. Jeffery RW, Wing RR. Long-term effects of interventions for weight loss using food provision and monetary incentives. *Journal of Consulting and Clinical Psychology*. Oct 1995;63(5):793–796.

30. Rolls BJ, Rowe EA, Rolls ET. How flavour and appearance affect human feeding. *The Proceedings of the Nutrition Society*. Jun 1982;41(2):109–117.

31. Johnson J, Vickers Z. Factors influencing sensory-specific satiety. *Appetite*. Aug 1992;19(1):15–31. See also: Rolls BJ. Experimental analyses of the effects of variety in a meal on human feeding. *The American Journal of Clinical Nutrition*. Nov 1985;42(5) Suppl:932–939. See also: Wansink B. Environmental factors that increase the food intake and consumption volume of unknowing consumers. *Annual Review of Nutrition*. 2004;24:455–479.

32. Raynor HA, Epstein LH. Dietary variety, energy regulation, and obesity. *Psychological Bulletin*. May 2001;127(3):325–341. See also: Rolls BJ, Van Duijvenvoorde PM, Rolls ET. Pleasantness changes and food intake in a varied four-course meal. *Appetite*. Dec 1984;5(4):337–348.

33. Hetherington MM, Foster R, Newman T, Anderson AS, Norton G. Understanding variety: tasting different foods delays satiation. *Physiology & Behavior*. Feb 28, 2006;87(2):263–271.

34. Temple JL, Kent KM, Giacomelli AM, Paluch RA, Roemmich JN, Epstein LH. Habituation and recovery of salivation and motivated responding for food in children. *Appetite*. May 2006;46(3):280–284.

35. Rolls ET, Rolls JH. Olfactory sensory-specific satiety in humans. *Physiology & Behavior*. Mar 1997;61(3):461–473.

36. Stubbs RJ, Johnstone AM, Mazlan N, Mbaiwa SE, Ferris S. Effect of altering the variety of sensorially distinct foods, of the same macronutrient content, on food intake and body weight in men. *European Journal of Clinical Nutrition*. Jan 2001;55(1):19–28.

37. Hirsch ES, Matthew Kramer F, Meiselman HL. Effects of food attributes and feeding environment on acceptance, consumption and body weight: lessons learned in a twenty-year program of military ration research (Part 2). *Appetite*. Feb 2005;44(1):33–45.

38. Gallo A. Fewer food products introduced in last 3 years. www.ers.usda.gov/publications/foodreview/sep1999/frsept99f.pdf. 1999. Accessed January 25, 2008.

39. Chartrand TL, Bargh JA. The chameleon effect: the perception-behavior link and social interaction. *Journal of Personality and Social Psychology*. Jun 1999;76(6):893–910.

40. Johnston LU. Behavioral mimicry and stigmatization. *Social Cognition*. Feb 2002;20(1):18–35.

41. de Castro JM, Brewer EM. The amount eaten in meals by humans is a power function of the number of people present. *Physiology & Behavior*. Jan 1992;51(1):121–125.

42. Tanner R, Ferraro R, Chartrand T, Bettman JR, Van Baaren R. Of chameleons and consumption: the impact of mimicry on choice and preferences. *Journal of Consumer Research*. Apr 2008;34(6):754–766.

43. Ibid.

PART II: THE FOOD ENVIRONMENT
Chapter 5: Abundant and Cheap

1. Levitsky DA, Halbmaier CA, Mrdjenovic G. The freshman weight gain: a model for the study of the epidemic of obesity. *International Journal of Obesity and Related Metabolic Disorders*. Nov 2004;28(11):1435–1442.

2. Khush G. Productivity improvements in rice. *Nutrition Reviews*. Jun 2003;61(6) Pt 2:S114–116.

3. Ibid.

4. USDA-ERS. Food CPI, prices and expenditures: food expenditures by families and individuals as a share of disposable personal income. www.ers.usda.gov /data-products/food-expenditures.aspx#26636. 2013.

5. Ibid.

6. Drewnowski A, Darmon N. The economics of obesity: dietary energy density and energy cost. *The American Journal of Clinical Nutrition*. Jul 2005;82(1) Suppl:265S–273S.

7. Jeffery RW, Utter J. The changing environment and population obesity in the United States. *Obesity Research*. Oct 2003;11 Suppl:12S–22S.

8. Goodwin BK, Mishra AK, Ortalo-Magne F. The buck stops where? The distribution of agricultural subsidies. National Bureau of Economic Research, NBER Working Papers: 16693; 2011.

9. Rickard BJ, Okrent AM, Alston JM. How have agricultural policies influenced caloric consumption in the United States? *Health Economics*. Mar 2013;22(3):316–339. See also: Alston JM, Okrent AM, Rickard BJ. Impact of agricultural policies on caloric consumption. *Trends in Endocrinology & Metabolism*. Jan 18, 2013. See also: Alston JM, Sumner DA, Vosti SA. Farm Subsidies and Obesity in the United States. *Agricultural and Resource Economics Update*. 2007;11(2).

10. Ibid.

11. Leibtag E. Where you shop matters: store formats drive variation in retail food prices. *Amber Waves*. www.ers.usda.gov/AmberWaves/November05 /Features/WhereYouShop.htm. 2005.

12. Krebs-Smith SM, Reedy J, Bosire C. Healthfulness of the U.S. food supply: little improvement despite decades of dietary guidance. *American Journal of Preventive Medicine*. 2010;38(5):472–477.

13. CSPI. Pestering parents: how food companies market obesity to children.

2003; www.cspinet.org/new/pdf/pesteringparentsnopictures.pdf. Accessed Nov 9, 2004.

14. Institute of Medicine. *Food Marketing to Children and Youth: Threat or Opportunity?* Washington, DC: National Academies Press; 2005.

15. Speers SE, Harris JL, Schwartz MB. Child and adolescent exposure to food and beverage brand appearances during prime-time television programming. *American Journal of Preventive Medicine.* 2011;41(3):291–296.

16. Tirodkar MA, Jain A. Food messages on African American television shows. *American Journal of Public Health.* Mar 2003;93(3):439–441.

17. Ibid.

18. FTC. *A Review of Food Marketing to Children and Adolescents.* www .ftc.gov/os/2012/12/121221foodmarketingreport.pdf. 2012.

19. Ibid.

20. Nestle M. The era of ads: food marketing to kids goes viral. www.the atlantic.com/health/archive/2011/04/the-era-of-ads-food-marketing-to-kids-goes -viral/237727/. *The Atlantic.* April 22, 2011.

Chapter 6: A Food Desert? Try a Swamp

1. USDA-ERS. *Access to Affordable and Nutritious Food: Measuring and Understanding Food Deserts and Their Consequences.* www.ers.usda.gov/Publications /AP/AP036/AP036fm.pdf. 2009.

2. Ibid.

3. Sorenson H. *Inside the Mind of the Shopper.* Upsaddle River, NJ: Pearson Education; 2009.

4. Farley TA, Baker ET, Futrell L, Rice JC. The ubiquity of energy-dense snack foods: a national multicity study. *American Journal of Public Health.* Feb 2010;100(2):306–311.

5. Price C. Trends in eating out. www.ers.usda.gov/publications/foodreview /sep1997/sept97c.pdf. *USDA ERS.* 1997.

6. Sharpe KM, Staelin R. Consumption effects of bundling: consumer perceptions, firm actions, and public policy implications. *Journal of Public Policy & Marketing.* 2010;29(2):170–188.

Chapter 7: Marketing Obesity

1. Slaton J. How slushy magic changed my mind on advertising to kids. http:// blogs.babycenter.com/mom_stories/08142012how-slushy-magic-changed-my -mind-about-kid-ads/?utm_source=dlvr.it&utm_medium=tumblr. *BabyCenter Blog; Mom stories.* 2012.

2. McAlister AR, Cornwell TB. Children's brand symbolism understanding: links

to theory of mind and executive functioning. *Psychology & Marketing.* 2010;27(3):
203–228.

3. Wedel M, Pieters R. *Visual marketing: from attention to action.* New York:
Taylor & Francis Group/Lawrence Erlbaum Associates; 2008.

4. Wedel M, Pieters R. Introduction to visual marketing. *Visual Marketing:
From Attention to Action.* New York: Taylor & Francis Group/Lawrence Erlbaum
Associates; 2008:1–8.

5. Childers TL, Jass J. All dressed up with something to say: effects of typeface
semantic associations on brand perceptions and consumer memory. *Journal of
Consumer Psychology.* 2002;12(2):93–106.

6. Doyle JR, Bottomley PA. Font appropriateness and brand choice. *Journal of
Business Research.* Aug 2004;57(8):873–880.

7. Kahneman D. A perspective on judgment and choice: mapping bounded
rationality. *American Psychologist.* Sep 2003;58(9):697–720.

8. Steinman RB. Projective techniques in consumer research. www.euro
journals.com/IBBA.htm. *International Bulletin of Business Administration.* 2009.

9. Laibson D, Zeckhauser R. Amos Tversky and the ascent of behavioral economics. *Journal of Risk and Uncertainty.* April 1998;16(1):7–47.

10. Dhar R, Wertenbroch K. Consumer choice between hedonic and utilitarian goods. *Journal of Marketing Research.* Feb 2000;37(1):60–71.

11. Khan U, Dhar R. Where there is a way, is there a will? The effect of future choices on self-control. *Journal of Experimental Psychology: General.* May
2007;136(2):277–288.

12. Kivetz R, Urminsky O, Zheng Y. The goal-gradient hypothesis resurrected:
purchase acceleration, illusionary goal progress, and customer retention. *Journal
of Marketing Research.* 2006;43(1):39–58.

13. Hsee Christopher K, Zhang J, Yu F, Xi Y. Lay rationalism and inconsistency
between predicted experience and decision. *Journal of Behavioral Decision Making.* Oct 2003;16(4):257–272.

14. Hsee Christopher K, Yu F, Zhang Y, Zhang J. Medium maximization. *Journal of Consumer Research.* Jun 2003;30(1):1–14. See also: Turley LW, Milliman
RE. Atmospheric effects on shopping behavior: a review of the experimental evidence. *Journal of Business Research Retail Atmospherics.* Aug 2000;49(2):193–
211.

15. Milliman RE. The influence of background music on the behavior of
restaurant patrons. *Journal of Consumer Research.* Sep 1986;13(2):286–289.

16. North A, Hargreaves D, McKendrick J. The influence of in-store music on
wine selections. *Journal of Applied Psychology.* Apr 1999;84(2):271–276.

17. North AC, Shilcock A, Hargreaves DJ. The effect of musical style on restaurant customers' spending. *Environment and Behavior.* Sep 2003;35(5):712–718.

18. Bargh JA. Losing consciousness: automatic influences on consumer judg-

ment, behavior, and motivation. *Journal of Consumer Research.* 2002;29(2):280–285.

19. Halford J, Gillespie J, Brown V, Pontin E, Dovey T. Effect of television advertisements for foods on food consumption in children. *Appetite.* Apr 2004;42:221–225.

20. Harris JL, Bargh JA, Brownell KD. Priming effects of television food advertising on eating behavior. *Health Psychology.* 2009;28(4):404–413.

21. Ibid.

22. Shapiro SU. When an ad's influence is beyond our conscious control: perceptual and conceptual fluency effects caused by incidental ad exposure. *Journal of Consumer Research.* Jun 1999;26(1):16–36. See also: Law S, Braun KA. I'll have what she's having: gauging the impact of product placements on viewers. *Psychology & Marketing.* Dec 2000;17(12):1059–1075. See also: Baker W. When can affective conditioning and mere exposure directly influence brand choice? *Journal of Advertising.* 1999;28(4):31–46.

23. Berridge KC, Winkielman P. What is an unconscious emotion? (the case for unconscious "liking"). *Cognition and Emotion.* 2003;17(2):181–211.

24. Goetz MC, Goetz PW. What's the use of being happy? mood states, useful objects, and repetition priming effects. *Emotion.* Aug 2007;7(3):675–679.

25. Shah JY, Kruglanski AW. Priming against your will: how accessible alternatives affect goal pursuit. *Journal of Experimental Social Psychology.* Jul 2002;38(4):368–383.

26. Ibid. See also: Shah JY. The automatic pursuit and management of goals. *Current Directions in Psychological Science.* Feb 2005;14(1):10–13. See also: Shah JY, Kruglanski AW. When opportunity knocks: bottom-up priming of goals by means and its effects on self-regulation. *Journal of Personality and Social Psychology.* Jun 2003;84(6):1109–1122.

27. Till BD, Stanley SM, Priluck RP. Classical conditioning and celebrity endorsers: an examination of belongingness and resistance to extinction. *Psychology & Marketing.* Feb 2008;25(2):179–196.

28. Cohen D. *J. B. Watson: The Founder of Behaviourism: A Biography.* London: Routledge, Kegan & Paul; 1979.

29. Zajonc RB. Mere exposure: a gateway to the subliminal. *Current Directions in Psychological Science.* Dec 2001;10(6):224–228.

30. Ibid.

31. Law and Braun. I'll have what she's having. See also: Auty S, Lewis C. Exploring children's choice: the reminder effect of product placement. *Psychology & Marketing.* Sep 2004;21(9):697–713.

32. Auty and Lewis. Exploring children's choice.

33. Grossman R, Till BD. The persistence of classically conditioned brand attitudes. *Journal of Advertising.* 1998;27(1):23–31.

34. Irwin R. Painting South Africa Red. 2001. www.brandchannel.com/features_effect.asp?fa_id=40. Accessed Nov 14, 2008.

35. Abramson E. A review of behavioral approaches to weight control. *Behaviour Research and Therapy.* Nov 1973;11(4):547–556.

36. Ibid.

37. Foreyt JP, Kennedy WA. Treatment of overweight by aversion therapy. *Behaviour Research and Therapy.* Feb 1971;9(1):29–34.

38. Abramson, A review of behavioral approaches.

39. Ibid.

40. John LK, Loewenstein G, Troxel AB, Norton L, Fassbender JE, Volpp KG. Financial incentives for extended weight loss: a randomized, controlled trial. *Journal of General Internal Medicine.* Jun 2011;26(6):621–626. See also: Paul-Ebhohimhen V, Avenell A. Systematic review of the use of financial incentives in treatments for obesity and overweight. *Obesity Reviews.* Jul 2008;9(4):355–367.

41. Wing RR, Phelan S. Long-term weight loss maintenance. *The American Journal of Clinical Nutrition.* Jul 2005;82(1) Suppl:222S–225S.

42. Papies EK, Hamstra P. Goal priming and eating behavior: enhancing self-regulation by environmental cues. *Health Psychology.* Jul 2010;29(4):384–388.

43. Stunkard AJ, Wolff HG. A mechanism of satiety: function and disorder in human obesity. *Psychosomatic Medicine.* 1956:515. See also: Stunkard A, Fox S. The relationship of gastric motility and hunger: a summary of the evidence. *Psychosomatic Medicine.* Mar 1971;33(2):123–134.

44. Schachter SCU, Gross LP. Manipulated time and eating behavior. *Journal of Personality and Social Psychology.* Oct 1968;10(2):98–106.

45. Herman CP, Olmsted MP, Polivy J. Obesity, externality, and susceptibility to social influence: an integrated analysis. *Journal of Personality and Social Psychology.* Oct 1983;45(4):926–934.

46. Ibid.

PART III: AN ALTERNATE VISION

Chapter 8: A Plea for Change: We Are All in This Together

1. Hamlin C. Providence and putrefaction: Victorian sanitarians and the natural theology of health and disease. *Victorian Studies.* 1985;28:381–411.

2. Landers J. *Death and the Metropolis: Studies in the Demographic History of London, 1670–1830.* Cambridge: Cambridge University Press, 1993.

3. Hamlin. Providence and putrefaction.

4. Hamlin C. Edwin Chadwick, "mutton medicine," and the fever question. *Bulletin of the History of Medicine.* 1996;70(2):233–265.

5. Ibid.

6. Hamlin C. Could you starve to death in England in 1839? the Chadwick-Farr controversy and the loss of the "social" in public health. *American Journal of Public Health*. 1995;85(6):856–866.

7. Hamlin. Providence and putrefaction.

8. Hamlin C. Muddling in bumbledom: on the enormity of large sanitary improvements in four British towns, 1855–1885. *Victorian Studies*. 1988;32(1): 55–83.

9. Hamlin C. Edwin Chadwick and the engineers, 1842–1854: systems and antisystems in the pipe-and-brick sewers war. *Technology and Culture*. 1992;33(4):680–709.

10. Ibid.

11. Hamlin C. "Cholera forcing": the myth of the good epidemic and the coming of good water. *American Journal of Public Health*. 2009;99(11):1946–1954.

12. Hamlin. Edwin Chadwick and the engineers.

13. Hamlin C. Sanitary policing and the local state, 1873–1874: a statistical study of English and Welsh towns. *Social History of Medicine: The Journal of the Society for the Social History of Medicine*. 2005;18(1):39–61.

14. Olmstead F. Public Parks and the Enlargement of Towns. In: LeGates RT, Stout, eds. *The City Reader*. Second ed. London: Routledge; 1870:314–320.

15. USDA. Profiling food consumption in America. *Agricultural Fact Book, 2001–2002*; Mar 2003.

16. Senauer B, Gemma M. Why is the obesity rate so low in Japan and high in the U.S.? Some possible economic explanations. The Food Industry Center, University of Minnesota; 2006.

17. NRDC. Wasted: how America is losing up to 40 percent of its food from farm to fork to landfill. www.nrdc.org/food/wasted-food.asp. 2012. See also: Levis JW, Barlaz MA, Themelis NJ, Ulloa P. Assessment of the state of food waste treatment in the United States and Canada. *Waste Management*. 2010;30(8–9):1486–1494. See also: Levis JW, Barlaz MA. What is the most environmentally beneficial way to treat commercial food waste? *Environmental Science & Technology*. 2011;45(17):7438–7444.

18. Jones CM, Kammen DM. Quantifying carbon footprint reduction opportunities for U.S. households and communities. *Environmental Science & Technology*. 2011;45(9):4088–4095.

19. Joyce A, Dixon S, Comfort J, Hallett J. Reducing the environmental impact of dietary choice: perspectives from a behavioural and social change approach. *Journal of Environmental and Public Health*. 2012;2012:978672.

20. Ibid.

21. USDA. Report of the Dietary Guidelines Advisory Committee on the Dietary Guidelines for Americans. www.cnpp.usda.gov/DGAs2010-DGACReport .htm. 2010. See also: Daniel CR, Cross AJ, Koebnick C, Sinha R. Trends in meat consumption in the USA. *Public Health Nutrition*. Apr 2011;14(4):575–583.

Chapter 9: A Safer Food Environment

1. Elbel B. Consumer estimation of recommended and actual calories at fast food restaurants. *Obesity.* Oct 2011;19(10):1971–1978. See also: Swartz JJ, Braxton D, Viera AJ. Calorie menu labeling on quick-service restaurant menus: an updated systematic review of the literature. *International Journal of Behavioral Nutrition and Physical Activity.* 2011;8:135.

2. Yi HY, Chen CM, Williams GD. Trends in alcohol-related fatal traffic crashes, United States, 1982–2004. http://pubs.niaaa.nih.gov/publications/surveil lance76/fars04.htm-fig2a2006. See also: Yoon YH, Yi HY. Surveillance report #88: liver cirrhosis mortality in the United States, 1970–2007. http://pubs.niaaa.nih .gov/publications/surveillance.htm. 2010.

3. Rorabaugh WJ. *The Alcoholic Republic.* New York: Oxford University Press; 1979.

4. Levine H. The Discovery of Addiction. *Journal of Studies on Alcohol.* 1978;15:493–506.

5. Rorabaugh. *The Alcoholic Republic.*

6. Ibid.

7. Theobald MM. When whiskey was the king of the drink. www.history.org /foundation/journal/summer08/whiskey.cfm. *Colonial Williamsburg Journal* (online). 2008.

8. Calman K. Beyond the "nanny state": stewardship and public health. *Public Health.* 2009;123(1):e6–e10.

9. Sloan FA, Chepke LM. *The Law and Economics of Public Health.* Hanover, MA: NOW Publishers; 2007.

10. O'Malley PM, Wagenaar AC. Effects of minimum drinking age laws on alcohol use, related behaviors and traffic crash involvement among American youth: 1976–1987. *Journal of Studies on Alcohol.* 1991;52(5):478–491. See also: Wagenaar AC, Toomey TL. Effects of minimum drinking age laws: review and analyses of the literature from 1960 to 2000. *Journal of Studies on Alcohol Supplement.* Mar 2002;(14):206–225.

11. Voas RB, Fell JC. Preventing alcohol-related problems through health policy research. *Alcohol Research & Health.* 2010;33(1–2):18–28.

12. Volkow ND, O'Brien CP. Issues for DSM-V: should obesity be included as a brain disorder? *The American Journal of Psychiatry.* May 2007;164(5):708–710.

13. Todd J, Mancino L, Lin B-H. The impact of food away from home on adult diet quality. www.ers.usda.gov/Publications/ERR90/ERR90.pdf. 2010.

14. Geier AB, Rozin P, Doros G. Unit bias. A new heuristic that helps explain the effect of portion size on food intake. *Psychological Science.* Jun 2006;17(6):521–525.

15. Wansink B, Painter JE, North J. Bottomless bowls: why visual cues of portion size may influence intake. *Obesity Research.* Jan 2005;13(1):93–100.

16. Young LR, Nestle MS. Portion sizes in dietary assessment: issues and policy implications. *Nutrition Reviews*. 1995;53(6):149–158.

17. Johnson RK, Appel LJ, Brands M, et al. Dietary sugars intake and cardiovascular health: a scientific statement from the American Heart Association. *Circulation*. 2009;120(11):1011–1020.

18. Wansink B. Environmental factors that increase the food intake and consumption volume of unknowing consumers. *Annual Review of Nutrition*. 2004;24:455–479. See also: Wansink, Painter, and North. Bottomless bowls.

19. Jeffery RW, Wing RR. Long-term effects of interventions for weight loss using food provision and monetary incentives. *Journal of Consulting and Clinical Psychology*. Oct 1995;63(5):793–796. See also: Wing RR, Phelan S. Long-term weight loss maintenance. *The American Journal of Clinical Nutrition*. Jul 2005;82(1) Suppl:222S–225S.

20. Babor TF, Caetano R, Casswell S, et al. *Alcohol: No Ordinary Commodity: Research and Public Policy*. Oxford: Oxford University Press; 2003. See also: Ludbrook A, Godfrey C, Wyness L, et al. *Effective and Cost-Effective Measures to Reduce Alcohol Misuse in Scotland: A Literature Review*. Aberdeen, Scotland: Health Economics Research Unit. 2002. See also: Norstrom T, Skog O-J. Saturday opening of alcohol retail shops in Sweden: an impact analysis. *Journal of Studies on Alcohol*. 2003;64(3):393–401.

21. Sorenson H. *Inside the Mind of the Shopper*. Upsaddle River, NJ: Pearson Education; 2009.

22. Downs JS, Loewenstein G, Wisdom J. Strategies for promoting healthier food choices. *American Economic Review: Papers & Proceedings*. 2009;99(2):159–164. See also: Dayan E, Bar-Hillel M. Nudge to nobesity II: menu positions influence food orders. *Judgment and Decision Making*. 2011;6(4):333–342.

23. Dayan and Bar-Hillel. Nudge to nobesity II.

24. Sharpe KM, Staelin R. Consumption effects of bundling: consumer perceptions, firm actions, and public policy implications. *Journal of Public Policy & Marketing*. 2010;29(2):170–188. See also: Harris J, Blair EA. Consumer preference for product bundles: the role of reduced search costs. *Journal of the Academy of Marketing Science*. 2006;34(4):506–513.

25. Anderson P, Chisholm D, Fuhr DC. Effectiveness and cost-effectiveness of policies and programmes to reduce the harm caused by alcohol. *Lancet*. 2009;373(9682):2234–2246. See also: Jones CM, Kammen DM. Quantifying carbon footprint reduction opportunities for U.S. households and communities. *Environmental Science & Technology*. 2011;45(9):4088–4095. See also: Joyce A, Dixon S, Comfort J, Hallett J. Reducing the environmental impact of dietary choice: perspectives from a behavioural and social change approach. *Journal of Environmental and Public Health*. 2012;2012:978672.

26. Shiv B, Fedorikhin A. Heart and mind in conflict: the interplay of affect

and cognition in consumer decision making. *Journal of Consumer Research.* Dec 1999;26(3):278–292.

27. Dhar R, Wertenbroch K. Consumer choice between hedonic and utilitarian goods. *Journal of Marketing Research.* Feb 2000;37(1):60–71.

28. Lapham SC, Gruenwald PJ, Remer L, Layne L. New Mexico's 1998 drive-up liquor window closure. Study I: effect on alcohol-involved crashes. *Addiction.* 2004;99(5):598–606. See also: Lapham SC, Skipper BJ. New Mexico's 1998 drive-up liquor window closure. Study II: economic impact on owners. *Addiction.* 2004;99(5):607–611.

29. Nestle M. Food marketing and childhood obesity—a matter of policy. *New England Journal of Medicine.* Jun 15, 2006;354(24):2527–2529. See also: Harris JL, Brownell KD, Bargh JA. The food marketing defense model: integrating psychological research to protect youth and inform public policy. *Social Issues and Policy Review.* Dec 2009;3(1):211–271.

30. Warner KE. The effects of the anti-smoking campaign on cigarette consumption. *American Journal of Public Health.* Jul 1977;67(7):645–650.

31. Vergnaud AC, Norat T, Romaguera D, et al. Fruit and vegetable consumption and prospective weight change in participants of the European Prospective Investigation into Cancer and Nutrition—Physical Activity, Nutrition, Alcohol, Cessation of Smoking, Eating Out of Home, and Obesity study. *American Journal of Clinical Nutrition.* Jan 2012;95(1):184–193.

32. Dijksterhuis A, Aarts H. On wildebeests and humans: the preferential detection of negative stimuli. *Psychological Science.* 2003;14(1):14–18. See also: Dijksterhuis A, Corneille O, Aarts H, Vermeulen N, Luminet O. Yes, there is a preferential detection of negative stimuli: a response to Labiouse. *Psychological Science.* 2004;15(8):571–572.

33. Kahneman D. A perspective on judgment and choice: mapping bounded rationality. *American Psychologist.* Sep 2003;58(9):697–720.

34. Kuo M, Wechsler H, Greenberg P, Lee H. The marketing of alcohol to college students: the role of low prices and special promotions. *American Journal of Preventive Medicine.* 2003;25(3):204–211.

35. Hammond D, Fong GT, McDonald PW, Brown KS, Cameron R. Showing leads to doing: graphic cigarette warning labels are an effective public health policy. *European Journal of Public Health.* Apr 2006;16(2):223–224; author reply 225. See also: Hammond D, Fong GT, McNeill A, Borland R, Cummings KM. Effectiveness of cigarette warning labels in informing smokers about the risks of smoking: findings from the International Tobacco Control (ITC) Four Country Survey. *Tobacco Control.* Jun 2006;15 Suppl 3:iii19–25.

36. Anderson, Chisholm, and Fuhr. Effectiveness and cost-effectiveness.

37. O'Malley PM, Wagenaar AC. Effects of minimum drinking age laws on alcohol use, related behaviors and traffic crash involvement among American

youth: 1976–1987. *Journal of Studies on Alcohol.* 1991;52(5):478–491.

38. Ruggless R. Calif. city links building permits to nutrition. http://find articles.com/p/articles/mi_m3190/is_22_44/ai_n56287820/. *Nation's Restaurant News.* 2010.

39. Cohen D, Rabinovich L. Addressing the proximal causes of obesity: the relevance of alcohol control policies. *Preventing Chronic Disease.* May 2012;9:E94.

Chapter 10: The Supermarket of the Future

1. Lin B, Frazao E. Away-from-home foods increasingly important to quality of American diet. *ERS/USDA.* 1999. www.ers.usda.gov/Publications/AIB749/.

2. Ibid.

3. Kant AK, Graubard BI. Eating out in America, 1987–2000: trends and nutritional correlates. *Preventive Medicine.* Feb 2004;38(2):243–249. See also: French SA, Harnack L, Jeffery RW. Fast food restaurant use among women in the Pound of Prevention study: dietary, behavioral and demographic correlates. *International Journal of Obesity and Related Metabolic Disorders.* Oct 2000;24(10):1353–1359.

4. Finkelstein EA, Trogdon JG, Cohen JW, Dietz W. Annual medical spending attributable to obesity: payer- and service-specific estimates. *Health Affairs.* 2009;28(5):w822–w831. See also: Mokdad AH, Marks JS, Stroup DF, Gerberding JL. Actual causes of death in the United States, 2000. *JAMA.* Mar 10, 2004;291(10):1238–1245.

5. Boffetta P, Nyberg F. Contribution of environmental factors to cancer risk. *British Medical Bulletin.* 2003;68:71–94. See also: Huxley RR, Ansary-Moghaddam A, Clifton P, Czernichow S, Parr CL, Woodward M. The impact of dietary and lifestyle risk factors on risk of colorectal cancer: a quantitative overview of the epidemiological evidence. *International Journal of Cancer.* 2009;125(1):171–180. See also: Fung T, Hu FB, Fuchs C, et al. Major dietary patterns and the risk of colorectal cancer in women. *Archives of Internal Medicine.* 2003;163(3):309–314.

6. Waganingin UR. Restaurant of the future. www.restaurantvandetoekomst .wur.nl/UK/. 2009.

7. Clarke P, Evans SH, Hovy EH. Indigenous message tailoring increases consumption of fresh vegetables by clients of community pantries. *Health Communication.* Sep 2011;26(6):571–582.

8. Cialdini R. *Influence: Science and Practice.* Boston: Allyn & Bacon; 2001.

9. Thaler R, Sunstein C. *Nudge: Improving Decisions About Health, Wealth, and Happiness.* New York: Penguin Group; 2008.

10. Fielding JE, Aguirre A, Spear MC, Frias LE. Making the grade: changing the incentives in retail food establishment inspection. *American Journal of Preventive Medicine.* Oct 1999;17(3):243–247.

11. Fielding JE, Aguirre A, Palaiologos E. Effectiveness of altered incentives in a food safety inspection program. *Preventive Medicine.* Mar 2001;32(3):239–244. See also: Simon PA, Leslie P, Run G, et al. Impact of restaurant hygiene grade cards on foodborne-disease hospitalizations in Los Angeles County. *Journal of Environmental Health.* Mar 2005;67(7):32–36, 56; quiz 59–60.

12. Ibid.

13. Jin G, Leslie P. The effect of information on product quality: evidence from restaurant hygiene grade cards. *Quarterly Journal of Economics.* 2003;118(2):409–451. See also: Jin G, Leslie P. The case in support of restaurant hygiene grade cards. *Choices* 2005;20(2):97–102.

14. Cohen DA, Bhatia R. Nutrition standards for away-from-home foods in the USA. *Obesity Reviews.* Feb 13, 2012.

Chapter 11: Fit and Fat: What About Physical Activity?

1. Troiano RP, Berrigan D, Dodd KW, Mâsse LC, Tilert T, McDowell M. Physical activity in the United States measured by accelerometer. *Medicine and Science in Sports and Exercise.* Jan 2008;40(1):181–188.

2. Gutin B. How can we help people to develop lean and healthy bodies?: a new perspective. *Research Quarterly for Exercise & Sport.* Mar 2013;84(1):1–5.

3. Blundell JE, Caudwell P, Gibbons C, et al. Role of resting metabolic rate and energy expenditure in hunger and appetite control: a new formulation. *Disease Models & Mechanisms.* Sep 2012;5(5):608–613.

4. World Health Organization. *Global Health Risks: Mortality and Burden of Disease Attributable to Selected Major Risks.* www.who.int/healthinfo/global _burden_disease/global_health_risks/en/index.html. Geneva: WHO; 2009.

5. Centers for Disease Control. Physical activity trends—United States, 1990–1998. *Morbidity and Mortality Weekly Report.* Mar 9, 2001;50(9):166–169. See also: Sturm R. Childhood obesity—what we can learn from existing data on societal trends, Part 2. *Preventing Chronic Disease.* Apr 2005;2(2):A20. See also: Swinburn BA, Sacks G, Lo SK, et al. Estimating the changes in energy flux that characterize the rise in obesity prevalence. *The American Journal of Clinical Nutrition.* 2009;89(6):1723–1728. See also: Carlson SA, Densmore D, Fulton JE, Yore MM, Kohl HW, 3rd. Differences in physical activity prevalence and trends from 3 U.S. surveillance systems: NHIS, NHANES, and BRFSS. *Journal of Physical Activity & Health.* 2009;6 Suppl 1:S18–S27. See also: Westerterp KR, Speakman JR. Physical activity energy expenditure has not declined since the 1980s and matches energy expenditures of wild mammals. *International Journal of Obesity.* 2008;32(8):1256–1263.

6. Church TS, Thomas DM, Tudor-Locke C, et al. Trends over 5 decades

in U.S. occupation-related physical activity and their associations with obesity. *PLoS One.* 2011;6(5):e19657.

7. Herman WH, Hoerger TJ, Brandle M, et al. The cost-effectiveness of lifestyle modification or metformin in preventing type 2 diabetes in adults with impaired glucose tolerance. *Annals of Internal Medicine.* 2005;142(5):323–332.

8. McKenzie TL, Marshall S, Sallis JF, Conway TL. Student activity levels, lesson context, and teacher behavior during middle school physical education. *Research Quarterly for Exercise and Sport.* 2000;71:249–259.

9. Tudor-Locke C, Lee SM, Morgan CF, Beighle A, Pangrazi RP. Children's pedometer-determined physical activity during the segmented school day. *Medicine and Science in Sports and Exercise.* Oct 2006;38(10):1732–1738.

10. Heady JA, Morris JN, Kagan A, Raffle PA. Coronary heart disease in London busmen: a progress report with particular reference to physique. *British Journal of Preventive and Social Medicine.* Oct 1961;15:143–153.

11. Marshall S, Gyi D. Evidence of health risks from occupational sitting: where do we stand? *American Journal of Preventive Medicine.* Oct 2010;39(4):389–391.

12. Ibid. See also: van Uffelen JG, Wong J, Chau JY, et al. Occupational sitting and health risks: a systematic review. *American Journal of Preventive Medicine.* Oct 2010;39(4):379–388.

13. Katzmarzyk PT, Church TS, Craig CL, Bouchard C. Sitting time and mortality from all causes, cardiovascular disease, and cancer. *Medicine and Science in Sports and Exercise.* May 2009;41(5):998–1005.

14. Ibid. See also: Katzmarzyk PT, Lee IM. Sedentary behaviour and life expectancy in the USA: a cause-deleted life table analysis. *BMJ Open.* 2012;2(4).

15. Barr-Anderson DJ, AuYoung M, Whitt-Glover MC, Glenn BA, Yancey AK. Integration of short bouts of physical activity into organizational routine: a systematic review of the literature. *American Journal of Preventive Medicine.* Jan 2011;40(1):76–93. See also: Lara A, Yancey AK, Tapia-Conye R, et al. Pausa para tu salud: reduction of weight and waistlines by integrating exercise breaks into workplace organizational routine. *Preventing Chronic Disease.* Jan 2008;5(1):A12.

16. Ewing R, Schmid T, Killingsworth R, Zlot A, Raudenbush S. Relationship between urban sprawl and physical activity, obesity, and morbidity. *American Journal of Health Promotion.* Sep/Oct 2003;18(1):47–57.

17. Senauer B, Gemma M. Why is the obesity rate so low in Japan and high in the U.S.? Some possible economic explanations. The Food Industry Center, University of Minnesota; 2006.

18. MacDonald JM, Stokes RJ, Cohen DA, Kofner A, Ridgeway GK. The effect of light rail transit on body mass index and physical activity. *American Journal of Preventive Medicine.* 2010;39(2):105–112.

19. Sturm R, Cohen DA. Suburban sprawl and physical and mental health. *Public Health.* Oct 2004;118(7):488–496.

20. Environmental Protection Agency. Sources of Greenhouse Gas Emissions. www.epa.gov/climatechange/ghgemissions/sources.html. 2010.

21. Malta DC, Barbosa da Silva J. Policies to promote physical activity in Brazil. *Lancet.* Jul 21, 2012;380(9838):195–196.

22. Granovetter MS. The Strength of Weak Ties. *American Journal of Sociology.* 1973;78(6):1360–1380.

23. Time Spent Watching TV. http://adage.com/article/media/time-spent -watching-tv/227022/. *AdAge Media News.* 2011.

24. Vuori I, Lankenau B, Pratt M. Physical activity policy and program development: the experience in Finland. *Public Health Reports.* May/Jun 2004;119(3):331–345.

25. Ibid.

26. Cohen DA, Lapham S, Evenson KR, et al. Use of neighborhood parks: does socioeconomic status matter? a four city study. *Public Health.* 2013;in press.

27. Cohen DA, Han B, Derose KP, et al. Neighborhood poverty, park use, and park-based physical activity in a Southern California city. *Social Science & Medicine.* 2012;75(12):2317–2325.

Chapter 12: In the Meantime: What Individuals Can Do

1. Wegner DM. Ironic processes of mental control. *Psychological Review.* 1994;101(1):34–52.

2. Spiegel TA, Kaplan JM, Tomassini A, Stellar E. Bite size, ingestion rate, and meal size in lean and obese women. *Appetite.* Oct 1993;21(2):131–145.

3. Rolls BJ, Roe LS, Halverson KH, Meengs JS. Using a smaller plate did not reduce energy intake at meals. *Appetite.* Nov 2007;49(3):652–660.

4. Coelho do Vale R, Pieters R, Zeelenberg, M. Flying under the radar: perverse package size effects on consumption self-regulation. *Journal of Consumer Research.* 2008;36:380–390.

5. Shapiro J. *No Pity: People with Disabilities Forging a New Civil Rights Movement.* New York: Crown; 1993.

6. Ibid.

7. Ibid.

Chapter 13: Conclusion

1. Spiegel CN, Lindaman FC. Children can't fly: a program to prevent childhood morbidity and mortality from window falls. 1977. *Injury Prevention.* Sep 1995;1(3):194–198.

2. Ibid.

3. Arndt M. McDonald's 24/7. www.businessweek.com/stories/2007-02-04/mcdonalds-24-7. *Bloomberg's Business Week Magazine*. Feb 4, 2007.

4. Centers for Disease Control. CDC estimates of foodborne illness in the United States. www.cdc.gov/foodborneburden/2011-foodborne-estimates.html. 2011. See also: Mokdad AH, Marks JS, Stroup DF, Gerberding JL. Actual causes of death in the United States, 2000. *JAMA*. Mar 10, 2004;291(10):1238–1245.

Index